WARS IN THE CAUCASUS, 1990–95

THE CAUCASUS
Capital city
Other towns & cities
International boundary
National boundary
Other boundaries
Railway
Caucasus Mountains
0 50 100 miles
0 50 100 kilometres
RUSSIAN FEDERATION
KAZAKHSTAN
STAVROPOL KRAI
INGUSHETIA
Mozdok
CHECHENYA
Znamenskoye
Tolsoy Yurt
Argun
Gudermes
Grozny
Shali
Urus-Martan
Achoi-Martan
Vedeno
Nazran
NORTH OSSETIA
Vladikavkaz
KABARDINO-BALKARSKAYA
DAGESTAN
Makhach Kala
Sochi
Gagra
Gudauta
Sukhumi
ABKHAZIA
Zugdidi
MINGRELIA
Khobi
Kutaisi
Poti
Samtredia
Batumi
ADHARIA
SOUTH OSSETIA
Tskhinvali
GEORGIA
Telavi
Tbilisi
Black Sea
Caspian Sea
TURKEY
Spitak
Kumairi
ARMENIA
Yerevan
Sadarak
NAKHICHEVAN
Gyandzha
AZERBAIJAN
Sumgait
Baku
NAGORNO-KARABAKH
Agdam
Stepanakert
Shusha
Lachin
Fizuli
Sabrail
Lenkoran
IRAN
Tabriz
N

Wars in the Caucasus, 1990–1995

Edgar O'Ballance

First published 1997 by
MACMILLAN PRESS LTD
Houndmills, Basingstoke, Hampshire RG21 6XS
and London
Companies and representatives
throughout the world

ISBN 0–333–67100–7

A catalogue record for this book is available from the British Library.

This book is printed on paper suitable for recycling and made from fully managed and sustained forest sources.

10 9 8 7 6 5 4 3 2 1
06 05 04 03 02 01 00 99 98 97

Printed and bound in Great Britain by
Antony Rowe Ltd, Chippenham, Wiltshire

Also by Edgar O'Ballance

ARAB GUERRILLA POWER
CIVIL WAR IN BOSNIA: 1992–94
CIVIL WAR IN YUGOSLAVIA
ISLAMIC FUNDAMENTALIST TERRORISM: 1979–95
NO VICTOR, NO VANQUISHED: The Middle East War 1973
TERRORISM IN IRELAND: The Story of the IRA
TERRORISM IN THE 1980s
THE ALGERIAN INSURRECTION: 1954–62
THE ARAB-ISRAELI WAR: 1948–9
THE CYANIDE WAR
THE ELECTRONIC WAR IN THE MIDDLE EAST: 1968–70
THE FRENCH FOREIGN LEGION
THE GREEK CIVIL WAR: 1944–49
THE GULF WAR
THE INDO-CHINA WAR: 1946–54
THE KURDISH REVOLT: 1961–70
THE KURDISH STRUGGLE: 1920–94
THE LANGUAGE OF VIOLENCE
THE MALAYAN INSURRECTION: 1948–60
THE RED ARMY OF CHINA
THE RED ARMY OF RUSSIA
THE SECOND GULF WAR: THE LIBERATION OF KUWAIT
THE SECRET WAR IN SUDAN: 1955–72
THE SINAI CAMPTAIN: 1956
THE THIRD ARAB–ISRAELI WAR: 1967
TRACKS OF THE BEAR: US–USSR Relations in the 1970s
WAR IN YEMEN: 1962–69
WARS IN AFGHANISTAN: 1839–1992
WARS IN VIETNAM, 1954–60

Contents

List of Maps

Preface

The saga of the Caucasus republics during the period 1990–95 is one of clashing warlord militias, coups and attempted coups, assassinations, terrorism, treachery, intrigue and avid ethnic cleansing, which still simmers uneasily. Previously a strategic backwater, international attention has increasingly focused on that region since the discovery of Azerbaijan's offshore Caspian oilfields, reputed to exceed in volume those of Kuwait. The present problem is how this oil is to be moved across unstable territories from Baku to Black Sea or Mediterranean terminals. We are told that the West will be looking to this Caspian oil reservoir in the first part of the next century, when the Arabian oilfields will be drying up.

The recent evolution of Caucasian republics from tightly integrated components of the USSR to independent republics free of the shackles of Communism, should be set against the even more dramatic dissolution of the Soviet Union, which forms the background to their fortunes and misfortunes.

It all began in 1985 when Mikhail Gorbachev, a well-meaning reformer, was appointed general secretary of the Communist Party of the Soviet Union (CPSU) and launched his two major reforms – perestroika (restructuring) and glasnost (openness) – which sent shivers of political anticipation throughout the Soviet Union and horrified the CPSU. In June 1988 he achieved sweeping political reforms and multicandidate elections were held in March 1989, when the CPSU surrendered its monopoly on political power – before its later demise it also abandoned its Marxist–Leninist principles.

The Berlin Wall was breached in November 1989 and the Cold War ended in July 1990. Massive political change was in motion in the USSR. The proceedings of the newly elected Congress of Peoples' Deputies in Moscow were televised live for all Soviet citizens and the world in general to see. Estonia, Latvia and Lithuania, constituent Soviet Union republics, were in the vanguard of the rush towards independence. The USSR was splitting asunder, even though an all-Union referendum held in March 1991 indicated that 74 per cent wanted it to remain as it was. Gorbachev's vision for the new USSR did not include dissolution, so he strove to keep it intact but democratically enlightened. His popularity began to wane as the promised capitalist benefits did not materialise.

The crunch came in August 1991, when a hastily planned and badly managed coup was mounted against him by diehard communists who were reluctant to see their old order, power, prestige and perks snatched from them. To Gorbachev's rescue appeared the bear-like figure of Boris Yeltsin, leader of the Russian Federation, the largest Soviet republic, whom Gorbachev had previously dismissed from office. This unlikely champion obtained the support of elements of the army, based himself in the 'White House' (the Russian Federation Assembly building) and rallied support for Gorbachev. Yeltsin's activities caused the coup against Gorbachev to collapse, but his price was the transfer of certain political powers and resources from the USSR to his Russian Federation.

Gorbachev desperately tried to stem the disintegration of the USSR, fumblingly trying to stitch together a Commonwealth of Independent States (CIS) from former Soviet republics, but this had indifferent success, the prize of independence being too great an attraction. Gorbachev was losing out to Yeltsin, who came to dominate the situation. The Minsk Declaration brought the CIS into being in early December 1991 as a loose alliance of several former Soviet republics, without any central governing bodies. The USSR had indeed fragmented. The Russian Federation assumed the status and dignity of the former USSR in most respects, including its permanent seat on the UN Security Council and control of the major part of the nuclear arsenal.

On 25 December 1991 Gorbachev resigned as president of the Soviet Union and handed over the nuclear codes to Yeltsin. Yeltsin had won and Gorbachev had been shouldered aside. However Yeltsin inherited massive problems as he had to dismantle the overcentralised Soviet political structure, reform the economy and create a new democratic system on the Western pattern. Opposition came from the Congress of Peoples' Deputies, which refused to approve some of his ministerial appointments and economic reforms, but he survived motions of no confidence.

Although a Russian Federation referendum in April 1993 supported Yeltsin's leadership, arguments still raged over the proposed new constitution, causing him to suspend the Congress of People's Deputies. Active confrontation erupted in Moscow in August between Yeltsin, this time based in the Kremlin, and the rump of the Congress of Peoples' Deputies, besieged in the White House. The armed forces mostly stood aside waiting to see who would win, but once again Yeltsin obtained the support of certain military units, and eventually mounted an attack with guns and armoured vehicles in an all-day battle against the 'rebels' in the White House, forcing them to surrender.

Yeltsin published his new Russian Federation Constitution in November, following it with elections for a new Federal Assembly, to consist of a Federal Council (upper house) and a State Duma (lower house). Although 'reformers' held the middle ground in the elections and mainly supported Yeltsin, extreme right-wing and left-wing parties made considerable gains. Watching Western leaders were horrified and disappointed that such a large number of Russian people were reluctant to accept change, overlooking the fact that the Russians were not enjoying the new 'non-superpower' status the West was patronisingly trying to impose on them.

In January 1994 Yeltsin reshuffled his cabinet, and in April assumed direct control over the Ministries of Defence, Foreign Affairs and the Interior. As his personal control tightened, new problems appeared. The introduction of a market economy brought with it the ills that have dogged capitalism everywhere, including unemployment, shortages, inflation, crime and corruption. Both beggars and expensive foreign cars could now be seen in the streets of Moscow.

Beset by enemies and problems, Yeltsin continued unsteadily in power, his relationship with individual fellow CIS republics varying from uncertain to acrimonious, some being reluctant to deal with a former 'colonial' power, others wanting beneficial trade and resources agreements, while factions within some of them wanted Moscow's political support. All the CIS republics were beholden to the Russian Federation to some degree, as former Soviet policy had been that of 'divide and administer', ensuring that no Union republic could become economically self-sufficient.

This brief outline of major events in the USSR and the Russian Federation forms the backcloth to the story of the confused, co-related struggle for national independence in the three Trans-Caucasus Soviet Socialist Republics of Armenia, Azerbaijan and Georgia, and to the North Caucasus autonomous republic of Chechenya's attempts to free itself from the Russian Federation.

For many centuries the mountainous Caucasus region was a strategic backwater inhabited by inward-looking peoples and tribes, the Caucasus Mountain range dividing the region into two parts where the raw edges of the Christian and Muslim empires rubbed abrasively together. Most of the Caucasus was absorbed into the Russian Empire in the nineteenth century, and when the Bolsheviks came to power their Red Army forcibly subjected it to communism. Lenin and Stalin implemented a policy of divide and administer, rearranging boundaries so that large ethnic groups were counterbalanced by smaller ones.

The mass resettlement of people and banishment to labour camps were Stalin's answer to acts of dissidence, and tight communist control smothered former interethnic hostility. All the 112 recognised nationalities were regarded as 'communist brothers', working together – the only hostile attitude permitted was that of socialism against capitalism. Gorbachev's glasnost caused this tight containment to be relaxed, thus allowing ethnic expression and political discontent to emerge.

Age-old enmity between Christian Armenians and Muslim Azeris, quiescent under communist rule, suddenly erupted in two small ethnic massacres in February 1988, which quickly developed into full-scale warfare between the Armenian and Azerbaijan republics, both of which contained scattered groups of each other's ethnic minorities. As Armenia and Azerbaijan shed communism and became independent republics, the war between them developed and intensified, initially with Armenia winning some one fifth of Azeri territory, which it still more or less retains.

Two tinderboxes were firmly planted by Stalin when redrawing the map of the Caucasus. One was Nagorno-Karabakh, a small, mountainous, mainly Armenian-inhabited enclave isolated within the Muslim Azerbaijan Republic but claimed by Armenia. The other was Nakhichevan, a border enclave inhabited mainly by Muslim Azeris and isolated within Armenia, but under the overlordship of Azerbaijan.

Landlocked Armenia (population just over three million), with its sparse economy, has been and still is subjected to a hard economic embargo by its Muslim neighbours, despite its successes in battle. The economy of adjacent Azerbaijan (population just over seven million) has run down badly since its oil-boom days. Neither country can buy sufficient sophisticated arms to achieve a military victory over the other. Both sides have carried out ethnic cleansing with a vengeance, so that both are now almost ethnically pure.

Across the Caspian Sea, Iran initially supported Azerbaijan (having some nine million Azeris), but this support has now waned, as Iran is upset by the cries for a Greater Azerbaijan that are emanating from Baku, and alarmed by the hordes of Azerbaijan Azeris, some politically minded, flooding in as refugees. Muslim Iran now supplies aid to Christian Armenia in order to perpetuate its war with Muslim Azerbaijan, and to smother aspirations of a Greater Azerbaijan.

Muslim Turkey, which is in competition with Iran for influence in the region, also comes into this equation, alternating between enforcing embargoes against Armenia and providing sufficient aid to prevent its economic collapse.

In Armenia, Levon Ter-Petrossian has been president since October 1991, despite considerable opposition as his pro-Turkey policy has upset returning Armenian exiles and others who remember the Turkish massacres of the First World War. He has gradually accumulated greater power, his new constitution giving him almost dictatorial status, but he is also beset by problems arising from semiloyal armed militias and frequent protest demonstrations.

Azerbaijan has been plagued by warlord rivalry and a series of coups and attempted coups. Gaidar Aliyev became president in October 1993, but is none too secure as predatory warlords are lurking in the background waiting to oust him and take his place. Like Ter-Petrossian, his new constitution gives him almost dictatorial powers. A ceasefire between Armenia and Azerbaijan came into effect in May 1994 and has held precariously, with only minor breaches. As the tinderboxes of Nagorno-Karabakh and Nakhichevan are irremovable, both republics are concentrating on building up their armed forces in preparation for resumed hostilities. The number of casualties so far in this war have been estimated at more than 30 000, with almost one million refugees and displaced persons.

Georgia (population about 5.5 million), a laterally enlongated

Black Sea country, is studded with discontented nationalities and factions. In the north-west are the Abkhazis, in the north the Ossetes and in the south-west the Adzharis, all wanting independence, as well as other tiny minorities wanting a special status. Although an oil pipeline (disused) and a rail link cross Georgia between the Caspian and Black Seas, its economy has stultified, but the entrepreneurial spirit that survived even under communism has gained the Georgians the dubious reputation of being the most active black-marketeering operatives in the former USSR.

An ancient Christian kingdom, Georgia was absorbed into the Russian Empire in the nineteenth century, and after a brief spell of independence (1918–21) became part of the USSR. Responding to perestroika and glasnost, Georgia quickly shrugged off its communist overlordship by rowdy demonstrations, replacing it with a fragmented, multiparty nationalism. In the first multiparty elections in October 1990, Zviad Gamsakhurdia, having considerable dissident credentials and some sympathy amongst Western statesmen, was elected president. A referendum in March 1991 confirmed the people's desire for independence, which was duly proclaimed. The snag was that in August 1990 the Abkhazis had also declared their independence, as had the Ossetes in February 1991, causing two civil wars to erupt simultaneously. Gamsakhurdia's dictatorial attitude and inability to control the warlords and their militias led to him being driven from the country by military force in January 1992, being replaced by a Military Council.

In March 1992 Eduard Shevardnadze, a former Soviet foreign secretary and the darling of Western statesmen as he had 'handed over Eastern Europe' to them, returned to his native Georgia and became head of the Georgian State Council. He has precariously survived as leader of his country, despite opposition, difficulties, dangers and assassination attempts. He arrived when the fight with the Abkhazis was at its height, going forward into the battle area and narrowly escaping death on several occasions.

Georgia was the adventure playground of several semi-independent warlords with changing allegiances, most of whom also indulged in 'bandit patriotism' for subsistence. A Zviadist revolt erupted in November 1992, directed by Gamsakhurdia from Chechenya, but was put down severely and several leaders were executed. Gamsakhurdia died in the last days of 1993 in mysterious circumstances. Assassinations had become frequent, while the age-old Georgian practice of hostage taking was rampant.

After hesitating, Georgia joined the CIS in October 1993, and in February 1994 a Russian–Georgian Friendship Treaty brought Russia into the equation. A Declaration of Unity grouped most Georgian factions together, and the Moscow Accord technically ended the fighting in Abkhazia, which gained 'independence' within Georgia: over 40 000 people having been killed in this three-year struggle, which only slowly simmered down. Russian peacekeeping troops appeared in Georgia, as did a UN presence.

During 1995 the Georgian economic situation improved to some extent, as the warlord militias were gradually disarmed. Turkmenistan resumed its gas supplies, Turkey began to supply electricity and Iran agreed to supply gas and make other economic arrangements. Georgia avoided becoming entangled in the problems of neighbouring Armenia, despite their mutual Christian heritage. On the political side, the dismissal of ministers and arguments between them continued, many being former warlords who still thirsted for power. Political assassinations and terrorist explosions became commonplace. Under Georgia's new constitution, in the elections in November 1995 Shevardnadze at last became president of Georgia, previously only holding the title of chairman.

On the north side of the Caucasus Mountain range an ex-Soviet air force general, Dzhokhar Dudayev, a Muslim, stirred up separatist Chechen emotions in the Russian Federation's autonomous republic of Ingushetia–Chechenya. The Ingush (numbering about 350 000 and living contiguously with the Chechens) split away as they wished to remain within the Russian Federation, leaving the republic with just under one million Chechens. Dudayev seized power, ousted the communist authorities and declared independence.

The economy of landlocked Chechenya is fairly weak, its main asset being its strategic position as an oil pipeline corridor and oil refining centre, having only a small reserve of oil itself.

Dudayev barricaded himself in his republic, charged a tariff on the oil passing through his pipelines, syphoned off large amounts and presided over a bandit state, illegal arms and drugs being on open display in market places. It was also a haven for Chechen mafia groups operating in the Russian Federation. Dudayev was left alone for a while as Yeltsin was preoccupied with his own survival.

It was not until December 1994 that Yeltsin took the military option and sent a Russian expeditionary force to bring Dudayev to heel. However he had underestimated the Chechens, as his troops ran into unexpectedly stiff opposition and put up a poor show. A major assault with aircraft, tanks and guns had to be mounted to seize and hold Grozny, the capital. The Chechens withdrew into the countryside, fighting back hard throughout 1995. An uneasy ceasefire went into effect in July, whereupon the incidence of urban terrorism increased.

In October, the 11-member international oil consortium that had gained the contract to extract and distribute the Caspian offshore oil decided it should have two overland oil pipelines to take the oil to the export terminals, one through Georgia (which already had a disused one) and the other through Chechenya, but admitted that more negotiations were needed.

The future is dark, and promises the continuation of intermittent outbursts of dissidence within the republics, as well as open warfare between them. Certain external powers, now interested in the Caspian offshore oil fields (which technically belong to Azerbaijan), may indulge in proxy warfare in the Caucasus for their own benefit, or to thwart rivals. Wheeling, dealing and political intrigue continues. Russia, which has plenty of oil itself, wants to gain a stranglehold on the distribution of Caspian offshore oil in order to regain its former influence in the Caucasus region. The international media spotlight will increasingly focus on this region.

EDGAR O'BALLANCE

Acknowledgements

Since 1992 I have been involved in the Caucasus region producing political analyses and commentary, during which time I have visited all the republics at least once, some several times, attended numerous briefing sessions and interviewed a wide range of personalities, including VIPs, politicians, military leaders, combatants, officials and others involved or interested in this subject. Where material has been obtained from other sources, due credit is given within the text. All comments, deductions and opinions are my own, and at times may differ from the current, generally perceived wisdom.

Map sources include the United Nations, NATO, *The Times Atlas of the World, The Times,* the *Daily Telegraph,* and the *Financial Times.*

Material from the following broadcasters, periodicals and news agencies was consulted, and some extracts appear in translation in this book.

UK:
BBC TV and radio
Channel Four
Daily Telegraph
Financial Times
Guardian
ITN
ITV
Middle East
Reuters
The Sunday Times
The Times

United States:
CNN
Helsinki Watch
International Herald Tribune
Newsweek
New York Times
Time magazine

Washington Post
USA Today

France:
Agence France Presse

Russia/Soviet Union:
All Russia State TV
Independent NTV
Inter-Fax news agency
Itar-Tass
Izvestiya
Komsomolskaya Pravda
Nezavisimaya Gazeta
Ostanko TV
Pravda
Tass

Armenia:
Local TV
SNARK news agency

Azerbaijan:
Assa-Irasa news agency
State TV
Turan news agency

Georgia:
State TV
Zarya Vostoka

Turkey:
Sabah

List of Abbreviations

ANA	Armenian National Army
ANM	Armenian National Movement
APF	Azerbaijan Popular Front
CIS	Commonwealth of Independent States
CNC	Chechen National Congress
CPSU	Communist Party of the Soviet Union
CSCE	Conference on Security and Co-operation in Europe
DMZ	Demilitarised zone
EC	European Community
FSB	Federal Special Services (successor of the FSK)
FSK	Federal Counter-Intelligence Service (from 1991)
GRU	Military Intelligence Service
IISS	International Institute for Strategic Studies
IMF	International Monetary Fund
KGB	State Security Committee
KSK	Counter-Intelligence Service (from April 1995)
MoD	Ministry of Defence
MVD	Internal Security Service
NATO	North Atlantic Treaty Organisation
NDC	National Defence Committee (Azerbaijan)
NSDA	National Self Determination Association (Armenia)
OPON	Special Purpose Militia (Azerbaijan)
OSCE	Organisation of Security and Co-operation in Europe (new title of the CSCE as from December 1994)
RSFSR	Russian Socialist Federative Soviet Republic
SCSE	State Committee for the State of Emergency
SSR	Soviet Socialist Republic
UN	United Nations
UNHCR	UN High Commissioner for Refugees
USSR	Union of the Soviet Socialist Republics

Chronology A: USSR

1917	(November)	Bolshevik Revolution in Russia
1939	(August)	Russian Non-Aggression Pact with Germany
	(September)	Second World War begins
1941	(June)	Germany invades the USSR
1945	(April)	War in Europe ends
1949		NATO formed
1955		Warsaw Pact formed
1985	(March)	Gorbachev appointed first secretary of the CPSU
1987	(May)	Perestroika and glasnost declared
1988	(June)	Political reforms in the USSR; CPSU loses some powers
1989	(March)	The first multicandidate elections in the USSR
	(May)	New Congress of Peoples' Deputies meets
	(November)	Berlin Wall breached
1990	(March)	Lithuania declares in dependence from the USSR
	(July)	London Declaration: end of the Cold War
	(August)	Estonia and Latvia declare independence from the USSR
1991	(March)	Referendum on preservation of the USSR
	(August)	Attempted coup against Gorbachev
	(December)	Minsk Declaration: the end of the USSR; CIS established; Gorbachev resigns as president of the USSR
1992	(March)	Russian Federation Treaty signed
1993	(April)	Referendum in the Russian Federation
	(September)	Yeltsin suspends the Congress of Peoples' Deputies
	(October)	Siege of the White House revolt
	(December)	Elections in the Russian Federation for a new Federal Assembly
1994	(January)	Yeltsin forms new government in the Russian Federation
	(July)	Investigative journalist killed in Moscow

1995 (July)	Yeltsin hospitalised
(October)	Yeltsin attends UN 50th Anniversary in New York
	Yeltsin again hospitalised

Chronology B: Armenia-Azerbaijan

Ar	= Armenia(n)(s)
Az	= Azerbaijan(i)(s)
NK	= Nagorno-Karabakh
N	= Nakhichevan

1870	Oil boom in Baku
1890	Dashnak founded
1895	Massacre of Armenians in Turkey
1905	Massacre of Armenians in Baku
1915	1.5 million Armenians massacred in Turkey
1918–1920	Dashnak Republic of Armenia
1919–1920	The Baku Soviet – massacre of Muslims
1920	Allied Peace Conference, Paris
	Treaty of Sèvres
	Treaty of Kars
1923	Treaty of Lausanne
	Oblast of Nagorno-Karabakh formed
1924	Oblast of Nakhichevan formed
1987 (October)	(Ar) First political demonstration in Yerevan
1988 (February)	(NK) Regional Soviet demand union with Armenia – vetoed by the USSR; political demonstrations in Stepanakert
	(Ar) Political demonstrations in Yerevan; Soviet troops arrive in Yerevan
	(Az) Sumgait riots
(March)	(Ar) Yerevan mass 'stay at home' demonstration
(May)	(NK) Regional Soviet again demands union with Armenia
(July)	(NK) Regional Soviet once again demands union with Armenia
(September)	(NK) Soviet Special Status order
(November)	(Ar) (Az) and (N) Intercommunal fighting
(December)	(Ar) Earthquake
1989 (January)	(NK) Placed under direct Moscow rule

	(May)	(NK) Wave of strikes
	(August)	(Az) Strikes in Baku; attacks on Armenians
	(September)	(Az) Economic blockade mounted against Armenia; new Sovereignty Law approved
	(October)	(Az) Soviet troops brought in to run the railways
1989	(November)	(NK) Direct rule from Moscow ceases; inter-communal fighting
	(December)	(NK) Nagorno-Karabakh declares itself part of Armenia
		(Ar) Outbreak of guerrilla warfare
		(Az) General strike resumed
		(N) Frontier fence torn down; guerrilla warfare
1990	(January)	(Az) Battle for Baku (13th–24th)
	(May)	(Ar) First multiparty elections
	(August)	(Ar) Armenia declares its 'independent statehood'
	(September)	(Az) First multiparty elections
1991	(January)	(Ar) Referendum on independence
	(October)	(Ar) Ter-Petrossian elected executive president
	(December)	(N) Declaration of independence
1992	(March)	(Az) President Mutalibov resigns, replaced by Mamedov
	(May)	(NK) Armenian military offensive
	(June)	(Az) Elchibey elected president
		(Az) Azeri counteroffensive
	(July)	(Az) Azeris consolidate gains
	(August)	(NK) Defence Committee takes over
	(October)	(Az) Attack on Lachin Corridor repulsed
		(Az) Attempted Mutalibov coup
1993	(March)	(Az) Armenian offensives
	(May)	(Ar) (Az) (NK) Tripartite Peace Plan
	(June)	(Ar) Mardakert falls to Armenia
		(Az) President Elchibey ousted
	(July)	(NK) Armenian successes
	(August)	(Az) Fizoli, Jebrail and Kubatly seized by Armenia
	(September)	(Ar) Economic siege
		(Az) Goradiz taken by Armenians

	(October)	(Az) Gaidar Aliyev becomes president
		(Ar) (Az) (NK) Iranian-sponsored ceasefire
	(November)	(Az) Armenia offensive
	(December)	(Az) Azeri counteroffensive
1994	(January)	(Az) Agdam, Goradiz and Kelbajar retaken
	(February)	(Az) Turkish–Azerbaijani agreement
	(March)	(Ar) (Az) (NK) Another cease-fire agreement; yet another in July
	(April)	(Az) Azeri offensive
	(June)	(N) Armenians attack
	(October)	(Az) First OPON revolt
		(Az) The Gyandzha revolt
	(November)	(Az) Caspian offshore oil agreement initialled
1995	(March)	(Az) Second OPON revolt
		(Ar) (Az) Ceasefire agreement
	(May)	(Ar) Energy agreement with Iran
		(Az) Call for a Greater Azerbaijan
	(July)	(Ar) Multiparty elections
	(August)	(Az) Another plot against President Aliyev
	(October)	(Az) Oil consortium decision
	(November)	(Az) Elections

Chronology C: Georgia

1801	Georgia becomes part of the Czarist Empire
1918–21	Georgian Democratic Republic
1988 (November)	Georgian nationalist demonstration
1989 (March)	Georgian nationalist rallies
	Abkhazian 'Lykhny' incident
(April)	Georgian 'Tbilisi' incident
(November)	Georgian 'sovereignty' declared
1990 (August)	Abkhazia declares independence from Georgia
(September)	South Ossetia declares itself a Union republic
(October)	Georgia's first multiparty elections
1991 (March)	Georgia's referendum on independence,
	Gamsakhurdia elected president of Georgia
(June)	Elections in Abkhazia
1992 (January)	South Ossetia: Georgian disturbances
	South Ossetia: referendum
(March)	Georgian State Council formed
	Shevardnadze returns to Georgia
(April)	Formation of the Georgian army
(June)	Trinational talks begin
(July)	Abkhazia proclaims 'state sovereignty'
(October)	Abkhazian counteroffensive
	Elections in Georgia
(November)	South Ossetia votes to secede from Georgia
	Shevardnadze confirmed as Georgian head of state
1993 (January)	Abkhazians attack Sukhumi
1993 (January)	Georgia asks for UN intervention
(March)	Abkhazians again attack Sukhumi
(May)	Georgian defence minister dismissed
(June)	Georgian–Abkhazian peace talks
(July)	Battle for Sukhumi
(August)	Mingrelian revolt begins
(September)	Georgians driven from Sukhumi
	Shevardnadze suspends Georgian State Council

	(October)	Georgia agrees to join CIS – receives Russian aid
	(November)	Russian–Ukrainian peacekeeping troops land in Georgia
		Mingrelian revolt crushed
	(December)	Georgian–Abkhazian agreement
		Death of Gamsakhurdia
1994	(January)	Peacemaking
	(February)	Georgian–Russian Friendship Treaty
		Abkhazian independence declared
	(April)	The Moscow Agreement
	(May)	Georgian National Unity and Accord
	(July)	Demonstrations in Tbilisi against Shevardnadze
	(September)	Russian peacekeepers in action
	(November)	Boutros Ghali visits Tbilisi
		UN approve Russian peacekeeping contingent
		Abkhazia adopts a new constitution
1995	(January)	Impromptu Georgian foray into Abkhazia thwarted
	(February)	Shevardnadze visits Britain
		Russian armed forces to have bases in Georgia
1995	(May)	Attempts to disarm the Rescue Corps
	(August)	New Georgian constitution
		Abkhazia rejects being part of Georgia
		Assassination attempt on Shevardnadze
	(November)	Elections in Georgia: Shevardnadze becomes president

Chronology D: Chechenya

1823		Oil discovered in Chechenya
1864		Russia annexes the Caucasus Mountain range
1921–24		Mountain Autonomous Republics formed (Chechenya included)
1923		Chechenya becomes an autonomous province
1934		Ingushetia–Chechenya autonomous republic formed
1944–57		Mass deportation of Chechens by Stalin
1960	(November)	Dudayev founds the Chechen National Congress
1991	(August)	Dudayev organises demonstrations in support of Yeltsin
	(September)	Dudayev seizes the presidential palace in Grozny
	(October)	Dudayev holds elections: becomes 'chairman'
	(November)	Russia imposes economic blockade on Chechenya
1992	(March)	Ingush opt out from the republic
		One-day revolt in Grozny
		Russian Federation Treaty comes into effect
	(April)	Dudayev announces Chechen independence
	(October)	Congress of the Confederation of Peoples of the Caucasus
1993	(April)	Dudayev impeached
	(June)	Dudayev launches a preemptive strike
	(December)	Chechen Provisional Council formed
1994	(July)	Internecine fighting in Grozny
	(September)	Chechen Government of National Renaissance formed in Moscow
		Secret KSK war in Chechenya
	(November)	Dudayev attacked by opposition in Grozny
		Yeltsin's 'secret war'

	(December)	Russian 'Operation Wave' military invasion of Chechenya
1995	(January)	Russian 'Operation Wave' continues
	(February)	First ceasefire
		Yeltsin's press conference
	(March)	Argun, Gudermes and Shali fall
	(April)	Ackhoi-Martan and Samashki fall; Bamut holds out
		Yeltsin declares unilateral ceasefire
	(June)	Chechen raid on Budennovsk (Russia)
	(July)	Peace Accord signed
	(August)	Chechen Government of Renewal appoints a prime minister
	(October)	Attack on military commander, Grozny
		Decision of oil consortium to have twin oil pipelines
	(December)	Increased autonomy granted to Chechenya
		Chechen elections
		Attack on Gudermes

1 Dissolution of the Soviet Union

To appreciate developments in the Trans-Caucasus from 1990 to 1995 it may be helpful to know something of the momentous events that took place in Moscow just before and during that period. In March 1985 Mikhail Sergeyich Gorbachev, a reformer, was elected first secretary of the Communist Party of the Soviet Union (CPSU) and, as it had a monopoly on political power, his office was the most powerful in the Union of Soviet Socialist Republics (USSR).

At that time the USSR, which covered an area of almost 22 million square miles and had a population of about 285.7 million, was a federal union of 15 states encompassing a multiplicity of nationalities. There were 112 officially recognised languages, and it was thought that less than 50 per cent of the people spoke Russian.

The nineteenth-century Czarist Russian Empire had been gained and exploited by use of the 'divide and rule' strategy. The USSR, the eventual successor of the old Russian Empire, supported a different policy, one that smothered national differences in line with Lenin's principle that all Soviet citizens were 'brothers in communism', and that the only permissible struggle was that of socialism against capitalism.

The centralised communist doctrinal stamp settled on the USSR, and with few exceptions managed to repress individual national aspirations by arranging administrative boundaries so that no one nationality became too powerful, and by merging minority nationalities within some of them to counterbalance the national majorities. When Stalin ruled the USSR, by divorcing the manufacturing processes from resources and consumers he ensured that none of the states of the Union were able to become economically viable.

The largest state was the Russian Socialist Federated Soviet of Russia (RSFSR), the 'Russian Federation', which consisted of 21 autonomous republics, 67 krais, oblasts and autonomous regions, and two cities with administrative status, but they had little political significance (Nevers, 1994).

The USSR was governed by its 1977 constitution as a one-party state, with a bicameral Supreme Soviet, consisting of the Soviet (Committee) of the Union and the Soviet of Nationalities. Each union state had a unicameral Supreme Soviet, a Council of Ministers (cabinet), its own constitution, and a political and governmental structure based on the central Moscow model. Political committees were watched over and guided by parallel government and administrative ones at all levels, the latter having the power of veto.

Gorbachev's reforms began slowly and somewhat timidly, and in 1986 he urged local legislatures to take more responsibility. The following year the first experimental multicandidate elections were held in some districts. Then at a plenary session of the CPSU in May 1987 he dropped two policy bombshells in connection with his organisational reform and democratisation programme.

The first was 'perestroika', which is usually taken to mean the restructuring of a system or organisation, or in this case political, social and economic reform. The other was 'glasnost', variously translated as 'publicity' or 'openness', which encouraged public scrutiny of governmental organisations and placed an emphasis on individual citizens' rights. Both were completely contrary to the USSR's established communist doctrines and practices, as well as its secretive way of working.

Glasnost in particular loosened tongues across the USSR, and nationalist tensions and frictions began to reappear after years of repression. While this was held in check for a while by loyal communist apparatchiks – time-serving administrators and political officers whose jobs and way of life were being threatened – Soviet communism began to falter.

A special CPSU conference in June 1988 approved sweeping political reforms, with a shift of power from the CPSU to the government. In October, constitutional amendments proposed to turn the 'rubber-stamp' USSR Supreme Soviet into a full-time legislature and provide for multicandidate elections.

To the watching world the first overt signs of internal weakness and the approaching dissolution of the Soviet Union were the dramatic breaching of the Berlin Wall on 9 November 1989, followed on 6 July 1990 by the London Declaration that the Cold War between the North Atlantic Treaty Organisation (NATO) and the Warsaw Pact forces was over.

THE SOVIET UNION

The Soviet Union stemmed from the Bolshevik Revolution of November 1917 in St Petersburg, led by Lenin. Lenin withdrew Russia, which had been fighting on the Allied side, from the First World War and turned his attention to vanquishing anti-Bolshevik forces and the Russian White Army. Gaining control of the whole of the former Czarist empire took the newly formed Red Army until 1928 to complete. The Bolsheviks formed the 'All Russian Communist Party'.

Lenin died in 1924 and in 1928 was succeeded by Stalin, who became notorious for his agricultural collectivisation projects and political purges. In August 1939 Stalin, intending to remain neutral in the Second World War, signed a non-aggression pact with Nazi Germany. Caught by surprise when Hitler's armies suddenly invaded the Soviet Union in June 1941, the USSR was roughly jostled into the Second World War on the Allied side. Stalin led the Soviet people through their 'Patriotic War' to victory in Europe, which cost over 25 million Soviet lives and left Stalin in control of Eastern Europe.

At once major differences surfaced between the Western Allies and the USSR, which led to the formation of NATO in 1949 and the opposing Warsaw Pact in 1955. This split Europe into two hostile camps divided by the 'Iron Curtain'. The two major superpowers – the USSR and the United States – each developed massive nuclear armouries.

The name of the All Russian Communist Party was changed in 1952 to the Communist Party of the Soviet Union (CPSU). Stalin died in 1953, to be succeeded by Nikita Khrushchev. In a secret speech Khrushchev denounced Stalin, but was himself ousted in 1964 and replaced by Brezhnev and Kosygin in a collective leadership. Brezhnev died in 1982, and was followed in quick succession by Andropov and Chernenko, both old and ailing men. Mikhail Gorbachev came on to the scene at a time when it seemed that the government of the Soviet Union was in danger of becoming overcentralised, fossilised and smothered by the communist ethos.

In June 1987 the Supreme Soviet adopted the Law on Nationwide Discussion on Important Matters of State Life, and March the following year saw the establishment of the first Soviet Public Opinion Research Centre, based in Moscow and with branches in 25 major cities in the Soviet Union. These were enlightening, speech-freeing and ultimately destabilising moves.

Not all rushed to embrace Gorbachev's reforms. For example in early September 1988, when visiting industrial centres in Siberia, Gorbachev was heckled by workers who complained that his perestroika had failed to improve their living standards or eliminate food shortages.

DECOMMUNISATION

In June 1988 a special CPSU conference approved major political changes that involved a shift of power away from the CPSU. Totalitarism was rejected, and Gorbachev suggested that candidates for office should compete in open elections. This was in stark contrast to the customary CPSU-produced 'lists' of nominated candidates, for whom people were expected to vote without question.

At a hastily arranged plenary meeting of the CPSU central committee on 30 September, much of Gorbachev's reorganisation programme was approved. It involved a drastic reduction in the size of the central committee, many other cuts and dismissals, the closure of some departments and the bringing of others under firmer control. Both the CPSU politboro and its secretariat were reshaped.

These momentous proposals and decisions were followed by the first multicandidate elections for the new Congress of Peoples' Deputies on 26 March 1989, which resulted in a humiliating defeat for many long-serving communist leaders across the country. Most authorities agree that these elections were reasonably free and fair. A run-off was held on 14 April in about 70 constituencies where a clear majority winner had not emerged for one reason or another.

One notable victor was Boris Yeltsin, the candidate for the constituency of Moscow, who polled some 89 per cent of the votes. Yeltsin had previously been first secretary of the CPSU of Moscow, but after delivering a speech that upset Gorbachev, who had appointed him in 1985, he had been dismissed from that post in November 1987. A personality clash developed between these two leaders as Yeltsin bounced back into the limelight in flamboyant style.

The newly elected Congress of Peoples' Deputies met on 25 May, when the deputies enthralled the Soviet Union – indeed the whole world – with their televised critical speeches. Also elected was a new USSR Supreme Soviet, still in two parts – the Soviet of the Union, and the Soviet of Nationalities – each with 271 seats. Gorbachev was elected chairman of the USSR Supreme Soviet. As yet there were no individual political parties, and the first Soviet congressional 'opposition', the 'Interregional Group', did not appear until July.

In December the Lithuanian Soviet Socialist Republic (SSR) approved the multiparty system of voting, and thus the Lithuanian communists created the first split within the CPSU by voting to break away from it. In January 1990 Gorbachev dropped his opposition to a multiparty system, and reformist communists met in Moscow to produce an alternative programme, threatening to start a new, completely independent party unless political reforms were made. At the second session of the Congress of Peoples' Deputies there was pressure to end the CPSU's monopoly on power.

Early in February hundreds of thousands of people marched through the streets of Moscow demanding democratic changes, and on the 5th the CPSU central committee agreed to surrender its monopoly on power. On 11 March Lithuania unilaterally declared independence from the USSR, however the following month the USSR blockaded that country to prevent it from breaking away.

On 15 March provisions were made by the USSR Supreme Soviet for an executive president. Gorbachev was elected to that office by secret ballot, but on the annual May Day parade in Moscow the crowds in Red Square demonstrated against communist rule and against Gorbachev, who was heckled. The Russia Federation Supreme Soviet (of 1086 deputies) elected Boris Yeltsin as its president on 16 May, and the much-publicised tussle for power between Gorbachev and Yeltsin escalated. Both operated in Moscow – Gorbachev having his base at the Kremlin and Yeltsin at the Palace of Congresses, the latter known locally as the 'White House' because of its appearance – and both men exploited the TV cameras to their own advantage.

The Russian Orthodox Christmas, held on 7 January 1991, became a public holiday for the first time since Soviet rule began, and a Christmas tree once again appeared in Moscow's Red Square. The previous evening the bells of St Basil's Cathedral had rung out for the first time since 1917.

That month Gorbachev ordered the Soviet military to intervene in the republics of Lithuania and Latvia, and on 19 February Yeltsin called upon Gorbachev to resign. An all-union referendum was held on 17 March on the 'preservation of the USSR', in which 74.4 per cent of those voting indicated they were in favour of the motion. Gorbachev then tried to formulate a new agreement amongst the union states to persuade them to cooperate, but had little success as several were agitating for independence from the USSR.

Gorbachev was losing popularity – in April he was confronted with a 'no confidence' motion, but he survived. Previously (on 28 March) he had sent 5000 Soviet troops on to the streets of Moscow to try to prevent a pro-Yeltsin demonstration in favour of the establishment of an 'executive presidency', but he had withdrawn them hastily and backed away from open violence. Yeltsin's hand was strengthened in June when he became executive president of the Russian Federation Supreme Soviet. The following month the CPSU adopted a new draft programme replacing Marxist–Leninist principles with social-democratic ones.

ATTEMPTED COUP

The pace of political change in the USSR was racing ahead, to the alarm of the 'conservative' element, as they came to be called (an odd name to Western ears for diehard communists), who, fearing the loss of their authority and jobs, were reluctant to see the old order change.

At about 6 a.m. on 19 August 1991 armoured vehicles suddenly appeared on the streets of Moscow and a few other major cities in the USSR. It was announced that, 'as President Gorbachev is unable to perform his duties for health reasons', presidential power had been transferred to Vice President Gennady Yanayev, in keeping with the constitution; a state of emergency would prevail for six months in Moscow and Leningrad; and an eight-man State Council for the State of Emergency (SCSE) had been formed to run the country in this interim period. This declaration was signed by Gennady Yanayev, Prime Minister Valentin Pavlov and Oleg Baklanov, deputy chairman of the Defence Council and also in charge of the Soviet armaments industry. All were opposed to the perestroika reforms and the proposed Union Treaty – due to be signed by representatives of the Russian Federation, Byelorrusia, Kazakstan, Tajikstan and Uzbekistan – which would effectively rend asunder the USSR. The SCSE also included Marshal Dmitri Yazov, the defence minister, and Vladimir Kryuchkov, chairman of the KGB (State Security Committee).

A 'Message to the Soviet People' was broadcast in the morning, ordering local authorities to obey the SCSE's regulations or face suspension, and banning political parties, demonstrations and strikes; TV and radio broadcasts were restricted, and only a few 'conservative' newspapers and *Izvestiya* (the organ of the CPSU) were allowed to be published. A statement by Anatoly Lukyanov, chairman of the USSR Supreme Soviet, saying there would be further discussions on the Union Treaty, was distributed by Tass. The timing of the coup was intended to preempt the signing of the Union Treaty. The motivating force behind the coup was said to be Yanayov, of whom Gorbachev was reputed to have said, when he appointed him in 1990, 'I want someone around me I can trust'.

In retrospect pundits said that signs of an imminent coup had been more than obvious, so it should have been expected, but certainly most of the top and intermediate level Soviet leaders had been taken by surprise. The plotters had been very circumspect but, as it later turned out, they had been neither thorough nor far-reaching.

One of those most surprised had been Gorbachev, who had been holidaying with his family near Sevastapol in the Crimea since 4 August, prior to which he had held a summit meeting with US President George Bush and signed an agreement on the reduction of nuclear arms. Gorbachev had been expected to return to Moscow by the 20th to sign the Union Treaty. On the evening prior to the coup a delegation had unexpectedly visited Gorbachev to present him with an ultimatum. Gorbachev, whose telephonic communications with Moscow had been severed, had been alone but for a small bodyguard. The delegation had included Oleg Baklanov, Yuri Plekhanov (a KGB chief), General Valentin Varennikov (commander of the Soviet Ground Forces) and Valery Boldin (Gorbachev's personal chief-of-staff). The delegation had demanded that he sign their state of emergency declaration and stand down, falsely claiming that an armed revolt was in progress in Moscow. When Gorbachev refused the delegation had placed him under arrest, but his bodyguards had remained loyal and he had been left alone for the time being, although divorced from events in Moscow. He may have pondered on the fate of a predecessor, Nikita Khrushchev, who had also tried to change the course of events in the USSR and had been arrested while on holiday – and deposed.

In Moscow the man who came to the fore to oppose this coup was Boris Yeltsin, president of the Russian Federation. This surprised many because of his apparent animosity towards Gorbachev. Yeltsin, like Gorbachev, had been out of Moscow when the coup was launched, but sufficiently close to reach the White House by about 11 a.m., just as the armoured vehicles had pulled up outside. Yeltsin had rushed towards the the vehicles and stood dramatically on one of them to harangue the crowd, in full focus of the TV cameras. Yeltsin had demanded the reinstatement of the Gorbachev government and called upon the armed forces in Moscow to obey him. The Soviet armoured commander had been won over and had refused to attack Yeltsin's supporters. The plotters' first mistake had been to fail to arrest Yeltsin, an obvious and dangerous opponent of any reversion to the *status quo*, but perhaps they had not been able to find him in time.

On the 20th, a huge number of demonstrators amassed around the White House – which had become a 'resistance centre' – to protect it from attack. Yeltsin called for a general strike, but this was only indifferently responded to, especially in Moscow where the people, unless very politically motivated, seemed largely indifferent to these events and many simply became curious spectators of whatever action was in progress. Marshal Dmitri Yazov, the defence minister, ordered General Leonid Zoltov, commander of the Soviet troops in Moscow, to send two divisions into the city. Zoltov hesitantly obeyed, but was given no positive orders as to what the troops were actually supposed to do.

More armoured vehicles arrived outside the White House, but those manning them refused to fire on Soviet citizens and seemed to be in support of Yeltsin. Likewise the Alpha KGB antiterrorist group refused an SCSE order to storm the building. In the evening Yeltsin declared himself to be in command of all Soviet security forces in Russian Federation territory, and would remain so until the restoration of constitutional rule. In Leningrad, resistance to the SCSE was organised by the mayor of the city in opposition to its military commander.

Crowds outside the White House were addressed by Yelena Bonner (a human-rights campaigner and widow of Andrei Sakharov), Eduard Shevardnadze (a former foreign minister) and other prominent personalities. Defying the curfew, the crowds remained, built barricades and formed 'defence units'. The White House itself was held by armed KGB units and police loyal to Yeltsin. Two men were crushed to death by tanks travelling along the Moscow ringroad towards the White House, but a tank attack did not materialise. General Pavel Grachev, a paratroop commander, disobeyed the SCSE's order for his division to attack the White House, and instead withdrew from the city.

Yanayev had been counting on a swift, almost silent victory, so that Lukyanov would be able to rubber-stamp the change of regime during the USSR Supreme Soviet meeting scheduled for 26 August. However, on the morning of the 21st the Defence Ministry Collegium decided to withdraw all troops from Moscow. Hence the coup collapsed and the SCSE members disappeared from their Kremlin stronghold. This victory had largely been due to the efforts of Yeltsin, but he had his price, and the death knell of Soviet communist rule rang out over the USSR. Yeltsin not only defeated the communist hardliners, but also took over from them.

Considerable concern had been shown in this crisis by certain Western leaders, who fondly regarded Gorbachev as the Soviet leader who had ended the Cold War. They had refused to recognise the SCSE as they dreaded the USSR slipping back under tight communist control. President Bush had cut short his own vacation and returned to Washington to telephone Yeltsin, the man he had once refused to meet. Bush had pledged his support and threatened to end all economic aid to the Soviet Union if the coup succeeded. Other Western leaders had also rushed back to their offices from vacation in a similar mood, causing the Moscow crisis to be dubbed 'The day the world was looking the other way'. The plotters had known that August is an international vacation month for statesmen and that foreign affairs would have been put on hold. When the coup collapsed Yeltsin became a Western democratic hero.

Gorbachev returned to Moscow in the evening of the 21st, and an investigation into the coup began. Meanwhile Yeltsin, who had been supported throughout by Ruslan Khasbulatov, acting chairman (speaker) of the Russian Federation Supreme Soviet, and General Aleksandr Rutskoi, its vice president, had been awarded additional powers of dismissal by that body, which strengthened his hand when he met Gorbachev. Seemingly dazed by his traumatic experience, Gorbachev agreed that he or Yeltsin would take over the other's responsibilities should a similar crisis take place in the future. Yeltsin collected more power as his reward, and jurisdiction over all Union State enterprises and natural resources was transferred to him as its president, as were governmental communications.

Those chairmen of regional Soviets who had supported the coup or sat on the fence were removed, and 'presidential representatives' (virtually governors) were appointed to replace the executive committees in the Soviet republics. Yeltsin formally announced that he had taken control of all Soviet armed forces and their assets, excluding nuclear ones, and banned CPSU activities. Publications that had supported the coup were also banned.

At a press conference on the 22nd Gorbachev voiced his support of the CPSU, but two days later he reversed his position and resigned from his post as CPSU secretary general, saying it should dissolve itself. Yeltsin's supporters forced the USSR Council of Ministers to resign after a no confidence motion. Gorbachev then formed an interim committee to manage the economy, which included several of Yeltsin's nominees. More ministerial responsibility and two of the main Soviet banks were transferred over to the Russian Federation. Yeltsin's star was beginning to eclipse that of Gorbachev.

General Yevgeny Shaposhnikov, the air force commander, was appointed defence minister in place of the dismissed Dmitri Yazov, and General Grachev, the paratroop commander, was appointed deputy defence minister (later, in May 1992, he was promoted to defence minister). At a session of the Supreme Soviet on 26 August Gorbachev admitted he had been wrong to appoint 'conservatives' to head organisations that controlled the security forces. On the 29th the CPSU's activities in the USSR were suspended by the Supreme Soviet. By the end of the month 14 people had been charged with treason and placed in detention.

So ended the plans of the small group of 'conservative' plotters, hardliners that opposed the activities of the 'radicals', led by Gorbachev. Quite unexpectedly they had run head-on into another radical, the ambitious Yeltsin, who had held most of the cards and played them in a shrewd and calculating manner. It had been a scanty, ill-prepared plot, and seemingly its perpetrators had taken for granted the support of the many key figures upon whom its ultimate fate rested, rather than sounding them out beforehand. The plotters had also been taken by surprise by the Western leaders' close interest in the possible change of Soviet government.

Another major reason for the failure of the coup was the recent growth of media freedom in the USSR and the increased use of fax machines and computers, which contributed to the evasion of media restrictions. The findings of the investigation into the August 1991 coup attempt were made known in January 1992, and resulted in the charge of treason being dropped against most of the accused. No evidence was found to incriminate Gorbachev, but it was noted that his actions might have led the conspirators to think they could count on his support.

COMMONWEALTH OF INDEPENDENT STATES

The signing of the oft redrafted Union Treaty was briefly postponed, but the problem would not go away. By the end of August a majority of the republics of the USSR had declared their independence, notably Lithuania (on 11 March 1990), Estonia (on 20 August) and Latvia (on 21 August), the three so-called 'Baltic States'. This seemingly uncontrolled dissolution brought the realisation that there was an urgent need to create common economic structures.

The Congress of Peoples' Deputies met on 2–6 September to consider the future, and after a heated discussion and pressure from Gorbachev it virtually voted itself out of existence. It was replaced by a new State Council, consisting of those heads of republics who were prepared to sign the new Union Treaty; a Supreme Soviet, with the right to alter the constitution; and an Inter-State Economic Committee. Gorbachev also established a Political Consultative Council.

Yeltsin had wanted to form a Union Treaty of independent states, linked in some loose way with the Russian Federation, and one of his first proposals was that it should consist of 'Russia', the three Baltic states, Belarus (Byelorrusia) and Ukraine to form a Slavic bloc to solidify the Slav position in Europe. He also wanted to shed what he considered to be the burdensome Asian Muslim republics. But the Baltic states would not join, and other problems arose when the Central Asian republics refused to be abandoned, insisting on becoming members. Then Ukraine opted out. Gorbachev still wanted a substantial rump that could operate influentially in Europe and internationally.

In November the Soviet Foreign Ministry was reorganised and renamed the Ministry of External Affairs. On the 19th Eduard Shevardnadze was reappointed as external affairs minister.

Meanwhile the pace of dissolution quickened, and on 8 December 1991 the 'Minsk Declaration' was signed, stating that the Soviet Union was defunct and a Commonwealth of Independent States (CIS) would be established, open to all Union republics. On the 21st, in Alma Ata (Kazakstan) eleven former Soviet republics joined the CIS in a loose alliance, without any central governing bodies. Assurance was given to the international community that single control would be maintained over nuclear weapons, and that former Soviet Union treaty obligations and agreements would be respected.

The Russian Federation took over many of the former Soviet Union's functions, but there were many areas of uncertainty and disputes arose between states over economic issues and control of the armed forces. The Russian Federation assumed the Soviet Union's place in the United Nations forum and occupied its permanent seat on the Security Council; and the CIS members began to be accepted as individual UN members.

On 25 December 1991, Gorbachev resigned as president of the Soviet Union and handed over the nuclear codes to Yeltsin, president of the Russian Federation, then consisting of about 13.6 million square miles of terrain with a population of about 149 million people. The Soviet military chose to back the CIS project, so Yeltsin won his struggle in Moscow for total control and Gorbachev was shouldered aside.

However Gorbachev won praise from Western leaders for his achievements during the previous six years – that is, ridding the USSR of Communist central power and bringing about the dissolution of the once powerful and aggressive superpower, much to their secret satisfaction. Gorbachev's popularity within the former USSR declined accordingly.

Yeltsin was faced with massive problems as he had to dismantle the overcentralised Soviet structure, reform the economy and create a new democratic system on the Western pattern. At that time Yeltsin enjoyed wide popular support, but sections of the old, dispossessed communist elite, the so-called 'conservatives', were reluctant to cooperate.

In January 1992 Yeltsin launched a programme to create a basis for the market economy within 500 days, lift price restrictions, reduce central government expenditure and transfer state enterprises into private ownership, but this programme was adversely affected by the collapse of the Warsaw Pact Treaty countries and Soviet trading agreements. He also had economic arguments with CIS members. He had strategic problems too. He failed to establish a commonwealth defence force, nor could he decide whether to defend just the boundaries of the Russian Federation, or to extend his military reach to cover the extreme boundaries of the CIS.

Yeltsin's first mistake, according to some analysts, was neglecting to form his own political party, which would have provided him with a firm political base. Instead he said he would remain above party politics. In the Congress of Peoples' Deputies he was faced with increasing opposition. The loose power groupings of the 1989 election had fallen apart. In June his opponents formed the Civic Union. He also failed to make personnel changes within the bureaucracy, which neither liked nor understood the market economy; and hesitated to reorganise the political structure, putting off a confrontation for as long as possible, thus allowing resistance to his programmes to mount.

This stalemate in Moscow enabled regions within the Russian Federation to wrest more powers for themselves, making it increasingly difficult for Yeltsin to enforce his writ. His supporting reformists argued that the stringent International Monetary

Fund (IMF) conditions should be rigidly enforced so that further loans and aid could be obtained from Western sources, but this met opposition from a section of the population that was harassed by galloping inflation, rising prices and increasing lawlessness in Moscow. In addition there was a growing sense of humiliation and resentment at the West's blatant patronage.

Differences began to surface between the trio who had been mainly responsible for the collapse of the August 1991 coup attempt, when Ruslan Khasbulatov supported Aleksandr Rutskoi's criticism of Yeltsin's policies, which resulted in calls for Yeltsin's resignation. Yeltsin was rapidly losing his popularity. On 9 February in Moscow, rival groups of demonstrators amassed outside the White House in support of Yeltsin, and outside the Kremlin against him.

On 31 March 1992 the Russian Federation Treaty was signed by 18 of the 20 autonomous republics (Nevers, 1994). In May Yeltsin issued a decree establishing the Russian Federation armed forces, with himself as commander-in-chief. The forces not only embraced all the military within the Federation, but also included former USSR military personnel still deployed in other CIS republics.

Yeltsin continued to encounter hostility within the Congress of Peoples' Deputies, but in July the 'Democratic Choice', a grouping of some 40 political parties, was formed to support him against the oppositional Civic Union. That month the Constitutional Court formally banned the CPSU and the Supreme Soviet took control of *Izvestiya* – the former CPSU periodical, which had been banned for supporting the attempted August coup – and it began to publish again under a new editor.

In October there were rumours and warnings of an impending coup against Yeltsin, owing to his unpopular reforms and dictatorial manner, but nothing came of it. The following month Yeltsin again met opposition in the Congress of Peoples' Deputies when he tried to have Acting Prime Minister Yegor Gaidar confirmed in his post. Congress refused, and Yeltsin reluctantly accepted Viktor Chernomyrdin instead, under the mistaken belief he would slow down the rate of economic reform. Chernomyrdin had formerly been in charge of the Soviet gas industry.

By February 1993 Yeltsin was locked in dispute with his former close colleague, Ruslan Khasbulatov, over whether ultimate power in the Russian Federation lay with the presidency or the legislature. The Western media viewed this struggle in black and white terms of Yeltsin being the enlightened reformist leader, a radical who was introducing a market economy and Western-style democracy despite the difficulties this entailed; while those who opposed him were regarded as discontented 'conservatives', that is, old-time communists still longing for a return to the old way of life. This tussle between Yeltsin and Khasbulatov dragged on.

A federation-wide referendum was held on 25 April, in which Yeltsin gained support for his leadership and endorsement for his reforms, but he did not take immediate advantage of this to make key personnel changes. He continued to rule by decree, while arguments raged on over the proposed new constitution.

Politically motivated mob violence broke out on the streets of Moscow on May Day 1993 for the first time since the August 1991 crisis, and it was feared that this would be repeated, and escalate, on the 9th, which was Soviet Victory in Europe Day. However, although some 40 000 people were allowed into Red Square, the demonstration was a peaceful one.

The month of June was dominated by a constitutional conference, which dragged on from the 5th to the 16th and terminated without producing a draft constitution. Rutskoi, vice president of the Russian Federation, and others continued to make allegations of corruption against Yeltsin. On the 15th Yegor Gaidar formed the 'Democratic Bloc of Reformist Forces' party, which had a pro-Yeltsin stance. Yeltsin suspended Rutskoi on September, but this was vetoed by Congress.

Eventually, on 21 September Yeltsin issued his own version of the new constitution, which he called 'On Constitutional Reform'. He dissolved the Congress of Peoples' Deputies and its Supreme Soviet because they had consistently blocked his economic and constitutional reforms, promising new elections in December. At once Khasbulatov, chairman of the Supreme Soviet, demanded that armed service personnel should disobey all orders from Yeltsin, but Pavel Grachev (now a marshal) and other senior generals declared their loyalty to Yeltsin, who had been assiduously lobbying them for some time. Rutskoi denounced Yeltsin's decrees, claiming they were unconstitutional, and convened an emergency meeting of the 'dismissed' Congress of Peoples' Deputies. On the 24th they voted to impeach

Yeltsin and appointed Rutskoi as president of the Russian Federation. Rutskoi immediately attempted to dismiss ministers and replace them with his political allies. Once again Western leaders openly voiced their support of Yeltsin.

SIEGE OF THE WHITE HOUSE

Active confrontation suddenly erupted in Moscow, this time with Yeltsin in the Kremlin and his opponents in the White House. The 'dismissed' Congress Members and their supporters had taken over the buildings and were insisting that the Congress was the legal government. On the 22nd all telephonic communications with the White House were severed, and two days later the electricity and water supplies were cut off. From the 21st, the day Congress had voted to assume control of the media, crowds milled around the White House, some individuals being armed with light weapons.

On the 23rd some associates of Vladislav Achalov, who on the 21st, along with several others, had been elevated to ministerial positions by the 'dismissed' Congress, launched an attack on the military headquarters of the CIS, which reputedly possessed communications equipment capable of reaching all parts of the former USSR. Two people were killed in this incident, which resulted in Federation troops being authorised to open fire if similar attempts were made to take over government buildings. Offers to negotiate were made, but failed when Khasbulatov rejected any compromise with Yeltsin.

On the 26th large demonstrations took place outside the White House in support of the 'rebels'. Rutskoi boasted that 'We will fight to the last cartridge', while his colleague, Khasbulatov, added that if necessary his supporters were prepared to defend it 'for a whole year at least' (Tass). The following day the White House was sealed off by some 2000 troops. In clashes during the night of 28–29 September a senior police officer died when he was pushed under moving vehicles by the mob.

General Albert Makashov – a member of the National Salvation Front, which had a membership of 4000 and was led by Ilya Konstantinov – organised the defence of the White House against anticipated government assaults, and boasted he had sufficient ammunition to repel all attackers. The 'dismissed'

Supreme Soviet claimed that 527 deputies were present in the White House and were determined to remain there, but a Yeltsin spokesman claimed they numbered barely 150.

In general the Federation regions had been supportive of Yeltsin, but a Moscow meeting of representatives from 68 of the 89 regions and republics called for an end to the siege of the White House, implying that if the crisis was not resolved soon they might withhold taxes, and oil and gas supplies.

After a 13-day stand-off, on 3 October up to 10 000 demonstrators, some with firearms, repeatedly clashed with the police in Moscow, and by late afternoon had broken through the military cordon around the White House. Outside – buoyed up by reports of Yeltsin's failure to regain complete control of all the streets in central Moscow – Rutskoi sabre-rattled and urged the crowds to form into units, saying they would be given arms and telling them to seize the mayor's office and then the Ostankino, the TV complex. Khasbulatov urged that 'Today we must take the Kremlin'. Yeltsin declared a state of emergency in Moscow.

Demonstrators did seize the office of the mayor of Moscow (Yuri Luzhkov), while Yegor Gaidar, Yeltsin's first deputy prime minister and economics minister, urged Muscovites to rally to Yeltsin, but there were few, if any, popular demonstrations for either side, those involved in the mob tactics being politically motivated. Ordinary Moscow citizens seemed content just to stand and watch the unfolding events from the Kalinin Bridge across the Moskva river, which gave them a splendid view of the area in front of the White House.

That night an attack was launched on the Ostankino by some 300 men of the National Salvation Front militia, led by Ilya Konstantinov. In the gun battle that ensued, it was later reported, '62 people were killed and over 400 injured' (Tass). However the attempted seizure was unsuccessful, although TV broadcasting was interrupted for a few hours.

Very early the next day Rutskoi requested talks with Yeltsin, but the government was still demanding unconditional surrender. In any case, by this time Yeltsin's mind was made up, and at 7 a.m. tanks opened fire on the embattled White House, whose facade was soon blackened by gunpowder. Many millions of TV viewers watched as the bombardment continued until about noon, when it was claimed that Yeltsin's troops had seized the first four floors of the building. Fighting in the White

House continued during the afternoon, but in the evening the 'rebel' leaders surrendered. They were led from the burning building with their hands up and taken to the nearby high-security Lefortovo prison. Yeltsin had ordered his troops to fire on Russian citizens, and they had obeyed. Once again Yeltsin emerged as the victor in Moscow over the nationalists and communists. Or at least that was the official picture.

A telephone poll conducted by the Public Opinion Foundation reported on the 4th that 72 per cent had sided with Yeltsin, and only 6 per cent favoured the rebels. A later poll, released on the 7th, showed that 40 per cent thought Rutskoi was to blame, while 40 per cent thought that both Yeltsin and Rutskoi were equally to blame.

But it was not the simple and smoothly run operation that the Russian public, and the world at large, was given to understand. It appears that initially Yeltsin was hesitant, confused and indecisive, and did not recover his confidence until the arrival in the Kremlin of Mikhail Poltoranin, head of the Federal Information Centre, and Gennady Burbulis, a close associate, who took charge and began to take decisive action. Later 'leaks' seemed to confirm this picture.

On the 6th Marshal Grachev stated that 1300 troops from various units had been despatched to Moscow for the assault on the White House. Critics noted that many of these troops had been attached to the Interior Ministry, the Security Service Ministry and the presidential administration, and that very few had been 'army'. Later (on the 18th) General Dmitri Volkogonov, Yeltsin's senior military adviser, admitted that Yeltsin had had difficulty persuading Grachev to agree to mount a military assault, and that Nicolai Golushko, head of the Security Service Ministry, had been reluctant to take part in the assault.

On the 7th Yeltsin suspended the Constitutional Court, which he blamed for taking hasty decisions that had 'brought the country to the brink of civil war' (*Pravda*). The following day Marshal Grachev stated, being somewhat 'economical with the truth', that the military leadership had been persuaded to act decisively against the 'rebels'. It was said that Grachev felt humiliated when the 'dismissed' Congress appointed Vladislav Achalov as defence minister in his stead. The truth seemed to be that military support for Yeltsin had been rather uncertain and limited, and at times there had been hesitation, but none had defected to the 'rebels'.

It was reported on 15 October that 1452 people had been detained, of whom 200 were still being held, and that charges of 'organising disorder' had been brought against Rutskoi, Khasbulatov, Achalov and two others that had been raised to ministerial office by the 'dismissed' Congress. On the 20th the Russian Ministry of Health reported that 145 people had been killed and 240 injured in the 'revolt', some of whom had been civilian 'onlookers' (Tass).

A NEW FEDERAL ASSEMBLY

To bring an end to the long, confused argument, Yeltsin published his own version of the new constitution on 9 November 1993 and called for elections to be held. Thirteen political parties and groups were registered and eight were rejected. One of the accepted parties was 'Russia's Choice', led by Yegor Gaidar. Under the controversial new constitution the election took place on 12 December for a Federal Assembly of two chambers: the 178-member Federal Council (upper house), to which each of Russia's regions and republics elected two deputies; and the 450-seat State Duma (lower house), in which half the deputies were elected by single-member constituencies and half by proportional representation on a party basis.

The results were not as had been expected – although the 'reformers' held the middle ground, extreme right-wing and left-wing parties made considerable gains. For example the Liberal Democratic Party, led by the unpredictable right-wing Vladimir Zhirinovsky, won 59 seats, more than any other party, with Russia's Choice coming second with 40 seats. Watching Western leaders were horrified and disappointed, as it seemed to them that a large section of the Russian people were reluctant to accept change. They overlooked the fact that the Russians were not enjoying the 'non-superpower' status the West was patronisingly trying to force on them.

In January 1994 Yeltsin formed a smaller cabinet, a coalition of disparate views. Viktor Chernomyrdin remained prime minister, Pavel Grachev defence minister and Andrei Kozyrev foreign affairs minister. Yegor Gaidar resigned from the cabinet to concentrate on building up his Russia's Choice party, as did Boris Fedorov, who in April formed the 'Liberal Democratic Union', which claimed 39 seats in the State Duma. Yeltsin decreed that the 'power ministries' – that is Interior, Defence and Foreign Affairs – would be directly subordinate to himself. There remained in the State Duma a hardline rump of old 'conservatives', implacably hostile to Yeltsin's reforms.

The introduction of the market economy into Russia brought with it the ills that have dogged capitalism everywhere, including unemployment, poverty, crime and corruption. Mafia gangs and criminal syndicates began to operate in Moscow. Expensive Western cars could be seen in the streets of Moscow, as could beggars. Moscow retained an air of nervous uncertainty, both politically and economically, as few of the anticipated, glittering benefits of capitalism were filtering down to the Russian in the street.

On 17 October 1994 an investigative journalist, Dmitri Kholodov, was killed by an explosion in his Moscow office. As he had been investigating high-level military corruption the finger of suspicion pointed to military involvement. Retention of the unpopular Marshal Grachev as defence minister led the opposition to sneer that Yeltsin was being kept in power by military bayonets. By this time Yeltsin's popularity was at a low ebb.

On 10 July 1995 Yeltsin was struck down by a heart attack and was away from his office for over a month. Rumours abounded that he was near to death and that a coup was imminent. Viktor Chernomyrdin, former boss of the Soviet gas industry and a less charismatic man than Yeltsin, was heralded as his most likely replacement. Yeltsin shakily survived in office and in October attended the 50th anniversary meeting of the UN in New York. There he rejected American insistence that Russian peacekeeping troops in Bosnia be placed under NATO (meaning US) command, and the US-sponsored Partnership for Peace, which would have brought Western troops right up to the Russian border.

Yeltsin's conduct in New York and elsewhere led the world to speculate that his 'illness' was alcohol-related. On his return to Russia he assumed direct control over the Foreign Affairs Ministry, having previously pushed Andrei Kozyrev aside, but was soon hospitalised again. Commentators speculated that the seeds of a resumption of the Cold War were being planted. For the remainder of 1995 Russian foreign policy unfolded unsteadily under Yeltsin's helmsmanship.

* * *

This brief resumé of a few major events in the USSR and the Russian Federation forms the backcloth to the following account of the struggle for national independence in the Trans-Caucasus republics of Armenia, Azerbaijan and Georgia, as well as the North Caucasus autonomous republic of Ingush-Chechenya's fight to free itself from the Russian Federation.

2 Armenia and Azerbaijan

The Battle for Baku, capital of the Soviet Socialist Republic of Azerbaijan took place in January 1990 after an Azeri cleansing pogrom had been mounted against resident Armenians. After his efforts had failed to reconcile the Armenians and Azeris, who had been in active confrontation with each other for many months, President Gorbachev reluctantly decided to mobilise the military against these Soviet citizens and authorised the dispatch of Soviet armed forces to that city. There had been over 200 000 Armenians in Baku, according to the 1989 census, but owing to the hostilities many had since left. Nonetheless a few thousand remained. The main reason for this ongoing hostility was the disputed sovereignty of the autonomous oblast of Nagorno-Karabakh, an enclave with an Armenian majority population but situated within Azerbaijan.

Azeri anger had been rising in Baku since the beginning of the month, when rowdy demonstrations began, ostensibly because the unpopular leaders of the Azerbaijan Supreme Soviet had acquiesced to the USSR's decision to retain responsibility for Nagorno-Karabakh, even though sovereignty of it had been formally restored to the Republic of Azerbaijan in November 1989.

This opposition to the Azerbaijan Supreme Soviet had been sparked off by the Azerbaijan Popular Front (APF), a loose coalition of nationalist and Islamic opposition groups that had been formed in July 1989. Its varying agendas ranged from replacing the Azerbaijan Supreme Soviet and gaining independence from the USSR, to union with Iran. Initially the APF had called for the economic independence of Azerbaijan, political pluralism and the removal of old-style leaders. There were probably about 30 000 Azeri exiles in Baku, most of whom had been ejected from Armenia the previous year; many were homeless and unemployed. These Azeris hurried to support the APF, which was now calling upon the Azerbaijani authorities either to reassert sovereignty over Nagorno-Karabakh, or to resign.

On the 13th a meeting held by the APF ended acrimoniously, whereupon some of the leaders of its constituent groups rushed out on to the streets of Baku to join the '70 000 demonstrators' in the city centre (Tass). Violent attacks on resident Armenians suddenly erupted – blame for this was later mainly ascribed to homeless Azeri exiles, who had begun forcibly to take over Armenian residences, ejecting their occupants. The fury of the mob increased as a rumour spread that an Armenian had attacked two Azeris who had come to remove him from his apartment, killing one with an axe.

The violence gathered momentum and developed into what amounted to an attempt at ethnic cleansing, as it was generally Azeris attacking Armenians, some of whom were killed and many others injured. Armenian homes were burnt, destroyed or looted. One source (*Daily Telegraph*) reported eye-witness accounts of people being thrown from roofs and upper-storey windows, and of others being burnt to death. The frenzy took almost three days to burn itself out.

The local security forces allegedly did little to try to curb the violence, although some did their best to shelter Armenians in their barracks and government establishments, and to aid pancistricker, fleeing Armenians, ferrying many of them across the Caspian Sea to Krasnovodsk in the Republic of Turkmenistan. Whenever they could, fleeing Armenians escaped by land into the Republic of Armenia. Few Armenians remained at large in Baku. This explosion of ethnic hatred exacerbated intercommunal friction in other parts of the Azerbaijan and Armenian republics.

On the 14th President Gorbachev, perplexed by his vexatious Baltic republics' 'problem' and describing the Azerbaijani militants as 'rabble wanting to halt the democratic reforms' (*Pravda*), sent 6000 MVD troops (internal security personnel) to supplement the 5000 already in Azerbaijan, plus 5000 army personnel. This decision was very controversial within the Kremlin as the armed forces might have to open fire on Soviet citizens. Military reinforcements began to land at two military airbases in Azerbaijan – Yevlak and Gyandzha, both well over 100 miles from Baku – only to find that they were hemmed in by protesting Azerbaijani militants and that the routes into Baku were barred by a series of roadblocks.

As soon as the Soviet military reinforcements were ordered to Baku the political atmosphere changed, and the Azeri opposition groups began to demand the withdrawal of all Soviet forces from the republic. Rowdy militants harassed these in the

Azerbaijan Supreme Soviet buildings in the centre of the city – Abdul Rahman Vezirov, the first secretary, a dedicated Moscow man and not a native of Trans-Caucasia, had already decamped on the 12th. Azeri opposition groups began to form armed resistance militias, with the National Defence Committee (NDC) taking the lead.

On the 17th Soviet troops at the two airbases brushed aside the Azeri blockade and advanced towards Baku, using armoured vehicles to crash through roadblocks and helicopters to lift troops over them, only to be halted on the outskirts of the city by more barricades. The troops had been given permission to open fire, and had already done so at a place called Shamkor, where armed Azeris had tried to seize some of their armoured vehicles. This became known as the 'Shamkor Incident'.

A Soviet Ministry of Interior communiqué stated on the 18th that the death toll in Baku had reached 66, that 220 people had been injured, including 26 police and 31 soldiers, that over 200 homes had either been set on fire or ransacked, and that the rebels had made 66 raids on government armouries and buildings. It claimed the army had made over 100 arrests.

Marshal Dmitri Yazov, the Soviet defence minister, as a reinforcing gesture ordered the call-up of military reservists to guard roads and military bases in the Trans-Caucasus, to open the railway line into Armenia, and to strengthen detachments in regions bordering Turkey and Iran. Demonstrators in Baku's central square continued to demand the withdrawal of all Soviet troops and the resignation of the Azerbaijan Supreme Soviet. Some Azeris tried to offer expressions of regret and sympathy for what had happened to the Armenians, but local Azeri newspapers refused to publish their words and insisted their regret should instead be directed at Azeris killed by Armenian gunmen. Foreign journalists were barred from Baku, and although the few official Soviet ones reported activities as they saw them, as far as their editors would allow, there was a dearth of factual news, the vacuum being filled by wild, unsubstantiated rumours.

Azeri militants seized the Baku TV station, which for a short time enabled them to broadcast their version of events and to appeal for the sympathy and help of adjacent Soviet republics and foreign countries, but they were silenced when the station's power plant was blown up. Later the station was surrounded by Soviet troops, who were forbidden to enter. The CPSU-controlled radio station continued to broadcast and local newspapers were still published. As the Soviet military action progressed, the APF began to raid government armouries to obtain weapons for its fledgeling militias. It also took over as many government buildings and offices as possible, ejecting the occupants.

On the 19th Gorbachev declared a state of emergency in Baku. Moving in by land and sea, Soviet troops forced their way into the city, cleared the streets and pushed back the impromptu Azeri militias. By the 21st they were in control of much of the central area and resistance lapsed into sullen civil disobedience. It was officially stated that 83 people had been killed in this phase of the fighting (*Pravda*), but outraged Azeri nationalists insisted that their death toll exceeded 600. A rumour spread like wildfire that, in order to conceal the casualty rate, the Soviet military was dumping bodies into the Caspian Sea at night.

Defying the ban on rallies and demonstrations under the emergency regulations, huge funeral processions were held in Baku on the 22nd for about 60 of the dead, many of whom were buried in a common grave. It was claimed that over '75 000 people took to the streets to mourn their Martyrs killed by Soviet soldiers' (Tass). A general strike was declared by the APF, which brought things to a standstill in Baku and newspapers ceased to publish.

About 50 Azeri ships, oil tankers and oil barges began a blockade of Baku port, their leaders threatening to destroy oil-rig terminals and to sink vessels to stop navigation unless all Soviet troops were withdrawn. A flotilla of small craft stopped two Soviet ships carrying Russian families – also anxious to quit Baku in a hurry by crossing the Caspian Sea – and searched them for 'Azerbaijan bodies': none were found. The port blockade continued.

The Communist Party leaders in Baku tried to redeem themselves by changing tack and openly identifying with the mood of the people. In an emergency session of the Azerbaijan Supreme Soviet, President Elmira Kafarova denounced the Soviet military action and declared a three-day period of mourning. He dismissed the absent first secretary and threatened that unless the Soviet troops withdrew within 48 hours, he would call for a referendum on secession from the USSR. Nonetheless the Azerbaijan Communist Party was, ousted from its offices by APF militants. Increasing support was given by apparatchiks for the NDC militias, and many disillusioned Azeri Communist Party members renounced their membership as the blossoming spirit of nationalism overcame communist loyalty. It was later admitted that over 20 000 party members in Baku had publicly destroyed their membership cards.

On the evening of 23 January the Soviet military authorities arrested over 40 key members of the APF and raided the offices of the NDC, where they severed telephone lines and took away communication equipment. More resistance leaders were detained the following day, it being suspected that Gorbachev wanted the major hardliners out of the way so that he could come to an arrangement with the moderates. The strike continued to paralyse Baku, and its port remained blockaded.

On the evening of the 24th Soviet armed forces suddenly launched a bombardment by tanks, guns and naval craft on the blockading vessels. This lasted some 40 minutes, sinking some craft and scattering many others. The blockade of Baku port was lifted, but no details of shipping losses were released. Encouraged, the Azerbaijan Supreme Soviet tried to reassume control, and at a meeting of its central committee elected Ayaz Mutalibov, a technocrat and engineer, as first secretary, but Baku remained strikebound.

The use of Soviet military force became a contentious issue in Moscow, and on 26 January Marshal Yazov, at a press conference in Baku, stated that the Kremlin authorities had ordered military intervention in Azerbaijan in order to preempt a meeting of the APF, scheduled for the 20th, at which its leaders would have announced they had seized power. Yazov demanded the annihilation of the APF. Later this was contradicted by the Soviet foreign minister, Eduard Shevardnadze, who insisted the object of sending military forces to Baku had not been to stifle dissent, but to end the bloodshed (*Pravda*). A military spokesman claimed that an APF attempt to take over the prisons and certain government buildings had been thwarted.

The following day the APF offered the Kremlin a peace pact (over the head of the Azerbaijan Supreme Soviet), saying it would guarantee civil order in Baku. This, its first direct contact with the Moscow authorities, was ignored. On the 30th the military made another 100 arrests in Baku, after which the APF went underground and an uneasy calm settled on the city, now under Soviet military occupation.

The Battle for Baku had an unsettling effect on the Soviet government in Moscow as it had given credence and authority to the APF, previously a very shadowy organisation that merely wanted local autonomy and economic freedom within the USSR. Now it had an armed militia, was in control of street mobs and was demanding complete independence. The war between Armenia and Azerbaijan, downplayed for so long, had become an inescapable, embarrassing fact of life. The Soviet military authorities had disliked this Baku mission, having the unspoken fear, influenced by the recent Romanian revolution, that soldiers might refuse to fire on their own people, and that officers might become involved in political dialogue with dissidents. Kremlin hardliners regarded the Battle for Baku as a triumph, and a lesson to other far-flung republics that might be entertaining separatist thoughts. To others it brought a cold realisation of the limits of effective Soviet central power. Gorbachev was criticised for taking military action so hurriedly and without first consulting the Azerbaijan Communist Party leadership, which was contrary to his perestroika doctrine of solving political problems by political means.

The Soviets admitted that during January over 200 people had been killed in Armenian–Azeri hostilities in the region, the majority in Baku. In Baku the Azerbaijan Supreme Soviet blamed the APF for the violence against the Armenians, and for attempting to seize power by mob violence, while the APF blamed the Azerbaijan Supreme Soviet for colluding with the KGB, claiming it had imported rabble-rousers to incite unrest. Azerbaijani militants equated the Battle for Baku of January 1990 with the Soviet invasion of Hungary of 1956.

TRANS-CAUCASUS

The expression Trans-Caucasus, or Trans-Caucasia, has come to include the three republics of Armenia, Azerbaijan and Georgia, which lie south of the diagonal Caucasus Mountain range on the isthmus between the Black Sea and the Caspian Sea. Without going too far back into the mists of antiquity, Islam was brought to the region in the eleventh century by the Seljuk Turks, the inhabitants previously having been predominantly Christian or Zoroastrian. In the eastern part, on the Caspian seaboard, the Turkic-speaking peoples came to be variously referred to as Turks, Tartars and eventually Circassian Muslims. In the twelfth century they began to fall under Persian influence and adopted the Persian Shia form of Islam. Persia divided its Trans-Caucasian territory into 'khanates', ruled either by hereditary khans or appointed governors.

To the west of this Persian-influenced sector lived the Armenians, with a long Christian heritage and governed by semi-independent princes. Farther to the west, alongside the Black Sea, lay the ancient Kingdom of Georgia, which more or less managed to retain its Christian sovereignty through the ages. The borders between these three ethnic regions, rather than countries, shifted over the centuries, depending on fortunes of war and other contingencies. The arrival of Islam had simply added another abrasive factor to the equation.

A period of Persian–Turkish rivalry began in the sixteenth century, and in 1555 the Trans-Caucasus was partitioned along a north–south axis, much of present-day Georgia falling under Turkish influence, and much of the terrain to the east of the axis under the Persian mantle. But there were exceptions. For example in 1639 a large part of present-day Armenia was ceded to the Turks. During the eighteenth century Persian colonial expansionist power waned and its outer possessions gradually obtained autonomy.

RUSSIAN COLONISATION

Early in the nineteenth century Russia decided to colonise Trans-Caucasia, and in 1801 it annexed Georgia. Then followed wars with Persia, in which Russia gained territory at Persia's expense. The first Russo–Persian war began in 1804 over the Circassian Muslim khanates, in which Persia lost more territory. A Persian armed force attacked the Russians in Karabakh (Armenia), but was routed and forced to hand over a huge wedge of terrain on the west side of the Caspian Sea, including much of present-day Azerbaijan and part of Armenia. The Treaty of Turkomchai (1826) defined the boundary between these two major powers on the western side of the Caspian Sea as the River Araxes (Araks), where it still remains. South of the River Araxes lies the present-day Iranian province of Azerbaijan (which means land of fire), said to be the birthplace of Zoroastrianism.

Russia organised all its newly won Trans-Caucasian terrain into four provinces, based on Baku (Azerbaijan), Yerevan (Armenia), Gyandzha (Armenia) and Tbilisi (Georgia), and worked to set its own stamp on the region and eradicate all traces of Persian influence.

OIL AND UNREST

The next milestone in the Trans-Caucasus was the discovery and exploitation of oil in Baku. The oil boom took off in 1870 and attracted international big business. As Russia had not yet reached an advanced stage of industrialisation, oil concessions were awarded to Belgian, British, Dutch, French and German companies, although some were gained by Armenians. This meant that the workforce in this rapidly expanding oil industry, especially the skilled element, was Christian, and it included a large number of Armenians. By this time the Armenians had developed a thriving, educated merchant class, and within 20 years they owned some 30 per cent of the Baku oil and allied industries. Armenians also ran most of the small businesses that proliferated as the population of Baku rapidly increased.

Circassian and other Muslims flocked to the new Baku oilfields, but lack of education, sophistication and ethnic prejudice generally debarred them from all but unskilled and menial jobs. This gave them a 'have not' complex, which bred envy and resentment. However the slow modernisation of Baku and some Muslim towns began to give Muslims a sense of identity as 'Azeri Turks'.

THE ARMENIAN DASHNAK

Persecution of the previously tolerated Armenians within the Ottoman Empire in the latter part of the nineteenth century resulted in the appearance of a number of Armenian political groups, some secret, mostly initially seeking some form of autonomy under Turkish sovereignty. One that gained prominence was the Dashnak Sution (Armenian Revolutionary Federation), usually referred to as the 'Dashnak', which was formed in 1890 in Tbilisi (Georgia), then Czarist territory. Initially it worked to achieve autonomy. More restrictions were placed on Armenians by the Turkish authorities – their religion and culture were repressed, their schools were closed, and Armenians were forbidden to learn or speak Russian, then the key to regional advancement. A wave of Turkish-led massacres hit the Armenians in 1895.

Political unrest came to the Caucasus in the wake of the Russian December Revolution (1904), when other revolutionary parties began to surface. In February 1905 a Muslim was murdered by the Dashnak in Baku, which caused a frenzy of Muslim rioting, in which roving gangs looted Armenian houses and shops. Simultaneously other Muslim–Armenian clashes occurred in the Nagorno-Karabakh region.

Ethnic confrontation and disturbances continued in several cities and towns, in which Armenian shops, businesses and oilfields were set on fire. The Dashnak, and other Armenian parties and groups, defended themselves as best they could, but it was estimated that the death toll of Armenians that summer in the Caucasus area exceeded 10 000. The causes included religious prejudice and envy. Dashnak's prestige was enhanced in 1907 when it joined the Second International, and the Young Turks revolution in Turkey in 1908 gave a further boost to Armenian political groups. However Muslim enmity remained.

THE FIRST WORLD WAR

Turkey entered the First World War in October 1914 on the side of the Central Powers, and thus was ranged against its traditional enemy, Russia. Talat Pasha, one of the triumvirate of Young Turks, offered the Armenians autonomy if they would openly side with Turkey against Russia and foment dissidence in Russian-held Armenia. The Armenians did not trust the Turks, and anyway by this time they were beginning to thirst for complete independence, so rejected the offer.

Infuriated by this refusal, Talat Pasha ordered the deportation of Armenians from Syria and Mesopotamia, then part of the Ottoman Empire, a process that began in April 1915. The massacre of Armenians began in Van, the traditional Armenian capital, followed by the notorious 'Death March'. Armenians claim that in this phase of genocide over 1.5 million perished. Those remaining in the Caucasus region gave their support to Russia. (In 1921, Talat Pasha was assassinated by an Armenian in Berlin.)

DASHNAK REPUBLIC OF ARMENIA: 1918–20

In 1915 Dashnak envoys visited Britain and France to lobby for an independent state 'within the Ottoman Empire', but Russia, one of the Allies, coveted Turkish Armenia and so the issue was put on hold. Russia created a special role for the Armenians on its Caucasus front and encouraged them to form their own battalions, which remained in action until 1916. On the other hand the Circassian Muslims were considered to be too politically unreliable and biased to be allowed to form armed forces.

Prior to the Armenian genocide the Allies had subsidised and assisted some Armenian dissident activity within Turkey and supported its political aspirations. Russian troops advanced into Turkey in September 1915 to find that the Armenian heartland around Van, Mush and Bitlis had been completely depopulated and devastated. In March 1916 Russian troops withdrew, leaving the remaining Armenians in a small barren sector of the Russian Trans-Caucasus.

The Bolshevik Revolution in Moscow occurred in November 1917, and the following January Russian troops completely withdrew from the Trans-Caucasus region, leaving the Armenians, Azeris and Georgians to their own devices. Under the Brest–Litovsk Treaty of March 1918 Russia withdrew from the First World War. In April a fragile Democratic Federative Republic of Trans-Caucasia was formed, but lasted only five weeks as the three ethnic groups rejected federation, now being hungry for individual independence.

THE BAKU SOVIET: 1918–20

Wartime deprivation and hardships caused old enmities to revive, and when Russian troops withdrew from Baku the city council declared for the Bolsheviks. With the help of the Dashnak the council formed the Baku Soviet, which in March 1918 mounted a series of pogroms against Muslims. The Bolsheviks took control of Baku and immediately nationalised the oil industry in the name of Revolutionary Russia.

Turkish troops resumed their advance in the wake of the retreating Russians, which prompted the Baku Soviet to invite British troops to help stave off the Turks. Dunster Force, comprising about 1000 men, arrived in August 1918, but quickly withdrew again in the face of the Turkish advance. Turkish troops arrived in Baku on 15 September, whereupon the 26-man leadership of the Baku Soviet, headed by Stepan Shaumian, took to the Caspian Sea. They had hoped to sail north to Astrakhan, but instead were landed at Krasnovodsk, then in the hands of rival social revolutionaries, who executed them all. The Soviets blamed the British for this, and in later years it was alleged that they could have prevented the executions. In Baku the Muslims took their revenge for the March pogroms, and in the process it was estimated that over 10 000 Armenians were killed.

In October 1918 Turkey sued for peace, and when the armistice marking the end of the First World War was signed in November, all Turkish and Germans troops were withdrawn from the Trans-Caucasus region, leaving a political power vacuum. In Armenia the Dashnak established a dictatorial regime that devolved into corruption. National independence was formally declared on 29 May 1919. In Baku the discredited Baku Soviet leadership was superseded by the Azeri 'Hemmet' organisation, which on 27 May formally declared its national independence.

Immediately after the First World War Americans strode on to the world stage for the first time as significant international statesmen. President Wilson's Fourteen Point Programme included a vague promise of independence for certain ethnic minorities within the former Ottoman Empire, including the Armenians, Assyrians, Azeris and Kurds. The Allied Peace Conference in Paris in January 1920, while more or less recognising the *de facto* independence of the Armenians and Azeris, did not admit them to the new League of Nations. The Treaty of Sèvres of August 1920 also mentioned this point. However the later (1923) Treaty of Lausanne made no mention of the issue at all. By that time the international situation had changed and Western statesmen had realised what a dangerous, destabilising factor the new Soviet Union was becoming. Allied policy switched from trying to weaken Turkey, to strengthening it as a bulwark against the insidious spread of communism.

In the meantime the Soviet Red Army, formed in April 1918, was ruthlessly enforcing Soviet sovereignty over all former czarist possessions. It entered the Trans-Caucasus, taking over over Baku by a simple show of force in April 1920, such was its reputation, and in November moved into Armenia, the Dashnak government collapsing before its advance.

NEW FRONTIERS

Anxious to be friendly to Turkey in the moment of its defeat, and owing to the limitations of the military expeditionary capability of the Red Army, under the Treaty of Kars in 1920 Russia ceded to Turkey the disputed Armenian 'Kars and Arshan' area, covering some 23 000 square miles. This was later confirmed by the Treaty of Lausanne and considerably reduced the size of Armenia.

The provisional Russian Soviet Federative Socialist Republic, which in 1923 became the Union of Soviet Socialist Republics (USSR), made other frontier agreements with Turkey. In October 1921 it established a common border with Turkey, which involved some devious and complicated bargaining. Turkey insisted that Russian Armenia, with a Christian majority, was to include the 'autonomous republic of Nakhicheven', which had a Muslim majority. Nachichevan lay alongside Persia, its southern tip touching Turkey, giving it a 12-kilometre mutual frontier with that country. Although completely inside the Armenian republic, authority over Nachichevan was awarded to Azerbaijan, thus making the enclave a major tinder box in the region. Turkey and Russia became guarantors this arrangement.

In December 1922 Armenia, Azerbaijan and Georgia, as autonomous republics, were amalgamated into the single Trans-Caucasian Federated Soviet Socialist Republic and Azeris were decreed to be of Soviet nationality. Lenin's policy of eliminating nationalism involved redrawing administrative boundaries so that the various nationalities would counterbalance one another.

NAGORNO-KARABAKH

The second major tinderbox was the Nagorno-Karabakh enclave. Although it had a large Armenian majority, it was situated within Azeri territory. The occupying British appointed a Muslim governor to Shusha, then its main city, which caused Armenian discontent that erupted into an armed rising. In April 1920 this was put down with great severity by Azeri troops. The ringleaders were executed and many other Armenians killed. Survivors fled to the nearby city of Khankende, which developed as the administrative centre of Nagorno-Karabakh, while devastated Shusha barely survived as an Azeri garrison town.

The arrival of the Red Army enabled the Bolsheviks to divide the multiethnic Trans-Caucasus into convenient administrative packages, with small national groups counterbalancing larger ones. In December 1920 Stalin, a Georgian and then 'commissar of nationalities', awarded Nagorno-Karabakh to Armenia, but this was later overruled and it was given instead to Azerbaijan, although it was to retain a large measure of autonomy. The reason given for this arrangement was that it would enable Armenians in the mountains to establish harmonious links with Azeris on the plains; even though the Armenians and Azeris were natural enemies and had fought a war against each other (1818–20), in which it was believed almost a third of their respective peoples had perished or were displaced (Goldenberg, 1994).

It was not until July 1923 that the 'autonomous region of Nagorno-Karabakh' formally appeared, shorn of the adjacent territories of Kelbajar, Lachin and Shaumian. It was claimed as Armenian, under Azeri overlordship. Khankende, the administrative centre, was renamed Stepanakert after the unfortunate Armenian hero of the ill-fated Baku Soviet. One explanation for the name of Nagorno-Karabakh was that 'kara' in Turkish means black, 'bagh' in Persian means garden and 'nagorno' in Russian means mountainous (Goldenberg, 1994).

Thus weakened, disadvantaged and shrunken, Armenia became the fifteenth and smallest autonomous republic in the USSR. The iron grip of communist rule now took hold on the Caucasus region, which managed to smother active ethnic hostility, with just a few unpublicised exceptions, for several decades.

By 1928 the Red Army had completed its subjugation campaigns in Central Asia, thus bringing all the peoples of the USSR firmly within its orbit. That year the Soviets launched an anti-Islamic propaganda campaign in Azerbaijan and attempted to prevent Azerbaijanis from visiting Shia shrines in adjacent Persia. Later Arabic was banned, and gradually most mosques and Islamic institutions in Azerbaijan fell into disuse.

THE EFFECT OF GLASNOST

President Gorbachev's reformist policies, especially that of glasnost, seemed to trigger the release of pent-up ethnic emotions in the Trans-Caucasus, allowing them to be aired in public. One of the first instances was a political demonstration in Yerevan, capital of Armenia, on 18 October 1987 by about 1000 people in support of the rights of Armenians living in the Nagorno-Karabakh autonomous region, and in the Republic of Azerbaijan generally. Nominally the protest was against changes to the regional school curriculum, which excluded the teaching of Armenian history, but this was just the tip of the iceberg. Nagorno-Karabakh, covering an area of about 1700 square miles, was mainly oak-forested and mountainous, and noted for sheep farming and its wine exports. It had a population of about 189 000 people (1989 census), some 75 per cent of whom were Armenian, 20 per cent Azeri and 5 per cent others.

The previous day there had been a much larger demonstration in Yerevan, where about 3000 people called for the closure of a nearby chemical plant and protested against the proposal to build another nuclear power station. There had been no police interference, nor official alarm. Protests about local economic matters were not unusual, but political ones were something quite different, so the local Communist Party authorities had to sit up and take notice.

A series of political demonstrations began on 11 February 1988 in Stepanakert, capital of Nagorno-Karabakh, coinciding with the voting (110 of the 140 members) of its regional Soviet for Nagorno-Karabakh, to be transferred from the authority of the Azerbaijan SSR to that of Armenia. This constitutional problem, one of several arising across the USSR, caused President Gorbachev to establish a USSR Central Committee Commission to examine the 'nationalities' problem, which he described as the 'most fundamental and most vital issue confronting Soviet society' (*Pravda*). He stressed that 'true internationalism and true friendship amongst peoples are possible only in conditions of profound respect for the dignity, honour, culture, language and history of every people'. Stirring words, but they meant little to the minorities that had suffered discrimination under the old 'divide and administer' policies of Lenin and Stalin. Even dedicated reformers thought that Gorbachev's reforms were perhaps going too far, and would merely confirm his opponent's jibes that 'conservatism (meaning the old communist order) was best after all'.

Political demonstrations began in Yerevan on the 15th in support of the Armenians in Nagorno-Karabakh, although at first they coincided with protest rallies against the construction of a synthetic rubber plant, an existing one being blamed for the high local incidence of infant mortality. Demonstrations continued daily in Opera House Square, and there was a huge one involving over 100 000 people on the 22nd. This caused the first secretary of the Armenian Supreme Soviet, Karen Dermirchyan, to appear on television to appeal for calm, explaining that while the factory project would be reconsidered, the political status of Nagorno-Karabakh was not open to discussion.

That day the CPSU Central Committee vetoed Nagorno-Karabakh's request to be transferred to the Armenian SSR. They criticised the demonstrations as 'provocations by national extremists', and called upon the Armenian and Azerbaijan authorities to safeguard public order and the strict observance of socialist laws. Prominent leaders of the CPSU Central Committee were hastily dispatched to the area on a fact-finding and temperature-cooling tour. On the 24th Soviet troops arrived in Yerevan to protect government buildings and installations, and all telephone links with the rest of the USSR were severed. The first secretary of the regional Soviet in Nagorno-Karabakh was dismissed. On the 26th, after personal intervention by Gorbachev, the situation in Yerevan became calmer.

THE KARABAKH COMMITTEE

The driving force behind the demonstrations and political unrest was the impromptu Karabakh Committee, led by a member of the Armenian Academy of Sciences, Dr Rafael Ghazarian, whose deputy was Ashot Manucharian. The committee had several scattered branches and its strength at that stage was unknown. Two members of the committee had a private meeting with Gorbachev, to the annoyance of the Azerbaijan Communist Party, who assured them a just solution would be found. The committee agreed to suspend demonstrations for a month in Armenia, but continued them in Nagorno-Karabakh, where an Armenian newspaper refused to print Gorbachev's appeal. By the end of February 1988, incidents in Armenia, Nagorno-Karabakh and adjacent areas had caused the displacement of several thousand people. The moratorium on demonstrations was broken on 8 March so that a large rally could be held in Yerevan to mourn the victims of the 1915 massacres. In addition some 1000 Armenians protested in Moscow.

THE SUMGAIT RIOTS

Rumours spread by Azeris fleeing from the southern Armenian town of Kafan provoked riots in Baku, from 24 February 1988, and a report that two Azeris had been killed in the town of Agdam near the Nagorno-Karabakh oblast led to a large anti-Armenian riot in Sumgait, a major Azeri Caspian port just north of Baku, on the 28th/29th, in which '32 people were killed and 197 injured' (Tass). The Armenians claimed that hundreds of their fellow countrymen had been killed and that many atrocities had been committed. A Soviet Foreign Ministry spokesman stated that troops had been brought in to curb the rioting in both cities and curfews had been imposed. It was later announced that the first secretary and mayor of sumgait had been dismissed. An Azeri man was sentenced to imprisonment for beating an elderly Armenian to death in the riots, and 80 others were awaiting trial. This provoked counterdemonstrations in Yerevan and Baku. Later, incidents in the Armenian town of Ararat caused some 7000 Azeris to flee from their homes.

The USSR Supreme Soviet ordered a seven-year package of economic and cultural reforms, including improvements in industry, housing and social services; the broadcasting of TV and radio programmes in Armenian; and the restoration of

Armenian monuments. (Armenia was an impoverished republic with indifferent farming land, apart from the wine-producing Ararat valley and plateau region. It lacked indigenous oil, gas or coal resources and was completely landlocked.) Light engineering, food-processing, vehicle-assembly and other plants were established; raw material was imported and the finished products exported. Armenia had to import some 95 per cent of its energy needs.

On 24 March the Karabakh Committee was ordered to disband and several of its members were detained. The response was a mass Armenian 'stay at home' protest on the 26th, after which the city was quiet until 12 May, when the Nagorno-Karabakh regional Soviet repeated its demand to be transferred to the Armenian SSR. A mass demonstration and general strike began in Stepanakert. By the end of June the authorities had to admit they had lost control of the situation, and troops were called in. Political unrest rumbled on in both Armenia and Azerbaijan throughout the summer and into the autumn of 1988. On 12 July Nagorno-Karabakh again called for immediate secession from Azerbaijan and incorporation into Armenia. This was again rejected by the USSR Supreme Soviet, and a protest rally followed in Yerevan.

Armed clashes reerupted in Nagorno-Karabakh on 18 September, when at least 25 people were killed. On the 22nd further casualties were caused by internal violence, and troops were deployed to guard government buildings and installations. That day a 'special status' order was decreed for Nagorno-Karabakh, effectively a step towards calling a state of emergency. In addition, further troop reinforcements were sent to Azerbaijan, which was beset by a rash of counterdemonstrations.

Renewed outbreaks of intercommunal fighting occurred in Baku, Kirovakan (Armenia) and the Nakhichevan strip on 22 November, mostly brought about by death sentences being pronounced on three Azeri 'Sumgait rioters'. Also, Azeris in Armenia were protesting against the building of an aluminium plant at Shusha, now its second largest city. Later (22 December) *Trud*, a local trade union periodical, stated that in a four-week period the military had 'seized 15 855 weapons in Armenia and Azerbaijan and that another 22 000 had been handed in'. This simply indicated that both republics were awash with illegal arms.

THE ARMENIAN EARTHQUAKE

A devastating earthquake measuring 7 on the Richter scale occurred on 7 December 1988. Its epicentre was near Spitak in western Armenia and thousands of buildings in that city and the adjacent ones of Kirovakan and Leninakan were destroyed. Villages in the surrounding countryside for miles around were devastated. Over 25 000 people were killed, although the final casualty figure remained vague. Many bodies remained buried in the rubble and over 400 000 people were made homeless. Rescue and aid efforts were hampered by harsh winter weather and the fact that the road and rail network, which had been sparse and rickety anyway, had been destroyed. Several accidents occurred, some fatal, at overcrowded airports and airfields.

Extensive publicity was given to the disaster both within the USSR and throughout the world due to Gorbachev's new glasnost policy, and offers of aid and help flooded in from the other Soviet republics and many foreign countries. (Previously such disasters would have been underreported, if reported at all.) Despite its dire circumstances Armenia refused the aid and assistance proffered by Azerbaijan, so, crippling though the Armenian disaster was, it did not seem to divert Armenia's attention away from its bitter quarrel with the Azeris.

The Armenian government subsequently announced its Community Reconstruction Programme, a monumental scheme for rehousing its homeless and restoring the economic superstructure within two years.

NAGORNO-KARABAKH UNDER MOSCOW RULE

In early January 1989, Armenian Nagorno-Karabakh delegates visited Moscow with a document demanding to be either incorporated into the Russian Federation, or put directly under Moscow rule. The petition had been signed by over 80 000 people, who would try anything to get away from Azeri overlordship. On the 12th Nagorno-Karabakh was placed under the USSR Supreme Soviet Central Committee, and a special commission with executive authority was appointed. This was a snub to the Azerbaijan government. There was a clampdown on opposition organisers, and martial law virtually settled over both republics.

By this time many members of the Karabakh Committee in Yerevan were in detention, which brought Armenian terrorist threats against the local KGB detachment unless they were released. Moscow tried to clean up its Caucasian party stables, and it was reported in *Pravda* that 97 senior Armenian party, government and security officials had been removed from office, and another 220 officials and over 100 police officers had been dismissed in the Azerbaijan republic.

In May 1989 a wave of strikes hit Nagorno-Karabakh. On the 5th, on the outskirts of Stepanakert, a small group of Armenians tried to steal the arms of a number of soldiers and several people were injured. The detained Karabakh Committee members were released on the 31st. In July there was a gunfight near Stepanakert between Armenian and Azeri shepherds over the scarce grazing, which escalated to include the construction of roadblocks and the ambushing of vehicles. Attacks on road and rail traffic were resumed. A USSR Supreme Soviet fact-finding mission toured the region, and the following month the local press reported near anarchy in Nagorno-Karabakh, where armed groups were clashing with each other daily. A carbomb exploded in Yerevan on 25 August.

THE AZERBAIJAN ECONOMY

It might be supposed that while Armenia was desperately poor, oil-rich Azerbaijan was correspondingly rich, but this was by no means the case. For many decades Baku, an historic trading centre, had enjoyed an oil boom, but almost all the riches that came with it were monopolised by the Soviet Union. Indeed during the Second World War Baku oil had fuelled the gigantic Soviet military machine.

After that war the Soviet Union had sought to diversify, discovering and exploiting other rich oilfields in Siberia and the central Muslim republics, as well as huge new reservoirs of natural gas, which further helped the Soviets in their 'divide and administer' policy of ensuring that no single republic could become self-sufficient. Oil and gas pipelines stretched across the USSR.

A malaise seemed to settle on the Azerbaijan 'Azarinet' oil company, which also operated two large refineries – it appears that these were allowed to run down to the point where they needed huge modernisation investment. By 1990 Baku's contribution to the Soviet Union's total oil pool had fallen to just 2 per cent. Just one oil pipeline ran from Baku into the Soviet system, while the pipeline to Georgia fell into disuse. Also it seems that the Azerbaijan railways were neglected and ramshackle. In short Azerbaijan had become a debtor republic.

ISLAMIC INFLUENCE

Glasnost enabled Azeris more openly to practice their religion, which had been discouraged by the CPSU. The Azeris now expressed their desire to repair or reopen their mosques, and to make pilgrimages to Shia shrines in adjacent Iran. In January 1989 Ali Akbar Rafsanjani, the Iranian speaker (later president), visited Moscow and took time out on his return journey to preach in the main mosque in Baku. Portraits of Ayatollah Khomeini were paraded in Baku amid a sea of green flags and Islamic chanting. Agreements were made for Azeris to visit Iranian *madrassahs* (Islamic colleges), and one was opened in Baku with Iranian help.

VIOLENCE IN AZERBAIJAN

Simmering disorder broke into violent rioting in Baku in August 1989, with Azeri groups raiding Armenian shops and homes. The Azerbaijan Popular Front (APF) took the lead in campaigning for political and economic autonomy, fresh elections and legal recognition for itself. It insisted that Nagorno-Karabakh should remain within the jurisdiction of Azerbaijan, and that direct rule from Moscow should cease. In the latter part of the month an APF-led general strike in Baku closed down half the city's industrial complex.

THE AZERI BLOCKADE OF ARMENIA

On 18 August 1989 an unofficial Armenian 'National Council' came into being in Nagorno-Karabakh to govern the *oblast* until constitutional government was restored. This was regarded as a direct challenge to USSR and Azerbaijani authority. Major protest demonstrations erupted in Baku that month, necessitating the dispatch of additional troops.

The APF was now calling the shots and manipulating the crowds, and on 2 September it organised a massive demonstration involving more than 500 000 people in the centre of Baku. Two days later it reactivated the general strike, which among other things disrupted the docks, railways and oil facilities. The effects of the strike spread beyond Azerbaijan into Armenia and Nagorno-Karabakh. Further large rallies forced the Azerbaijan Supreme Soviet into negotiations, and the APF suspended the strike action on the 10th. It was already estimated the strikes had cost over US$270 million in lost production (*Pravda*). On the 16th the Azerbaijan Supreme Soviet agreed to end the 'special commission' in Nagorno-Karabakh.

An Azerbaijani blockade of Armenia began, virtually as a side effect of the major strikes as the railways and much road transportation had been forced to a halt. By 14 September Armenia was suffering a serious fuel shortage and factories were closing due to a shortage of raw materials. The Community Reconstruction Programme, begun after the 1988 earthquake, came to a halt. Even when the APF called off the general strike, road and railway traffic into Armenia remained suspended. The APF was trying to starve Armenia into submission over the Nagorno-Karabakh issue. By the end of the month the volume of freight from Azerbaijan into Armenia had been reduced by 95 per cent (*Pravda*) and Armenia had to rely entirely on the single railway line from Georgia to import food and fuel.

The Armenian authorities appealed to Gorbachev for help, and he urged the leaders of Armenia and Azerbaijan to negotiate the lifting of embargoes and the removal of roadblocks. Failure to do so would result in the imposition of state of emergency regulations. Although the embargo was relaxed to some extent, Azeri railway workers uncoupled from the trains any wagons carrying fuel and foodstuffs, and there were complaints of food rotting due to the delayed transit.

On 3 October the USSR Supreme Soviet approved special measures for the army to run the railways in Azerbaijan, and troops arrived the following day to take over. On the 6th the Moscow authorities claimed that rail traffic was moving again, but on the 8th Tass reported that the few wagons that reached Armenia had either been looted or their contents deliberated sabotaged.

NAGORNO-KARABAKH SOVEREIGNTY

Mob rule prevailed, and on 13 September Abdul Rahman Vezirov, first secretary of the Azerbaijan Communist Party signed a protocol with the APF that lifted martial law, decreed a general amnesty for strikers and appointed a special commission to examine evidence against those already in detention. On the 23rd the Azerbaijan Supreme Soviet approved a new 'Sovereignty Law', confirming its authority over Nagorno-Karabakh, asserting its right to secede from the USSR and to veto any Soviet legislation, and proclaiming it had full control over all its natural resources. Azeri became the state language, and on 5 October the APF became an officially registered organisation.

Violence continued inside Nagorno-Karabakh. On 9 October, for example, an Azeri was shot dead by troops, and a substantial arms cache was found aboard a helicopter chartered by an Armenian humanitarian organisation to carry food aid. On the 18th a Soviet military plane carrying 'peacekeeping' troops to Azerbaijan crashed into the Caspian Sea – all on board perished.

The Congress of the Armenian National Movement (ANM) opened in Yerevan on 4 November. Some 900 delegates attended and called for sovereignty over Nagorno-Karabakh, as well as for the earthquake Community Reconstruction Programme to be restarted.

The USSR Supreme Soviet technically ended its direct rule over Nagorno-Karabakh on the 28th, but not completely as a Soviet 'Observation Commission' took over the supervision of Soviet troops remaining in the region. A joint meeting of the Armenian Supreme Soviet and the 'National Council' of Nagorno-Karabakh declared that the latter was now 'part of a unified Armenian Republic'. A massive rally in support followed in Yerevan. On the 29th a huge demonstration in Baku, again said to consist of over 500 000 people, insisted that Nagorno-Karabakh was theirs. The general strike was resumed.

The Armenian Supreme Soviet was in local difficulties as a result of its refusal to support radical proposals such as abolition of the Communist Party's leading role in government, elimination of the words 'Soviet Socialist' from the republic's title and the right to veto USSR legislation. The Assembly buildings in Yerevan were besieged by angry radicals. By January 1990 virtual guerrilla war had broken out in the Shaumian and Khanlar regions, wedged between Armenia and Nagorno-Karabakh, with rival groups stealing army weapons, armoured vehicles and even helicopters.

THE NAKHCHEVAN PROBLEM

In the meantime there had been friction in the Nakhichevan strip between the Azeri majority, motivated by elements of the Baku-based APF, and the Armenian minority supported by the ANM, which at times devolved into guerrilla skirmishes. Broadly, the Azeris wanted the removal of the restrictions that were preventing them from visiting their Azeri brethren in the Iranian Azerbaijan province. On 29 December 1989 armed groups of Azeris took control of Jalilabas and Lenkoran, two Nakhichevan towns.

During the last days of December 1989 and the first days of January 1990, several thousand Azeri rioters pulled down or set fire to a stretch of border fencing between the autonomous Soviet oblast of Nakhichevan and Iran. Mobs tried to push forward and construct a bridge across the Araxes river into Iran, whose government protested to the USSR. Nakhichevan farmers were protesting about the amount of rich agricultural land taken up by the frontier defences. However the Soviets' excuse was that the unrest had been caused by local residents who had received no response to their demands, made in November 1989, for freer access to fellow Azeris in Iran. The Tehran government did not want revolutionary-minded Azeris from the Soviet Union to penetrate its Azerbaijan province and peddle their 'Greater Azerbaijan' crusade as it was still in the process of bringing some of its own outer provinces back under central control, having almost prised themselves loose during the Iran–Iraq War (1980–88).

The Soviet KGB, which was responsible for this section of

Soviet–Iranian frontier, rushed reinforcements to the area, but by 3 January 1990 the attacks against the border fences had spread along the whole length of the joint frontier with Iran. The Moscow authorities blamed the APF, alleging it was planning to create a separate Muslim state.

On 7 January Azeris began to pull down the frontier fencing along the 12-kilometre Turkish–Nakhichevan border. This was a closed border, but on the 9th an informal crossing point was opened and tension in the sector relaxed somewhat. Turkey did not want to tangle with the Soviet Union over their tiny common frontier. On the 11th KGB detachments recovered possession of Jalilabas and Lenkoran. These were some of the main events that led up to the Battle for Baku, described at the start of this chapter.

3 Multiparty Politics: 1990–92

On 25 January 1990 in Nakhichevan, the two towns taken over by Azeri activists – Jalilabas and Lenkoran – were regained by KGB troops. In the meantime, on the 19th Nakhichevan nationalists had declared they intended to secede from the USSR and establish an independent Islamic republic. However, on the 25th representatives of the competing Azerbaijan Popular Front and the Armenian National Movement met in Riga (Latvia), under the auspices of the Latvian Popular Front, to bring about a ceasefire along part of the border between Armenia and Nakhichevan, where the death toll during the previous three weeks had exceeded 200. (The Armenian National Movement had been formed in July 1989 after the release from detention of the Karabakh Committee members who, with their supporters, were founder members. In August Levon Ter-Petrossian had been elected as its leader.)

On 1 February, also in Riga, it was agreed there would be an exchange of prisoners, a ceasefire and better relations between the two rival organisations. However the negotiations broke down when the ANM alleged Armenians were being forcibly removed from their villages in the Khanlar area of Azerbaijan. Nonetheless on 13 February the Azerbaijan railway resumed freight traffic between Baku and Yerevan.

Since the Yerevan and Sumgait incidents of February 1988 there had been a steadily growing exodus of Armenians from Azerbaijan, and of Azeris from Armenian-held territory. One estimate was that some 180 000 Armenians and 160 000 Azeris were involved in this ethnic-cleansing movement (*Guardian*).

Neither Armenia nor Azerbaijan had any formal armies to speak of at that stage as the USSR government still retained full military authority, so the protagonists began to form impromptu militias. Hungry for arms, the militias were forced to procure them by illegal means. Soviet servicemen still serving in the two republics became sources of procurement, through bribery or threat. On 27 May a small group of Soviet Interior Ministry troops, waiting at the Yerevan railway station to escort a train through Nagorno-Karabakh to Kafan in southern Armenia, were attacked by Armenian militants in search of arms. Six of the militant were killed, and ten soldiers and one civilian were injured.

Armenian roadblocks sprang up around the city and protest demonstrations were mounted. Amid this heightened tension the Armenians held a huge gathering, said to exceed 100 000 people, to celebrate the proclamation of the Dashnak Republic in 1918. Gorbachev censured the Armenian authorities on 25 July, ordering that the illegal militias be disbanded and disarmed by 9 August. Nationalist leaders warned that any attempt to disarm them forcibly would lead to a bloodbath.

ARMENIAN DECLARATION OF INDEPENDENCE

The first multiparty election in the Soviet Republic of Armenia was held in May 1990 with barely a 50 per cent voter turnout. The new Armenian Supreme Soviet met on 20 July and openly rejected Gorbachev's criticisms and his order. Levon Ter-Petrossian was elected 'president' (chairman), having defeated the Armenian Communist Party by 140 votes to 80, and his nominee, Vazgen Manukyan, became prime minister. Both men had been members of the proscribed Karabakh Committee, had spent time in political detention and were now leaders of the new Armenian National Movement.

Ter-Petrossian was considered by some to be too elderly to lead his country into independence. He was about 70 and was unprepared for such a task, being an academic Orientalist who had taught in Egypt for some years before returning to Armenia. Also, he tended to be pro-Turkish – not a popular stance in Armenia, especially the new Armenia that was emerging – and favoured retaining links with the USSR. He called on all Armenian militias to swear an oath of allegiance to his Supreme Soviet, and then rushed off to Moscow, where he persuaded Gorbachev to extend the deadline for two months to allow Ter-Petrossian himself to disarm the militias.

On 23 August the Supreme Soviet, by 183 votes to two, adopted a declaration of Armenia's 'independent statehood', proclaiming the new Republic of Armenia and deliberately omitting 'Soviet Socialist' from its title. As a sovereign state it claimed the right to form its own army and police force; Soviet troops could only be deployed on Armenian territory with Armenian permission; and it assumed control of its own natural resources and foreign relations. All Armenians living abroad had a right to citizenship. It firmly laid claim to Nagorno-Karabakh and re-surrected the old Dashnak Republic flag of 1918. However, cautiously, it did not declare immediate secession from the USSR.

THE ARMENIAN DIASPORA

President Ter-Petrossian had high expectations of support from the Armenian diaspora, it being said there were far more Armenians in exile than resided in Armenia. Estimates varied, although it was thought there were about 6.5 million Armenians in all – about 3.5 million in Armenia and the remainder scattered around the world (*Statesman's Year Book*, 1993), including some 400 000 in the United States, 500 000 in the Middle East, 160 00 in Turkey, 30 000 in Canada and a similar number in Western Europe. In Armenia, Armenians formed 93.3 per cent of the population, Azeris 4 per cent, Russians 1.5 per cent and Kurds 1.5 per cent.

The Armenians in exile had generally prospered and most were content with their lot, so while many were prepared to contribute morally, politically and financially, only just over 100 000 returned to their homeland. The returnees had strong anti-Turkish sentiments and came into conflict with the policies of President Ter-Petrossian. Several political organisations had developed within the Armenian diaspora, some of which could bring influence to bear on Western governments. Also, a few terrorist groups had been spawned, the most notorious being the Armenian Secret Army for the Liberation of Armenia, which had been active against Turkish targets.

In the latter part of August there was a sudden escalation of armed clashes along the Armenian–Azerbaijan border, with regular Soviet troops fighting Armenian guerrillas who had attacked villages inside Azerbaijan. On the 24th Ter-Petrossian agreed to the creation of a special security zone along the border, to be manned by Soviet Interior Ministry troops.

Ter-Petrossian had been serious when he told Gorbachev he would disarm and disband the Armenian militias, but this was because he needed the arms for his new national army and did not want armed maverick groups roaming at large. He did his best to rein them in, but his efforts were disrupted by an assassination. On the night of 29 August Viktor Aivanzian, a Supreme Soviet deputy, was killed in a shoot-out with rebel troops. Aivanzian had gone with a detachment of the Armenian National Movement (ANM) militia to the headquarters of the Armenian National Army (ANA), which claimed 60 000 members and was refusing to subordinate itself to the Ter-Petrossian government. Immediately Ter-Petrossian declared a state of emergency and ordered the ANA to disband by 10 p.m. When it failed to comply, ANM militiamen attacked the ANA headquarters and captured its entire command structure. Ter-Petrossian announced the dissolution of the ANA and called for all its arms to be handed it.

Incidents of terrorism began to occur, for example on 15 July the manager of the Stepanakert airport was killed in a bomb attack, while on 10 August a home-made bomb exploded on a bus near the Azerbaijan city of Gyandzha, in which nearly 20 people were killed and many others injured.

AZERBAIJAN ELECTIONS

For the first time, multiparty voting took place for the 360-seat Azerbaijan Supreme Soviet on 30 September and 14 October 1990. Public rallies and demonstrations were banned on polling days, and Baku was closed to all non-residents. Only 52 per cent voted in Baku, compared with the overall Azerbaijan average of 81 per cent. Polling did not take place in Nakhichevan and the Shaumian district for 'security reasons'. The result was surprising, showing a dramatic loss of public support for the APF since its peak in January, when it had controlled the mobs in Baku. In the first round, for example, communists won 220 of the 260 available seats. The victorious communists advocated keeping Azerbaijan within the USSR, but to placate Azeri nationalists they insisted on retaining authority over Nagorno-Karabakh. (The population of Azerbaijan had risen to about 7 145 000, Azeris forming 71.8 per cent, Armenians about 7.9

per cent and Russians about 7.9 per cent – *Statesman's Year Book,* 1994).

Due to disagreements the new Azerbaijan Supreme Soviet did not convene until 5 February 1991. Over 80 per cent of the deputies were members of the Azerbaijan Communist Party. Ayaz Mutalibov remained president, and Gasan Gasanov was reelected prime minister. The opposition consisted of Deputies from the Azerbaijan Popular Front (APF), Social Democrats (moderates hived off from the APF), Greens and the Union of Democratic Intelligensia, brought together under the umbrella of the Democratic Bloc of Azerbaijan. A few seats remained unfilled.

President Mutalibov, a technocrat with a reputation for being an able administrator, took Azerbaijan into the CIS upon its formation as he considered Azerbaijan would not be able to stand alone without the prior ratification of the Assembly. He hesitated to establish a Ministry of Defence and a national army as he feared the APF would take them over and topple him from power. The political parties formed their own militias.

BORDER VIOLENCE

On the evening of 30 April 1991 a unit of Azerbaijan Interior Ministry troops, supported by Soviet ones and supposedly acting under Gorbachev's decree of July 1990 that illegal militias should be disarmed, attacked the Armenian-populated villages of Getashen and Martunashen, inside Azerbaijan just north of Nagorno-Karabakh, allegedly bases for Armenian guerrillas. The Armenians later claimed that about 20 villagers had been killed and over 100 wounded, and that the troops had refused to allow the wounded to be evacuated for medical treatment. This sparked off a series of interethnic clashes along the border. This Armenian Supreme Soviet condemned the action and censured Gorbachev for permitting 'state terrorism'.

President Ter-Petrossian rushed to Moscow to demand the cessation of both Azerbaijan's aggressive actions against Armenia and the eviction of Armenians from Azerbaijan, and that the Armenian wounded be allowed hospital treatment. Gorbachev was unsympathetic, pointing out that the incidents had occurred on Azerbaijani territory and that his decree to disarm the illegal paramilitary groups still stood. Ter-Petrossian accused Gorbachev of colluding with the Azerbaijani leadership to punish Armenia and reward President Mutalibov, whose popularity in Baku was fast flagging, but who remained in favour in Moscow for supporting the projected CIS Treaty.

The Soviet Interior and Defence Ministries issued a joint statement on 4 May, saying responsibility for the violence lay with the Armenian leadership because it supported paramilitary groups, and threatening to take all necessary steps to stop it. They claimed that Armenia was waging an undeclared war on Azerbaijan, and that there had been over 300 cross-border attacks since January, in which over 60 Azeris had been killed. On the night of 5 May the village of Voskepar, in the north-east corner of Armenia, was attacked and razed to the ground by Azeri and Soviet troops. Subsequently the Yerevan authorities claimed that over 30 Armenians had been killed and 40 others taken hostage.

In the following days other villages in the area were attacked and at least 20 more hostages seized, most of them Armenian policemen. Hostage taking, an ancient custom in the region, had been revived for reprisal, insurance and exchange purposes. The village of Artzvashen, with some 5000 inhabitants, complied with the Azeri order to surrender all weapons and was left unscathed. Getashen and Martunashen, situated within Azerbaijan, were less fortunate, and on the 11th both were razed to the ground and their populations deported.

In mid July 1991 Gorbachev had apparently obtained an assurance from President Mutalibov that he would guarantee the safety of the people in Nagorno-Karabakh, and thus lifted the state of emergency in two of its areas. However, things were getting beyond control and on the 15th a KGB-instigated operation was mounted against Armenian-inhabited villages in Azerbaijan, in which several people were killed and others evicted. The following month about 40 Soviet Interior Ministry troops were seized by an Armenian paramilitary group to exchange for a captured militant Armenian leader and others detained by Soviet forces. The hostages were eventually freed. This type of hostage exchange procedure was more common than any of the authorities involved would admit.

AZERBAIJAN INDEPENDENCE

When the attempted coup against President Gorbachev began in Moscow on 19 August 1991 the Armenian leadership stood dispassionately aside, neither condemning nor supporting it. On the other hand President Mutalibov, who was in Iran at the time, welcomed it, being the only Soviet state leader openly to support the self-styled State Committee for the State of Emergency. On the 23rd a demonstration was mounted by the APF against Mutalibov's decision, but was broken up by Baku security forces. However, the Azerbaijan Communist Party backed out of the CPSU on the 29th with the intention of going it alone in their region.

The Azerbaijan Supreme Soviet declared independence on the 30th and lifted the state of emergency that had been imposed in Baku by the Soviets in January 1990. Popular presidential elections were held for the first time on 8 September. Ayaz Mutalibov gained the office, supposedly having received the support of 87 per cent of the electorate, a figure that was disputed by the opposition Democratic Bloc of Azerbaijan. The APF had tried but failed to muster a general strike and election boycott. On 10 October the Azerbaijan Supreme Soviet voted to establish a republican defence force, something that so far Mutalibov had been hesitant to do, and on the 18th confirmed its declaration of independence.

Turkey recognised Azerbaijan's independence, and in a speech Prime Minister Gasan Gasanov said he was hoping for increased commercial links with that country, and that Azerbaijan's planned adoption or the Latin alphabet would aid cultural cooperation.

NAKHICHEVAN

No elections were held in Nakhichevan as they had been banned by its Supreme Soviet, now headed by Gaidar Aliyev, leader of the APF. A bridge border crossing over the Araxes river was opened between Azerbaijan and Turkey on 31 October by Aliyev. Immediately about 10 000 asylum seekers rushed across into Turkey, two dying in the process. Aliyev accused the Azerbaijan leadership of blocking Turkish aid to Nakhichevan so as to thwart its struggle for independence.

ARMENIAN INDEPENDENCE

Meanwhile in Yerevan, a city of over one million people, the Armenian Communist Party was suffering ill fortune as on 17 April 1991 the Armenian Supreme Soviet had nationalised all its assets. Gorbachev declared that this was contrary to the constitution and countermanded the resolution. Gorbachev's protest was ignored and the Communist Party was evicted from all its premises. By the end of the month it was having to operate 'from three small rooms in a printing works' (Tass), and eventually it voted itself out of existence. The spirit of nationalism was growing even stronger in Armenia, and that of communism all but extinguished. On 30 June the Armenian Supreme Soviet voted to create the post of executive president.

In a referendum on independence on 21 September, for which it was claimed there was 95.5 per cent turnout, 94.39 per cent voted in favour of secession. On the 23rd President Ter-Petrossian formally declared Armenia's independence. On 16 October Ter-Petrossian was confirmed by popular vote as the executive president. However Armenia's quest for international recognition was unsuccessful. President Ter-Petrossian visited the United States and Canada, both with large Armenian communities, but was refused national recognition.

THE REPUBLIC OF NAGORNO-KARABAKH

On 2 September 1991 Nagorno-Karabakh declared itself a republic, incorporating the adjacent Shaumian district in accordance with joint decisions of the governing councils.

A CEASEFIRE

On 24 September 1991 a ceasefire agreement between Armenia, Azerbaijan and Nagorno-Karabakh was brokered by President Yeltsin of the Russian Federation and President Bursuktan Nazarbayev of Kazakstan. It was estimated that over 800 people had died in this conflict since 1988. This agreement provided for the withdrawal and disarming of all armed groups by the end of the year, excepting Soviet troops. Local self-government was to be restored by January 1992, hostages were to be freed, and refugees returned to the villages from which they had been ejected. The Russian Federation and Kazakstan were to provide monitors and act as guarantors. Delegations were to commence talks on 1 October.

Meanwhile the violence in the Nagorno-Karabakh area continued. For example on 25 September a missile attack was made on Stepanakert, and the following day six Armenians were killed in the Mardakert district. Relations between Armenia and Azerbaijan over Nagorno-Karabakh did not improve, and on 5 November Azerbaijan cut off the gas supply to Armenia. Relations further deteriorated on the 20th, when an Azeri helicopter carrying high-ranking republican and military officials crashed, killing over 20 people. Azerbaijan accused Armenia of shooting it down, while Armenia claimed the crash had been due to bad weather.

The Azerbaijan Supreme Soviet annulled the autonomous status of Nagorno-Karabakh on the 26th, decreeing that it would be governed by an Azerbaijan 'National Unity Council'. Gorbachev stepped in and persuaded Azerbaijan to postpone this order.

THE CIS

In December 1991 the USSR came to the end of its existence and the CIS appeared in its place, which both Armenia and Azerbaijan joined. On the 16th Turkey recognised all the newly independent former Soviet republics, as did other foreign countries selectively. On the 17th Nakhichevan demanded to join the CIS, but Azerbaijan objected. On the 24th Ali Akbar Vellayati, the Iranian foreign minister, after a tour of the former Soviet Muslim republics, visited Moscow and signed a number of agreements concerning communications and trade, one being to form a land route to link Nakhichevan with Azerbaijan by way of Iran. Both Armenia and Azerbaijan joined the Conference of Security and Co-operation in Europe (CSCE) and the United Nations.

By the end of 1991 the Soviet forces had already begun to pull out from Armenia, Azerbaijan, Nagorno-Karabakh and Nakhichevan, leaving behind chaos and violence – the CIS had no legal authority to intervene in any conflicts between member CIS states.

NAKHICHEVAN PROCLAIMS INDEPENDENCE

The Supreme Soviet in Nakhichevan held elections on 28 December 1991, in which eleven of the 81 seats were reserved for Azerbaijani deputies, but Baku boycotted the poll. The APF candidates swept the board. Nakhichevan declared its independence but was only recognised by Armenia.

WAR IN NAGORNO-KARABAKH

Nagorno-Karabakh issued casualty figures for the conflict in 1991: 270 Armenians, 216 Azerbaijanis and 15 servicemen killed; 400 Armenians, 180 Azerbaijanis and 34 servicemen wounded; and 599 Armenians taken hostage, of whom 226 had not yet been returned.

Nagorno-Karabakh was in a sorry state of civil war, communications and transport had broken down, and within towns and villages ethnic majorities had openly turned against minorities. The Armenians accused the Azeris of trying to ethnically cleanse the enclave by a combination of repression and terror, while the Azeris blamed Armenian gunmen for infiltrating the narrow strip of Azerbaijani territory for this purpose. Previously most cities, towns and villages tended to have a majority of either Armenians or Azeris, the legacy of historical changes where minorities had to accept their lot under communist rule.

One of the first effects of the formation of the CIS, and the nominal adherence of Armenia and Azerbaijan to it, was to hasten the Soviet military withdrawal as the Moscow authorities wanted to avoid involvement in regional squabbles. Previously (January 1991) it had been reported that Soviet military personnel would only serve on a voluntary basis in Trans-Caucasia, owing to 'difficult conditions' (Tass). This caused the proportion of regional personnel in Soviet units in the region to rise, especially as the approaching dissolution of the USSR became more obvious, although precise proportions can only be guessed at as Soviet military records on this issue remain blank. Many of these 'regional' soldiers, with homes in Armenia or Azerbaijan, were in sympathy with their ethnic cause, and many volunteered to become part of the national armies of Armenia and Azerbaijan that were trying to spring into existence.

The Azerbaijan government immediately laid claim to all Soviet military weaponry and establishments remaining within its writ (as did that of Armenia), including those in Nagorno-Karabakh. However the government was hesitant about taking actual possession of them as it was not sure that Russia had completely shed its colonial attitude and may yet delay its departure and conduct reprisals for any over-hasty actions.

The year 1992 began badly in Nagorno-Karabakh, as on 2 January President Mutalibov put the region under direct presidential rule, meaning that 'presidential representatives' would replace local councils. Salam Mamedov, deputy prime minister of Azerbaijan, was appointed as head of administration in Nagorno-Karabakh.

During January armed Azeri militias surrounded Stepanakert and periodically bombarded the city, which suffered a fuel shortage and the breakdown of its water and sewerage systems. The Armenians used seven helicopters to bring in relief supplies and fly out the wounded, but it was reported that only three remained airborne, the other four having been shot down by Azeri militias (*Guardian*). The Armenians concentrated on attacking Shusha, where on the 28th they shot down an Azeri helicopter, killing about 40 people. In reprisal, on the 31st the Azeris launched a rocket attack on Stepanakert.

CSCE INVOLVEMENT

Armenia, Nagorno-Karabakh and Russia called upon the CSCE to intervene to help solve the conflict, but this was vetoed on 5 February by Azerbaijan, which objected to the issue being 'internationalised'. However a CSCE representative was able to visit Nagorno-Karabakh on the 12th, and the prime minister of Azerbaijan, Hassan Hasanov, put his case to a NATO meeting on the 17th. He admitted that Azeri militiamen were attacking Armenian terrorists, but denied it was a full-scale military operation (Assa-Irasa, Azeri news agency). The foreign ministers of both Armenia and Azerbaijan met Boris Yeltsin in Moscow to discuss a ceasefire and access for humanitarian aid.

In Baku President Mutalibov was fast losing popularity. Demonstrations were held to call for his resignation, partly owing to his refusal to accept a peace plan that allowed Nagorno-Karabakh cultural autonomy. Belatedly, Mutalibov had established an Azerbaijan Ministry of Defence in September 1991, and a start had been made at selectively recalling some of the estimated 140 000 former Soviet Azeri reservists. In theory military manpower was available, although there was a shortage of trained officers as most Azeris had been drafted into construction and similar units. The APF and other groups were actively forming armed militias to fight in Nagorno-Karabakh and construct power bases.

On the other side of the fence, one authority estimated that Armenia had over 100 000 armed man (*The Times*). While a proportion of these were in the embryonic national army, several large, semi-independent militias existed, including that of the ANM, the Armenian National Army, the Armenian Popular Liberation Army of Artsakh and other smaller ones.

The governments of both Armenia and Azerbaijan had assumed responsibilities and functions previously held or exercised by the USSR, which included defence and internal security. The Armenian Ministry of the Interior already had a 1000-strong armed force, while that of Azerbaijan numbered about 20 000 men.

THE KHOJALI MASSACRE

The Iranian foreign minister, Ali Akbar Vellayati, visited Baku and Yerevan and brokered a ceasefire that was due to start on 27 February 1992 but failed to materialise. In mid February Azeris fired rockets on Stepanakert and launched other attacks against Armenian villages. Reprisal came on the 25th, when Armenian militias seized the Azeri town of Khojali in Nagorno-Karabakh and ejected the estimated population of 10 000. The following day Armenian militias attacked the retreating column of Azeri refugees moving towards Agdam (in Azerbaijan), allegedly killing over 1000 and committing other atrocities. This was a watershed event that caused ethnic cleansing to speed into a gallop in Nagorno-Karabakh.

Azerbaijan decreed a three-day mourning period. Armenia claimed the reports were exaggerated, and were intended to divert attention from major Azeri attacks on Armenian towns. Later the ousted and somewhat embittered President Mutalibov claimed that the casualties and atrocities had been deliberately exaggerated to discredit him. Whether control of the Armenian militias had been completely lost on this occasion, or whether it was a deliberate policy, is still debated. At that stage both sides were largely dependent on militias for their aggressive operations, but these had minds and motives of their own.

CIS WITHDRAWAL

A number of CIS servicemen were attacked or killed and robbed of their arms, and many others deserted with their weapons. On the last day of February, the volume of military *matériel* lost as a result of such theft and black market activities caused Marshal Yevgeny Shaposhnikov, the CIS commander-in-chief, to order the immediate withdrawal of this troops from Nagorno-Karabakh and along the Armenia–Azerbaijan border, as well as the destruction of all weaponry that could not be moved. On 9 March 1992 the '366 motorised regiment was air-lifted by helicopter from Stepanakert into Georgia'. The strength of this once '1800-strong regiment had sunk to 350, due to desertions and defections' to one side or the other. The '4th Army remained in Azerbaijan and the 7th Army in Armenia', both former Soviet formations (*Izvestiya*).

Before defecting a group of Armenian officers from the 336 Regiment in the Stepanakert area opened up their armouries, depots and stores to Armenian militias. A similar pattern of events occurred at CIS armouries and depots in the Gyandzha area, but this time the Azeris were the beneficiaries. A few Russian officers were held as hostages, including the commanding general, until they promised their troops would not be deployed to Armenia, Azerbaijan or Georgia. Hostages were also released in exchange for arms. Future Russian historians may no doubt skim quickly over this most embarrassing episode in Russian military history. Both Armenia and Azerbaijan were desperately anxious to get their hands on as much Soviet weaponry as possible to build up their national armouries, and threats, bribery, deceit and forcible seizure became commonplace.

On 2 February 1992 Armenia and Azerbaijan joined the Turkish-initiated Black Sea Economic Co-operation Project, which became the only multinational regional agreement to have Armenia, Azerbaijan and Georgia as members, neither Armenia nor Azerbaijan having a Black Sea seaboard. (The Black Sea was the main trade outlet to Europe.) The downside was that since the end of the Gulf War, West European interest in Turkey had distinctly waned, and the Caucasus were rarely on any Western political or economic agenda. Iran quickly founded a counter pact – the Caspian Sea Co-operation Zone – the members being Azerbaijan, Iran, Kazakstan, Russia and Turkmenistan.

RESIGNATION OF MUTALIBOV

All-night demonstrations were held on 6 March 1992 in Baku to call for the removal of President Mutalibov, who was accused of not protecting the Azeris. As a consequence Mutalibov resigned and was replaced by Yagub Mamedov. Mamedov appealed to Abdulfaz Elchibey, now leader of the APF, for cooperation. The APF only had 50 seats in the 260-seat Supreme Soviet, and Elchibey was demanding the transfer of government power to the 'National Council', on which his party had 50 per cent of the seats. On the 24th the APF was invited to join a coalition government. Mamedov ran headlong into a power struggle, for example when he tried to remove Prime Minister Gasan Gasanov his whole cabinet resigned. This was the start of an open struggle for power between half a dozen ambitious, prominent Azeris.

During March the conflict over Nagorno-Karabakh intensified. For example on the 3rd an Armenian helicopter evacuating wounded from Stepanakert was shot down and all on board were killed, an Armenian attack on the Azeri village of Kazanchi resulted in almost 30 deaths, and further rocket attacks were made on Stepanakert, as well as on the town of Askeran. On the other side of the fence, Agdam came under Armenian fire on the 12th and Shusha was surrounded. An economic state of emergency was declared in Yerevan on the 25th, it being alleged that Azeri rail workers were deliberately delaying oil supplies to Armenia. Extra gas supplies from Georgia were meeting part of the energy needs of its nominally Christian sister republic.

Meanwhile, on the home front the Armenian government was struggling with constitutional and economic problems, being reluctant to adopt President Ter-Petrossian's economic reform programme, which he hoped would attract more IMF aid. In April Ter-Petrossian refused to accept the resignation of his vice president and prime minister. The main opposition group was the National Self-Determination Union, led by Paruyr Ayrykian who, during a TV broadcast on 28 April, called for a new constitution.

In Nagorno-Karabakh, on 14 April 'President' Artur Mkrtchyan was shot dead in his home, and although Azeris were suspected of implication, it was insisted it had been an accident.

PEACEMAKING

Turkey and Iran, Muslim rivals in expanding their influence eastwards into former Soviet Muslim republics, began to show an interest in the Armenia–Azerbaijan conflict, wearing a peacemaking cloak. President Turgut Ozal of Turkey had given VIP treatment to Mutalibov when visiting Ankara, urging that support be given to Azerbaijan and suggesting a blockade of Armenia's export route to the Black Sea. Iran called on the UN to impose an arms embargo on both republics. The CSCE suggested that Nagorno-Karabakh should be given the right to self-determination, but both Armenia and Azerbaijan disagreed. All wished to participate in any ceasefire conference. The CSCE, the UN, NATO and other international organisations were vying with each other for business. Also, several countries and their statesmen, often at variance with each other, were jostling to get into the peacemaking act. None wanted to miss any opportunity to appear on an international peacemaking stage. There was backbiting, for example Armenia accused Iran of sending arms to Baku. In April Iran agreed to commence diplomatic relations with Azerbaijan, but not with Armenia. Muslim–Christian differences were accentuated in the hostile line-ups, to mingle with the mystic scent of oil and trade and the thirst for one-upmanship on the regional stage. Peace was elusive.

THE ARMENIAN OFFENSIVE

After intensive Azeri shelling of Stepanakert on the evening of 8 May 1992 Armenian armed militias began a massive assault on Shusha, the only remaining Azeri stronghold in Nagorno-Karabakh, which ended in victory the following day, leaving Armenia in undisputed control of the whole enclave. The Armenian armed forces then attacked the Azerbaijan city of Lachin, on the edge of Nagorno-Karabakh, in an attempt to force a corridor through Azeri territory into Armenia proper. From Agdam the Azeris tried to counter this by opening a new front to the east in the Askeran region, but failed. The Azeris lost Lachin on 17 May, causing Isa Kambarov, deputy leader of the APF, to say 'We have lost the first stage of this war' (*The Times*).

On 18 May Armenian militias launched a full-scale attack on the hills surrounding the city of Sadarak at the northern end of Nakhichevan. Turkey expressed its disapproval on the 19th, warning Armenia to halt its aggression, while President Turgut Ozal called for Turkish troops to be sent to Nakhichevan and for the return of Shusha and Lachin to Azerbaijani control. (Previously, in January, a bridge over the Araxes river between Turkey and Armenia, near Nakhichevan, had been reopened by Prime Minister Demirel and Gaidar Aliyev, head of the Nakhichevan Milli Majlis, who renamed it the Bridge of Hope.) Turkey still had its eyes on Nakhichevan.

This drew the attention of Boris Yeltsin as, under the Treaty of Kars (1921), Turkey and Russia were joint guarantors of the status of Nakhichevan. Anticipating such a situation, on 15 May Yeltsin had come to a collective agreement with certain CIS states, excluding Azerbaijan, to go to the aid of Armenia if it was in danger. He dispatched his defence minister, Pavel Grachev, to Armenia to discuss the role of the '7th Army', which was stationed in Armenia under Russian control, and to assure the Armenians he would not abandon them. This caused the Turkish prime minister to say that his country ruled out the use of force to settle the Nakhichevan problem, and thus backed away away from direct confrontation with Russia.

On 28 May Demirel arrived in Nakhichevan to attend the opening of another bridge across the Araxes river. Later Gaidar Aliyev visited Turkey and subsequently announced that Turkey had promised to provide assistance to construct a power station and power line from Turkey, a priority, since Armenia had imposed a blockade on energy supplies to Nakhichevan on 15 June. Azerbaijan complained that Armenia had attacked it the day after a ceasefire agreement had been made between the two countries, and of using the negotiations leading up to it as a cover for military preparations.

The Russian 7th Army began to withdraw from Armenia in June, as did the Russian 4th Army from Azerbaijan, and in the latter case there were further accusations of Russian arms and equipment being stolen for use by Azeri militias in the Nagorno-Karabakh conflict. On 18 June a one-month state of emergency was declared in Nagorno-Karabakh by the Armenian government, which also called up former Soviet reservists aged 35 and under.

THE APF'S RISE TO POWER IN BAKU

In Baku on 14 May 1992 an emergency session of the supreme Soviet blamed President Mamedov for the recent setbacks on the battlefield. Mamedov was dismissed and Ayaz Mutalibov reinstated, the latter then cancelled the elections scheduled for June, which had been widely expected to bring Abdulfaz Elchibey, leader of the APF, to power. The APF alleged that this amounted to a coup, and called for widespread civil disobedience.

On 15 May an estimated 20 000 APF supporters gathered outside the APF headquarters, and then marched to the Assembly building and the presidential palace. The APF mob overran both buildings with minimum loss of life. Mutalibov fled, and the APF established effective control over Baku. A special session of the National Council gave the APF a number of ministerial posts in the new coalition government. On the 18th Isa Kambarov was appointed acting president, pending elections.

The elections were held on 7 June and were won by Abdulfaz Elchibey, who gained 59.4 per cent of the votes cast in the 76 per cent turnout. Elchibey became president on the 16th. His policy was for his republic to remain in the CIS, a matter that had yet to be ratified.

To reverse its military setbacks, Azerbaijan launched a counteroffensive on 12 June against the town of Mardakert in the northern part of the Nagorno-Karabakh enclave, claiming to reoccupy about 15 villages. The Azeri militias were trying to force open a corridor through Armenian territory to Nakhichevan.

THE LACHIN KURDISH STATE

The founding assembly of the Kurdish Liberation Movement – meeting in Lachin (Azerbaijan) on 9 June 1992 with other informal Kurdish organisations – announced the revival of the autonomous Kurdish state that had existed from 1923 to 1928. It had been known as Red Kurdistan and had included parts of the Lachin and Kelbajar regions. Many Kurds had since been deported, although according to the 1989 census 152 952 Kurds remained in the area, a figure thought by some to be an underestimate. This project proved a non-starter.

THE LEZGHIN STATE

Another potential ministate sought to surface on 26 June 1992, when the Lezghin population – thought to number about 100 000, living partly in Dagestan (situated in the Russian Federation, which had eight official nationalities) and partly in adjacent northern Azerbaijan – demanded a unified Lezghin Muslim state. Talks were held in Makhachkala (Dagestan) on the Caspian Sea, and President Elchibey vaguely promised to try to meet the Lezghin people's 'cultural and other needs', but otherwise this was another non-starter.

ARMENIA

In Armenia the government was having trouble with the Dashnak organisation (then thought to have about 40 000 members, many living overseas), which had an armed militia. President Ter-Petrossian accused Dashnak of having cooperated with the KGB in Soviet times, and that it was directed from abroad. He feared its competitive, disruptive influence. However it was allowed to hold its '25th Congress' in Yerevan on 30 June 1992, but the Dashnak leader, Khrayr Marukhyan, a Greek citizen who had arrived in Armenia, was expelled.

On 8 July the Armenian Supreme Soviet pledged support for Nagorno-Karabakh, but insisted that it remain within the Armenian structure, which was a compromise reached by President Ter-Petrossian with the opposition National Democratic Bloc, which favoured recognition of Nagorno-Karabakh's compete independence.

AZERBAIJAN

In Azerbaijan on 2 July Musavat (the Muslim Democratic Party), founded in 1911, was revived. Led by Isa Kambarov, Musavat superseded the existing New Musavat Party. The following day the Istikla (National Independence Party) held its constitutional congress in Baku, and Etibar Mamedov was appointed as its leader. Its policy was to foster Azerbaijan's Islamic traditions and Turkish unity.

CSCE PEACE NEGOTIATIONS

Anxious to prove its existence and to gain credibility as an arbiter of quarrels, the CSCE plunged into the Nagorno-Karabakh controversy. In March 1992 it was decided to establish a 'Rome Commission', which met in June to prepare for a peace conference to be held in Minsk (Byelarus). However, this failed to materialise as Nagorno-Karabakh refused to cooperate, and at a later Summit of Black Sea States the presidents of Armenia and Azerbaijan refused to hold bilateral negotiations. The CSCE bumblingly persisted, and in July persuaded the Nagorno-Karabakh and Armenian representatives to return to the Rome Commission.

AZERI ADVANCES

In July 1992 Azeri armed militias consolidated the gains they had made in Nagorno-Karabakh the previous month by taking over the main town of Mardakert and renaming it 'Agdere'.

The Azeris, who now occupied the northern part of the strip, bombarded Stepanakert on the 20th. The following month Azeri armed militias continued to push back the Armenians in Nagorno-Karabakh, especially around Mardakert, and also took control of the Armenian-held Lachin corridor. Intermittent bombing raids were made on Stepanakert.

The Nagorno-Karabakh government ordered a six-month state of emergency and general mobilisation on 13 August, but in an emergency session two days later the Supreme Soviet accepted the resignation of Prime Minister Oleg Yesayan and his government, which was replaced by a defence committee that was invested with full governmental authority until the end of the war. This was led by Robert Kocharyan, a leading member of the ANM. President Georgi Petrossian was replaced by Karen Baguryan.

Just previously, on 10 August, President Ter-Petrossian, who was alarmed by the Azeri advances in Nagorno-Karabakh, had appealed to the signatories of the CIS Collective Security Treaty (signed in Tashkent in May) to 'carry out their obligations' and 'come to Armenia's aid'. The response had been cool, but on the 2lst a vague statement was made in Moscow that some support might be given by the Russian troops still in Armenia.

August and September were months of broken ceasefires and negotiations. The Kazakstan-brokered ceasefire of 28 August had little effect, nor did the Russian-brokered one of 19 September and the negotiations at Alma Ata, while the CSCE Rome Commission talks for the elusive Minsk conference fell apart. None of these peacemaking efforts seemed to be taken seriously by the combatants, who seemed to girding themselves up for more war. Russian military observers arrived in Baku on 1 October.

Armenia had hardly begun to establish a conventional defence force and relied on semi-independent armed militias that were fighting in Nagorno-Karabakh and elsewhere, being regarded as 'irregular volunteers'. A new post was created, that of minister of state for defence issues, headed by Vazgen Manukyan, a former prime minister. Manukyan was to be superior to the defence minister, Vazgen Sargsyan, but this caused confusion and had to be changed. Manukyan then became defence minister and Sargsyan was pushed aside to become a presidential aide. In October President Ter-Petrossian dismissed his foreign affairs minister, Raffi Hovhannesyan, for his anti-Turkish stance when Armenia had requested 100 000 tons of grain from Turkey. He was replaced by Arman Kirakosyan.

In Baku an attempt was again made by President Elchibey to expand the conventional army, which had hung fire for so long, alleged with Iranian and Turkish assistance. Colonel Nureddin Sadykhov was appointed chief of general staff and first deputy defence minister.

The Azeris launched two offensives in September, one centred on the Lachin corridor and the other around Mardakert, in which ethnic cleansing was prominent. However, on 4 October an Azeri attack on the Lachin corridor was repulsed by Armenia (SNARK, Armenian news agency), who claimed that over 100 Azeris had been killed and some tanks destroyed. Later the Azerbaijan Defence Ministry admitted that its troops had been forced to withdraw from the Lachin corridor. Fighting continued throughout October.

NAKHICHEVAN

Trouble flared up in Baku when President Elchibey appointed Siavush Mustafayev as interior minister on 24 October 1992, when 200 men of the APF militia occupied the Interior Ministry and the Milli Majlis because the Assembly refused to endorse the appointment. Gaidar Aliyev, head of the Nakhichevan Milli Majlis, denounced the action of the militia as an attempted coup. Local police ended the occupation amid pro-APF rallies, and Elchibey agreed to look for a compromise candidate. On 23 November Aliyev became leader of a new party, Yeni Azerbaijan (New Azerbaijan), designed to form a 'constructive' opposition (Itar-Tass). The Azerbaijan government accused former President Ayaz Mutalibov of organising a coup and demanded his extradition from Nakhichevan for trial.

ARMENIAN ECONOMIC PROBLEMS

Falling Soviet oil production had caused a progressive rundown of Armenian industry, and as 1992 drew to a close Armenia was swamped with economic problems, largely due to the Azeri blockade and Turkish intransigence. The fuel shortage caused the government to announce the reopening of the country's nuclear power station at Medzhmor – some 40 miles west of Yerevan near the border with Turkey and closed since the earthquake of 1989 – which previously had provided Armenia with 50 per cent of its electricity needs.

At that time Armenia required 7.5 million cubic metres of gas daily, but only received 4.0 million (Itar-Tass). The dispute over Nagorno-Karabakh had resulted in closure of the pipeline bringing Turkmenistan gas to Armenia via Azerbaijan, while gas from Russia via Georgia was reduced by one third due to pressure from Azerbaijan, pilfering and military devastation. Also, the Baku government had persuaded Turkey not to go ahead with its offer to supply electricity to Armenia.

Bread rationing was introduced in December as emergency grain deliveries from Syria and the United States were held up at the Turkish border. The UN High Commissioner for Refugees (UNHCR) established a six-month, $6 million emergency relief programme, but on the 15th President Ter-Petrossian declared a national emergency, warning that 30 000 people would die unless they received help soon (Itar-Tass).

4 Competing Warlords: 1993–95

January 1993 was a black month for Armenia, largely due to energy shortages. On the 16th the Ministry of Industry had to halt all industrial production for two weeks, and on the 23rd the entire republic was left without gas when Azeris in the Marneul region of Georgia blew up a section of the gas pipeline to Armenia. Yerevan was bereft of trees for miles around, all having been cut down for fuel. Negotiations were conducted with Turkey and Muslim CIS member states, but to no avail, although Russia did promise to increase its supplies of 'black oil, diesel fuel and petrol' (*Pravda*). The gas pipeline in Georgia was again sabotaged on 11 February and remained out of action for several days.

In contrast Azerbaijan's economic prospects seemed brighter, as on 4 January the government announced it was set to become Iran's most important trading partner, an agreement with that country having been concluded in Tehran for some 50 joint ventures, including the construction of a linking railway line. On the 7th the government approved the law on privatisation, which included shops, restaurants and cultural facilities.

After clashing with President Elchibey over policy, Prime Minister Rakhim Guseinov resigned. The Azerbaijan Movement for Democratic Reform, which had condemned the government's attitude towards a protest demonstration held in Baku on 24 December 1992, when over 400 people had been arrested, four being on hunger strike, called for President Elchibey to resign and for multiparty elections to be held. Its leader, Nemat Panakhov, was arrested.

On 3 January Presidents Yeltsin and Bush jointly called for an immediate end to the bloodshed in Nagorno-Karabakh and the resumption of peace negotiations under CSCE auspices. During that month, Azeri attacks concentrated on the heights to the north of the Lachin corridor. Attacks were also made on the Martuni area of Nagorno-Karabakh, and around Askeran and Mardakert. Armenia contented itself with shelling Azeri border villages and Agdam.

So far relatively little reliable information was available on the strength of the various armed forces involved in this war, but eventually one well-respected authority (the IISS) came up with some estimates. The Armenian government was said to have an army of about 50 000, split between two divisions and equipped with whatever ex-Soviet military matériel it had been able to obtain by devious means. Having introduced conscription, the long term-plan was that within 15 years its defence forces would number (with reservists) about 300 000. Non-government paramilitary forces numbered about 30 000, equipped with infantry weapons.

Azerbaijan also had a long-term plan to expand its defence forces to about 500 000 within a 15-year period through conscription. At the time the national army had only a hard core of some 5000 men, with a force of 30 000 in the process of formation. Again, weaponry had been obtained from the former Soviet armed forces. Five mine warfare vessels, flying the Azerbaijan flag, were part of the so-called Caspian Flotilla.

The Baku government claimed that its Popular Front Karabakh Peoples' Defence militia, consisting of Azeris, numbered 12 000. On the other hand it admitted that the 'armed rebels' in Nagorno-Karabakh exceeded 50 000, including volunteers from Armenia. The headquarters of the Russian 7th Army, some 32 000-strong, was still based near Yerevan, and that of the Russian 4th Army, some 62 000-strong, was still in Azerbaijan. Both were nominally thought of as having a peacekeeping role, but the Armenians and Azeris saw them as colonial remnants reluctant to depart.

The Russian minister of external affairs, Eduard Shevardnadze, rushed to Baku on 3 February to sign mutual agreements to improve trade and economic relations and overland communications with Azerbaijan.

On the 21st General Dadach Rzaev, who was described as a professional soldier but was virtually a mercenary warlord, was appointed as Azerbaijan's defence minister, replacing Rakhim Gaziyev, who was blamed for the poor showing of Azeri troops in Nagorno-Karabakh. The Azeris began an offensive in the Nagorno-Karabakh area, but they ran into difficulties and soon the Yerevan media was claiming that Armenia had recovered several villages and gained absolute control of the Sarsang reservoir. The main weakness of the Azerbaijani army was that after each successive defeat those local commanders and officers who were thought to have failed were ruthlessly removed, thus draining the officer corps. Both sides were short of good, medium grade regimental officers.

In Yerevan on 2 February, President Ter-Petrossian dismissed Prime Minister Khosrov Haroutunian for criticising government policy. This resulted in huge anti-Ter-Petrossian rallies by the National Self-Determination Association opposition parties, who demanded his resignation.

ARMENIAN OFFENSIVES

During the last week of March 1993 Armenian armed forces advanced from Nagorno-Karabakh and the Lachin corridor into Azerbaijani territory, and by 11 April they had overrun the Kelbajar district, thus seizing a whole wedge of Azerbaijani territory that had separated Armenia from Nagorno-Karabakh. At least 40 000 Azeri refugees fled from the Kelbajar district and another 15 000 were trapped. In the south Armenians also advanced towards the Azerbaijani town of Fizuli, near the Nakhichevan border and less than 20 miles from Iran, which had fallen to them on 2 April. President Elchibey called upon the Iranian government for military assistance: there was no answer.

Bitterly disappointed by the way the battle was going, on television President Elchibey reprimanded his troops for their over-hasty evacuation of the Kelbajar region, and 'for deserting their posts'. The Armenians had deliberately left open 'escape corridors' for the fleeing Azeris.

On 7 April the UN Security Council expressed its concern and piously called for the withdrawal of Armenian troops from Azerbaijan. The Armenian government countered by insisting it had no troops in Azerbaijan, as all involved were 'irregular volunteers'. President Turgut Ozal of Turkey made a state visit to Baku on the 13th, declaring Turkey would never allow a Greater Armenia, but he showed no inclination to intervene on the Azeri side. Nor did he mention that previously he had considered a military alliance with Azerbaijan. He merely murmured he would tighten up his embargo against Armenia.

The Muslim economic blockade was certainly having dire effects on Armenia. Bemoaning his country's economic woes, on 7 April President Ter-Petrossian stated that his unemployment figure was 90 per cent and his country was absorbing 300 000 Armenian refugees (*Guardian*). On the other hand his battle successes were alarming the Azeris and their allies, as his country and the territory obtained by war were becoming ethnically purified.

President Ozal was a shrewd manipulator who believed in having a foot in several camps. He also expected to be recompensed for the local political actions of his allies. For example he had been allowing Western, particularly American, humanitarian aid to reach Armenia through Turkey, but feeling he was not being sufficiently rewarded for these 'acts of neutrality', in March he had closed his border with Armenia and banned aircraft from flying to that country from Turkey. Ozal also began to send supplies to 'rebel' Azeris in Nakhichevan. On the other hand he persuaded the Turkish Grand National Assembly to ratify the 1992 Accord with Azerbaijan on mutual military assistance. Ozal died of a heart attack on 17 April and was succeeded by Suleiman Demirel.

CSCE efforts to negotiate a ceasefire again failed, as Azerbaijan insisted that all Armenian troops must first withdraw from its territory. On 30 April 1993 the UN Security Council adopted Resolution 822, demanding an immediate ceasefire and the withdrawal of Armenian troops.

TRIPARTITE PEACE PLAN

In May 1993 a peace plan was formulated by Russia, Turkey and the United States for the resumption of peace negotiations between Armenia and Azerbaijan through the auspices of the CSCE, which also aimed at bringing about a settlement on Nagorno-Karabakh. It called for the withdrawal of Armenian troops under international supervision, but failed as at that time Armenia regarded Nagorno-Karabakh as an independent entity. On 24 May Azerbaijan announced a unilateral six-day ceasefire to create the necessary conditions for implementation of the plan, which was eventually approved by Armenia and Azerbaijan but not by Nagorno-Karabakh, which demanded an end to the Azeri blockade and bilateral safety guarantees as a first step towards the resumption of negotiations.

RUSSIAN SOLDIERS ON TRIAL: BAKU

In September 1992 five Russians had been captured by the Azeris and accused of taking part in the battle of Mardakert on the Armenian side. They were eventually sentenced to death by Azerbaijan's Supreme Court and on 11 May 1993 Yeltsin appealed for clemency. Later it was said that Azerbaijan had offered to exchange them, plus one other captured Russian who had been sentenced to imprisonment, for six Azerbaijani prisoners of war. The Azerbaijani government continually alleged that many Russian soldiers were fighting with the Armenians. There was much truth in this, but an unknown number were also fighting on the Azeri side against Armenians.

MARDAKERT FALLS

Another Armenian offensive began on 12 June 1993 and led to the capture of Mardakert on the 27th, the last major town in Nagorno-Karabakh held by the Azeris. Armenians also attacked the strategic town of Agdam, penetrating several miles into Azerbaijan. A temporary Russian-brokered ceasefire came into effect. Meanwhile a revised peace plan, basically for the Armenians to withdraw from the Kelbajar region, was put to the Armenian Assembly on the 14th, which immediately requested a month's postponement to enable it to assert its control over maverick units in the battle area. Nagorno-Karabakh was not keen on this plan.

ELCHIBEY OUSTED

In early June 1993 a military rebellion suddenly erupted in Azerbaijan, led by Surat Guseinov, now a wealthy merchant but formerly a communist manager of a textiles plant. Guseinov had organised his own military force, with some government approval, to fight the Armenians. He was granted the rank of colonel but was soon deprived of his commission for disobeying orders and trafficking in illegal arms. Guseinov was probably the first of the ambitious Azeri warlords to declare his hand. Rumours circulated that he had obtained arms from the

Russian 104th division when it withdrew from Gyandzha in May. His rebellion began on 4 June in Gyandzha, his power base, after a violent clash between his force and the new Azerbaijan 'National Army', in which dozens were killed. Guseinov's militia then advanced towards Baku to bring down President Elchibey. They met little hindrance on the way and by 21 June had reached the suburbs of Baku.

The defection of government troops had actually smoothed Guseinov's speedy advance towards Baku. There was much resentment amongst frontline soldiers against the authorities in Baku, and they considered the city was packed with draft dodgers, that it was swamped with corruption and black market activities, and that the government was incompetent. President Elchibey was continually blamed for the failings of the army in battle. The following day he threatened to use force against Guseinov, but his acting defence and interior ministers refused to take action. Elchibey hurriedly left Baku for Nakhichevan, his home-town area and power base.

On 24 June the Milli Majlis voted to impeach Elchibey, and demanded that he hand over his powers to Gaidar Aliyev. Small demonstrations by Elchibey's APF took place in Baku on the 26th, followed by a larger one on the 29th, after which the APF suspended all activities until Elchibey reassumed authority. Elchibey was replaced by a joint administration headed by Gaidar Aliyev and Surat Guseinov. This compromise warlord arrangement proved brittle.

On 27 June the Milli Majlis appointed Surat Guseinov as prime minister and supreme commander of the armed forces of the republic, with control of defence, national security and the interior, following his formal nomination by Aliyev. Promising to unite the national army and solve the economic crisis, he called for the abolition of the presidency. Differences at once arose between the two warlords. Aliyev insisted he was head of state, and that elections should not be called prematurely.

On 16 July Aliyev claimed that an attempt on his life had been made the previous day by members of the APF, designed to reinstate Elchibey, who was still in Nakhichevan. Amongst those arrested were Isa Gambarov, leader of the APF, and former Prime Minister Panakh Guseinov. The next day there was mob violence in Baku as police moved to close down the APF's headquarters. Over 300 people were detained. There had been previous pro-Elchibey demonstrations, as the Azerbaijan Supreme Court had not yet decided on the legality of the Milli Majlis' decision of 24 June to strip Elchibey of his legal powers. On 29 August a referendum was held on 'Do you trust Abdulfaz Elchibey?' It was said that only 2 per cent of the votes were in his favour, out of a claimed turnout of 92 per cent. Isa Gambarov, after going on hunger strike, was released from detention. That day APF militiamen attacked the main TV station in Nakhichevan.

AZERI DEFEAT IN NAGORNO-KARABAKH

Meanwhile, on 5 July 1993 Armenian troops had moved against Azeri forces in Agdam, an Azeri bridgehead from which Nagorno-Karabakh towns, including Stepanakert, were periodically shelled. The Armenians seized Agdam on the 24th, after which the Azeri armed forces collapsed in disarray. Acting Defence Minister Safar Abiyev alleged that all major buildings in the town had been deliberately destroyed and over 500 people killed. A three-day ceasefire came into being; this was extended, but periodically broken. The June peace plan was still not acceptable, the Defence Committee of Nagorno-Karabakh refusing to commit itself while the political situation in Azerbaijan was so unstable.

On 29 July UN Security Council Resolution 853 condemned the Armenian seizure of Agdam and called on Armenia to withdraw. In Yerevan, Serzhik Sarkissian, a member of both the Armenian Assembly and the Nagorno-Karabakh Defence Committee, was appointed Defence Minister on 21 August.

The Azerbaijani Ministry of Defence admitted the loss of Jebrail on 18 August, and of Fizuli on the 23rd, while Armenia claimed it had also taken Kubatly, a town in southern Azerbaijan. Iran condemned the Armenian military incursion into southern Azerbaijan, especially as some 60 000 civilians from Jebrail and Fizuli had fled towards the Iranian border. The Iranian government feared it would be inundated with yet more refugees, as this latest Armenian advance had isolated a pocket of southern Azerbaijan that contained up to 250 000 Azeris. An air of despondency hit the Azerbaijani Defence Ministry, which stated on the 30th: 'so many of our men are missing, but we don't know if they have been killed, or are hiding with their families' (*Guardian*). On 3 September Armenian troops seized Goradiz.

ARMENIA BESIEGED

The Armenian prime minister, Hrand Bagration, declared on 17 September 1993 that the last remaining land supply route into the country had been closed due to the 'Zviadian rebellion' in Georgia, which had severed road and rail communications from the north; and that emergency supplies of rice and grain would have to be flown in by air. Although not yet seriously suffering from air attacks, Armenia was now firmly besieged by land, as neither Turkey, Iran nor Azerbaijan would trade with it.

The new prime minister of Turkey, Tansu Ciller, assumed office in June 1993, bristling over the security of Turkey's 12-kilometre frontier with Azerbaijan, warned the Yerevan government that if it attacked Nakhichevan she would ask the Grand National Assembly to declare war. However, after a meeting with Boris Yeltsin, she calmed down. Yeltsin had at last persuaded Azerbaijan to join the CIS.

Iran had promised to build facilities in southern Azerbaijan to house 100 000 of the estimated 800 000 Azeri refugees displaced by the war, but Russia became alarmed when about 1000 Iranian military personnel entered that country for this purposes. Russia wanted better relations with Iran, but was wary of its empirical gestures.

PRESIDENT ALIYEV

A Presidential election, held in Azerbaijan on 10 October 1993, returned Gaidar Aliyev to power. Reportedly Aliyev secured 98.8 per cent of the votes, but *Helsinki Watch* reported that the election had been undemocratic. Aliyev, a former Soviet VIP who had been a chief of the KGB in Azerbaijan, as well as a member of the Soviet Politburo and deputy prime minister, had been dismissed by Gorbachev in 1987, whereupon he had retired to Nakhichevan, his home territory, to busy himself with local affairs.

IRANIAN-SPONSORED CEASEFIRE

In a resumption of fighting on 23 October 1993, Armenian forces seized a sector of Azerbaijani territory in the Zangurian region adjoining the Iranian border, thus forcing another 20 000 or so Azeri refugees to flee south into Iran. An Iranian-brokered ceasefire came into effect on the 28th through the direct mediation of President Rafsanjani, who visited Baku. On 2 November the Azerbaijan Communist Party, which had been abolished in August 1991, reconstituted itself, with Sayad Sayadov as its new leader. Many of the old communist comrades were resurfacing as socialists or nationalists, but increasingly few were bothering to adopt such a political disguise.

ARMENIAN PROBLEMS

Meanwhile, on 12 October 1993 a minor digression had occurred when Ashot Sarkissian, president of the Armenian Chamber of Commerce and a senior figure in the security service, had been assassinated in Yerevan. This was linked to the case of Gagic Ter-Organisation, who on the 21st was convicted by a criminal court in London for the murder (in February) of Ruslan Outsiev, a senior official of the Russian Federation republic of Chechenya, and his brother Nazarbek, who had been buying arms. The case revealed interesting insights into the covert business of buying illegal weapons, and of denying them to opponents.

Another Armenian offensive in early November drove several thousand Azeri refugees across the Araxes river into Iran. At least 100 people, including women and children, drowned during the crossing. The offensive was condemned by the CSCE. Heavy fighting continued in south-western Azerbaijan into December. It was reported in the Turkish press (*Sabah*) that President Aliyev had contacted President Suleiman Demirel of Turkey to ask for Turkish volunteers, arms and ammunition so that he could retake lost Azerbaijani territory. It seems that Turkey made no response.

CASPIAN OIL AGREEMENT

An agreement was signed on 2 November 1993 between the Azerbaijani government and a consortium of international oil companies, led by the UK-based British Petroleum. (An earlier draft had been cancelled in June, when Elchibey, who had initiated the project, was ousted.) This envisaged the investment of some US$7500 million in three oilfields in the Caspian Sea, involving an initial $250 million payment to Azerbaijan upon ratification of the deal by the Milli Majlis. The consortium would be entitled to 20 per cent of the profits from the oilfields, which were thought to contain some 2000 million barrels of oil. This agreement was made after a visit to Baku by a British minister, Douglas Hogg. The political price of this favourable deal for British industry was that Hogg had to state openly that the UK government regarded Nagorno-Karabakh as an integral part of Azerbaijan, and condemned the use of force to change its status.

CENSORSHIP IN AZERBAIJAN

The Azerbaijan Milli Majlis approved legislation in December 1993 banning both the publication of military secrets and reports deemed to insult prominent officials, which would allow the suspension of offending publications and prosecution of the journalists responsible. President Aliyev dismissed two ministers who had held office under Elchibey but had been retained in the Surat Guseinov cabinet after the June coup.

AZERBAIJAN OFFENSIVE

A full-scale Azeri offensive began on 21 December 1993 that led to the recapture of some territory lost near Nagorno-Karabakh. The offensive continued throughout January 1994, but despite Azerbaijan's claims of victories and 'hundreds of Armenian dead', progress was very slow. Goradiz was retaken on 6 January, Agdam on the 8th, and towards the end of the month reports indicated that part of the Kelbajar region had been recovered. However, it was widely believed that the Azeri's advances and battle successes were not due to a newly found military prowess, but had only occurred when Armenian troops had withdrawn to more favourable defensive positions for the remainder of the winter. Even so it was estimated that there were probably about 8000 Azeri casualties (*Guardian*).

Fighting continued into February, until on the 18th a ceasefire was announced, to take effect on 1 March, after negotiations had taken place in Moscow. General Grachev announced that during the entire war over Nagorno-Karabakh a total of 18 000 people had been killed, a further 25 000 wounded and over one million had become refugees.

TURKEY–AZERBAIJAN AGREEMENT

President Aliyev visited Turkey on 8 February 1994 and was successful in obtaining a 10-year treaty of friendship and cooperation that pledged mutual military assistance in the event of attack by a third party. Both sides had Armenia in mind. President Demirel loudly condemned the presence of Armenian troops on Azerbaijan soil. President Ter-Petrossian visited London in an unsuccessful attempt to urge Britain to adopt a more balanced policy towards the Caucasus region.

Despite the ceasefire agreement fighting in disputed areas rumbled on during March, without either side seeming to gain any significant advantage. A proposal by Russia on the 4th for the creation of a demilitarised buffer zone between Armenian and Azeri troops was rejected by the Azerbaijan Milli Majlis as rewarding Armenians for aggression by solidifying their forward battle lines. On 17 March an Iranian C-130 aircraft crashed in Nagorno-Karabakh – over 30 people died, some of whom were relatives of Iranian embassy staff in Moscow. Iran claimed it had been shot down by an Armenian missile, while Armenia claimed it had crashed because of technical problems.

In Baku the crackdown on supporters of former President Elchibey and the APF continued, it being alleged on 28 February that weapons had been recovered from a building scheduled to act as a springboard for a coup to be mounted on 5 March. Many APF members were arrested, but the APF alleged the weapons had been planted by security forces. The Azeri warlords were jostling restlessly for position.

Then terrorism entered the equation – for example on 19

March a bomb explosion in a Baku underground railway station killed 12 people and injured 52, but no one claimed responsibility. Three men were convicted and imprisoned for attempting to assassinate former President Elchibey. The organiser of these terrorist incidents was said to be Aydin Gasymov, a relative of Elchibey. On 3 July a similar bomb explosion in the Baku underground railway killed seven people. President Aliyev blamed 'terrorist forces hostile to Azerbaijan'.

A renewed Azerbaijan offensive, mainly against the Mardakert region of Nagorno-Karabakh, began on 10 April, and two days later Armenia claimed that Azerbaijan aircraft had bombed Armenian towns – Goris and Kafan. This was probably the first incident of its kind on Armenian soil, but it was denied by the Azeris, as were air raids on Stepanakert. Another Russian-mediated ceasefire was negotiated but the fighting continued. Robert Kocharyan, leader of the Nagorno-Karabakh Defence Committee, called for autonomy within a united Armenia, a modification of recent demands for independence (Snark news agency).

In Baku on the 29th, in a televised address President Aliyev blamed the police for 'popular discontent within the capital' and accused them of corruption. He dismissed the interior minister, Vagif Novruzov, and appointed Ramil Usubov, a former Nakhichevan police chief, in his stead. In Nakhichevan, Natig Hasanov was elected president in place of Gaidar Aliyev.

The speaker of the Milli Majlis, Rasul Kuliyev, signed a controversial protocol on 9 May calling for a ceasefire with Armenia and the deployment of 'international forces as peacekeepers'. This had been negotiated by the CIS and already signed by Armenia and Nagorno-Karabakh. Some deputies, feeling that the protocol recognised the independence of Nagorno Karabakh, walked out and an opposition demonstration was organised in Baku, in which the Musavat party, whose headquarters was later raided by the police, played a major part. President Aliyev insisted the 'peace-keeping forces' would not be Russian, and so the deputies returned. Interior Minister Kuliyev closed down the only independent TV station in Baku.

Meanwhile, in Yerevan allegations were made that Azeri prisoners in Armenia were being beaten, starved and shot. On 18 June Gagik Ovanessian, leader of the Dashnak, was expelled from his party for criticising the Dashnak's 'Bolshevik methods'.

ARMENIANS ATTACK NAKHICHEVAN

A large crowd of Armenians attacked a village in the Sadarak area of Nakhichevan on 31 May 1994, killing four Azeri troops. Later the Azeris alleged that Armenia had bombed two other villages, while Armenia counterclaimed that Azeri forces in Nakhichevan were firing shells into Armenian territory. This caused Turkey some anxiety, as in September 1993 the Turkish prime minster had threatened to go to war with Armenia in defence of Nakhichevan. Eventually, on 27 July the defence ministers of Armenia, Azerbaijan and Nagorno-Karabakh signed an agreement giving legal status to, and indefinitely extending the ceasefire agreement reached in May.

TROUBLED BAKU

An APF opposition rally in Baku on 12 September 1994 ended in clashes with the police. Many arrests were made, including that of Ali Kerimov, who was accused of carrying a grenade. The protest was against government policies, especially its policy on Nagorno-Karabakh, which was thought to betray Azerbaijan interests. On the 21st four important Azeri 'rebels' escaped from Azerbaijan custody. One of these was former Defence Minister Rakhim Gaziyev, who had been blamed for the poor performance of the Azeri troops; another was Alikram Gumbatov, a rebel warlord. On the 30th Afiyaddin Jalilov (deputy speaker and a strong supporter of President Aliyev), Shamsi Ragimov (a top security official) and a vehicle driver were all shot dead in an attack in Baku – a warlord killing.

THE OPON REVOLT

The struggle between the warlords in Baku intensified on 2 October 1994, when the Azerbaijan Prosecutor General, Ali Omerov, ordered the arrest of three OPON (special purpose militia under the authority of the Interior Ministry) personnel in connection with the assassinations of 30 September. In response about 100 OPON troops, led by former Acting Interior Minister Ravshan Javador, seized Omerov and about 40 of his officials. Javador claimed that the OPON unit had been subjected to persecution and demanded the release of the detained men.

President Aliyev condemned the action and claimed that subversive internal and external forces opposed to the oil deal had been responsible for the escape of the four rebel leaders on 21 September. Omerov was released on the 4th, when OPON troops withdrew to their base in Baku, but Aliyev ordered his national troops to seal it off. Omerov addressed a crowd from the presidential palace and promised to use only legal means to resolve this dispute.

THE GYANDZHA REBELLION

On 4 October 1994 another, unconnected rebellion erupted in Gyandzha, the base of the Prime Minister Surat Guseinov, who had seized power in the coup of June 1993. Rebel forces captured key buildings, the railway station and the airport, but were driven out by pro-Aliyev troops by the 6th. Three government soldiers and seven 'rebels' were killed and 127 rebels arrested (Turan news agency).

Meanwhile Aliyev claimed that Russia was deliberately destabilising Azerbaijan by covert means in order to force him to permit the deployment of Russian troops along the Iranian border, and to gain a larger stake in the oil deal. Russia alleged that Aliyev was trying to extend his jurisdiction over certain sections of the Caspian Sea.

Aliyev further alleged that Ayaz Mutalibov, a former president, and Vagif Guseinov, a former director of the regional KGB, had orchestrated the violence in liaison with Russia, and that units involved in the Gyandzha rebellion were close to Surat Guseinov, still the serving prime minister. Guseinov denied all this, pledged his support for Aliyev, and the two men appeared in public together on the 5th. The following day Aliyev dismissed Guseinov, which was confirmed by the Milli Majlis, and assumed direct governmental responsibility.

Javador alleged that Omerov had planned a coup with Guseinov, and that the OPON action on the 2nd had in fact averted it and was not part of the plot. Omerov was dismissed by Aliyev on the 8th. Guseinov lost his deputy's immunity and disappeared to his power base, being charged in his absence with treason. Later, two other former ministers were arrested and charged with involvement in the attempted coup, while other suspects were dismissed for 'serious inadequacies' regarding the widespread bread shortages in Azerbaijan.

On 8 November Interior Minister Ramil Usubov stated that a large quantity of weapons, including 400 automatic rifles and two tanks, had been seized, or surrendered, since the alleged coup on the 2nd, and that over 5000 illegal weapons still remained in the hands of private citizens (Turan news agency).

WAVERING SUPPORT

Initially the Iranian government had automatically given support to Azerbaijan for ethnic and religious reasons, and had been hostile to Armenia for the converse ones. Turkey had also initially showed sympathy towards Azerbaijan and hostility towards Armenia, which had been strongly reciprocated. Now those attitudes seemed to be changing. Still recovering from its war with Iraq (1980–88), which it had lost, the Tehran government had been striving to reimpose central authority over its outer provinces, especially that of Azerbaijan, and was alarmed by the destabilising hordes of politically orientated Azeri refugees flooding into the country.

Occasional cries for a 'Greater Azerbaijan' also alarmed the Tehran government, reminding it that in 1946 there had been an independent Azerbaijan Republic, and that it would not take much provocation for its Azeri population to seek independence once again, noting that apart from the seven million Azeris in Azerbaijan, there were also two million in Turkey, all practically indigenous. Accordingly Iran modified its stance towards Armenia and offered some aid. The Nagarno-Karabakh issue diverted attention from visions of a Greater Azerbaijan.

Russia too had at first seemed to favour Azerbaijan over Armenia, but after the Battle for Baku it had changed its attitude, due to Azerbaijan leaving the CIS, the warlord struggle in Baku and the projected Caspian offshore oil exploration project.

CASPIAN OIL AGREEMENT

In June 1994 the question of the proposed Caspian offshore oil agreement cropped up again. Russia was not satisfied, a foreign affairs spokesman explaining that any maritime exploitation of resources must have the consent of all countries in the region, one of which was Russia. Nonetheless an agreement was signed on 20 September by the Western-led eleven-nation oil consortium. Britain was pleased, and so was Azerbaijan, but Russia was not.

At last, on 15 November the Azerbaijan Milli Majlis ratified the oil deal after three years of negotiations, and the 30-year contract was formally signed on the 20th to exploit the Azeri and Chirag offshore oilfields. Although the Russian company Lukoil had a 10 per cent stake, Russia was still not satisfied, arguing that the Caspian Sea was the joint possession of the five littoral countries (Russia, Kazakhstan, Turkmenistan, Iran and Azerbaijan), which should share all profits equally.

The next year, on 12 April 1995 an amendment to the agreement was signed, which increased Turkey's share to 6.75 per cent by transferring a 5 per cent stake from the Azerbaijan SOCAR oil company to the Turkish Petroleum Corporation (*Financial Times*). Turkey was not a Caspian country, which angered Iran as it was still angling for a share in the deal.

ARMENIA AND THE IMF

After consultating with the International Monetary Fund, on 19 November 1994 the Armenian government announced a programme of economic reforms. There had been several large demonstrations in Yerevan against poor living standards, as price liberalisation and inflation had caused huge increases in the cost of electricity, bread and other necessities. For example teachers were on strike, demanding a huge pay rise. The first instalment of the IMF loan, about $25 million, came though on 15 December, from a 'systemic transformation facility, to support the Armenian government's comprehensive programme of macroeconomic stabilisation and structural reform' (*Financial Times*) (one wonders how this translated into Armenian).

After the murder of Hambartsum Galtian, a former mayor of Yerevan and associate of Ter-Petrossian, on 29 December, the Dashnak was suspended by presidential decree, having been accused of organising a terrorist group, of committing political murders and of drug trafficking. In Baku on 6 February 1995, General Mamedrafi Mamedov, the Azerbaijani defence minister, was arrested and blamed for 'shortcomings in supplying and training the national army' (Tass). He was replaced by Safar Abiyev. State subsidies on bread and fuel were abolished, causing price rises.

SECOND OPON REVOLT

OPON (the Azerbaijani special purpose militia under the authority of the Interior Ministry) compromised about 3000 well-armed security troops, some 700 of whom were based in Baku. On 13 March 1995 OPON militiamen attacked a police station and other buildings in the Azerbaijani towns of Akstafa and Kazakh, where fighting continued for over two days. This revolt was led by Ravshan Javador, the deputy interior minister and another warlord. It was alleged that the attack had been provoked by a government investigation into OPON involvement in illegal trade in strategic materials, notably copper (Inter-Fax news agency).

The following day Interior Minister Ramil Usubov ordered the disbandment of OPON, but President Aliyev accused Javadov of starting a coup, warning that once again the country was on the brink of civil war. By the 16th the OPON units had withdrawn into their Baku headquarters, which was surrounded by government troops. Javadov demanded the resignation of President Aliyev and his own appointment as interior minister, in return for his OPON forces laying down their arms, as well as the appointment of his brother, Makhir Javadov, as prosecutor general. The Azeri warlords were bargaining with one another for power.

On 17 March government soldiers stormed the OPON headquarters and defeated the 'rebels'. The official casually figures were 36 dead, including Javadov, and 658 injured, but unofficial estimates were much higher. Some 200 'rebels' were arrested, including Javadov's brother, Makhir. In a televised address to the people of Azerbaijan, President Aliyev praised his new national army soldiers for their loyalty and accused Javador of conspiring with ex-President Ayaz Mutalibov, ex-President Surat Guseinov and former Defence Minister Rakhim Gaziyev, as well as foreign intelligence agencies and organised criminals.

CEASEFIRE

On 7 March 1995 it was agreed that disputes under the ceasefire agreement of May 1994 would be settled directly between the Armenian and Azerbaijani defence ministers. However, exchanges of mortar and small-arms fire continued along the northern stretch of the joint border. In April the Milli Majlis lifted the state of emergency that had been imposed on Gyandzha in October 1994 after the attempt by the then prime minister, Surat Guseinov, to seize power, but the state of emergency remained in being in Baku.

ARMENIAN AFFAIRS

In Yerevan on 6 April President Ter-Petrossian signed an electoral law for a 'National Assembly', to be elected every four years by two ballots, one to elect a deputy for each of the 150 single-member constituencies, and the other for a 'political party list' of 40 deputies, to be elected proportionally. A general election was scheduled for July. Members of the government, civil service, the armed forces and security services were barred from standing for election as deputies.

An indication of changing international allegiances occurred on 3 May in Tehran, when the Iranian government signed an energy agreement with Armenia for the supply of gas. This was to last for 20 years and required a 140 kilometre gas pipeline to be constructed by 1997. It was perhaps motivated by Iran's desire to upstage Turkey, which was currently discussing the exportation of electricity to Armenia. At times the electricity supply in Yerevan was limited to one hour per day.

On 21 May a bomb explosion in an Azeri region of Georgia severed the gas pipeline from Turkmenistan – the latest of a series of sabotage incidents. Vardan Oskhanian, the Armenian deputy foreign minister, claimed there was indisputable evidence that the Baku government had covertly sent agents to carry out terrorist attacks on the gas pipeline in Georgia. Armenia announced it would withdraw from the Nagorno-Karabakh peace talks.

In Yerevan on 27 May unknown gunmen opened fire on a car in which the leader of the National Self-Determination Union opposition party, Paruyr Ayrykian, was travelling – he was unharmed. The probable motive was to disrupt the new legislative procedures. The following month demonstrators clashed with police in Yerevan, protesting at the exclusion of certain political parties from the forthcoming elections. The offices of the progovernment Republican Party were bombed on 22 June.

The first multiparty elections in Armenia since its declaration of independence took place on 5 July 1995 (the second round being on the 20th), in which the ruling 'Republican Bloc', a pan-Armenian National Movement, won 119 of the seats in the 190-seat chamber. At the same time a new constitution was approved by a referendum (by an almost two-thirds majority). These elections were monitored by the Organisation of Security and Co-operation in Europe (the OSCE, which had replaced the CSCE in December 1994), which reported several irregularities. Several political parties had been barred from participating in the election, including the virile Dashnak, which mounted protest demonstrations. Ter-Petrossian became executive president and reappointed Hrand Bagration as prime minister. Although Ter-Petrossian had consolidated his constitutional power, his opposition was sharply defined, bitter and active.

THE CALL FOR GREATER AZERBAIJAN

On 6 May 1995 ex-President Abdulfaz Elchibey, leader of the APF, called for the creation of a Greater Azerbaijan, which would unify present Azerbaijan territory with parts of northern Iran. This upset Iran, which cut its electricity supplies to Nakhichevan, Elchibey's power base, ostensibly for non-payment of debt.

That month, despite pressure from Armenian exile organisations in the United States, President Clinton smiled on Azerbaijan and granted it 'most favoured nation' trading status. The scent of oil was in the air as this was the price the United States had to pay for its share of the British-led oil consortium's stake in the Caspian offshore oil agreement.

Azerbaijan also had a shortage of gas, as that supplied through the Turkmenistan pipeline had been cut off on 12 April for non-payment of previous supplies. The debt amounted to about $100 million. Azerbaijan had significant natural gas resources of its own, but its antiquated gas industry had deteriorated badly and only about one third of the country's domestic needs had been extracted in 1992–94. Several parts of Azerbaijan were deprived of their gas supplies (*Financial Times*).

AZERI WARLORDS

The Azeri warlords continued to jostle and quarrel. In Baku it was reported by Russian NTV that former Defence Minister Rakhim Gaziyev, whose trial had begun in August 1994, had been convicted of illegally surrendering the towns of Shusha and Lachin in early 1993, and was sentenced to death on 15 May.

Nakhichevan remained unstable, and on the 31st Shahmerdan Jafarov was killed in a clash with the police. A former deputy in the local Milli Majlis, he had been stripped of his immunity for establishing an armed group in Nakhichevan. The APF claimed that Elchibey's residence in Nakhichevan was continuously surrounded by Azerbaijan security forces, but this was blandly denied. Nakhichevan was certainly a hotbed of simmering revolt.

It was announced on 2 August in Baku that a plot had been discovered to assassinate President Aliyev, who on the 16th identified the plotters as a group of discontented army officers acting under the orders of former President Ayaz Mutalibov. Mutalibov, who was living in Moscow, denied the allegation. The Azerbaijan Security Minister (Namig Abbasov) later stated that the coup had been due to commence with the assassination of Aliyev as his motorcade passed under a bridge.

OIL CONSORTIUM DECISION

The Azerbaijan International Operating Company, the 11-member Caspian offshore oil consortium, met in Moscow on 9 October and decided to distribute the oil through two overland pipelines. One would cross Georgia, where a disused one already existed, to the Black Sea terminal of Suspa, and the other through Chechenya into Russia to the Black Sea oil terminal near Novorossiysk. The company hastened to stress that considerable negotiations would be required before the oil came on-stream. Across the Caspian Sea, Iran, which had been excluded from the consortium, gazed balefully and refused to accept the technicality that the offshore oil deposits belonged to Azerbaijan, insisting there should be joint ownership by all states with a Caspian seaboard.

AZERBAIJAN ELECTIONS

Elections were held in Azerbaijan in November. The results were predictable: the victor was the New Azerbaijan Party, formed by President Aliyev. At the same time a new constitution was approved, under which the one-chamber legislative body of 125 deputies was replaced by one of 181 seats, with a degree of proportional representation. In essence this provided the republic with a new pro-Western, secular, free-market stance. International observers commented on the exclusion of certain political parties and personalities and some critics complained of nepotism, while international human rights organisations pointed out that President Aliyev still held political prisoners, some of whom were alleging inhumane treatment and even torture.

Since the Moscow decision of the Azerbaijan International Operating Company, a mood of entrepreneurial buoyancy began to develop in Baku, invigorating its moribund oil and other industries, spurred on by international attention. Like all the CIS states, Azerbaijan was experiencing painful teething problems in its metamorphosis to a free market economy. Simultaneously, luxurious foreign cars and beggars were seen on the streets of Baku, which now teemed with an estimated 1.8 million people, many of whom were unemployed. Although

Azerbaijan's economic prospects seemed bright, one black cloud remained – its ongoing war with Armenia.

AN ARMED CAMP

By autumn 1995 both Armenia and Azerbaijan, and the two tinderboxes, Nakhichevan and Nagorno-Karabakh, had developed into armed camps, in which armies and militias were being equipped, trained and conditioned for battle, but most had the common weaknesses of unreliability and potential disloyalty. Ample ex-Soviet weaponry was available, but neither country had the means to buy the best, nor to buy in quantity, so military adventures were somewhat restricted. Armenia was plagued with unruly, semi-independent militias, while Azerbaijan was cursed with jostling rival warlords. The position of both executive presidents was tenuous.

The Armenian army, which was probably about 32 000-strong, now consisted of six brigades and half a dozen specialist regiments. It was equipped with just over 300 armoured vehicles, over 200 guns and mortars, and eight helicopters, but apparently no combat aircraft. The Azerbaijan army was about 56 000-strong and consisted of a probable 12 brigades and a few specialist regiments. It had over 600 armoured vehicles and more than 400 guns and mortars, some helicopters and probably 50 combat aircraft.

Each had hundreds of thousands of reservists, but mainly on paper; both had been slow to establish conventional Defence Ministries and general headquarters; and both had problems with ammunition and fuel supplies. The Defence Committee of Nagorno-Karabakh had about 20 000 men, including at least 8000 Armenian volunteers; the Azeri APF militia was about the same strength (IISS). Both seemed to be preparing for war.

So far states sympathetic to one side or another have been discrete in providing aid and arms, standing clear of the arena, but the danger is that instead of the embers of war dying due to lack of fuel, arms and money, they could blaze up again, stoked by interfering and interested nations that want to fight by proxy.

It is true that the May 1994 ceasefire has held, but until the matter of Nagorno-Karabakh is resolved, peace will be elusive, as neither Armenia nor Azerbaijan seem willing to compromise. It is probable that neither side, if it has to rely on its own resources, will be able to overcome the other in battle in the near future. Hope tends to focus on the continuing efforts of the 'Minsk group' of the OSCE, which has been involved in peacemaking in Nagorno-Karabakh since 1992. In September 1995 it sponsored talks that were attended by delegations from both Armenia and Azerbaijan. Both sides were urged to continue to observe the ceasefire, as well as to release all prisoners of war and detainees.

A NUCLEAR NOTE OF ALARM

Although in 1995 there were some signs of economic recovery in Azerbaijan, its enemy Armenia, beset by embargoes by neighbouring states, could see no such light at the end of the tunnel. Approaching winter left the citizens of Armenia shivering with cold and the apprehension of having to face yet another season of fuel deprivation. In early November this factor probably drove the Armenia government to restart its nuclear reactor at Medzhmor – disused since the earthquake of 1989 but which had previously provided up to half the country's electricity needs – against considerable international technical advice. Critics claimed that the nuclear reactor, commissioned in 1979, had several serious design faults and therefore should be decommissioned, and that to restart it after this length of time would endanger millions of lives as the Caucasus region is one of the most geologically unstable in the world.

Some were of the opinion that this was a deliberate ploy by Armenia to provoke international pressure on Turkey, Iran and Azerbaijan to lift their fuel embargoes. Drastic means for drastic ends indeed, bold but suicidal; but a gamble that may succeed as a Chernobyl-type nuclear disaster could affect Van in Turkey Tabriz in Iran, Baku in Azerbaijan, Yerevan in Armenia and the countless cities, towns and villages between them. Clearly this is an urgent task for the Minsk group to work on.

5 Georgia

During the evening of 8 April 1989 about 8000 Georgian protesters gathered for an all-night vigil in the grandly laid-out Rustaveli Prospekt in Tbilisi, capital of the Soviet Socialist Republic of Georgia. Above them towered the statue of King Vakhtang Gorgaslani, who won independence for Georgia at the end of the fifth century. Seated on horseback, the King's image looked out over Tbilisi and the Kura river.

In the early hours of the 9th the authorities ordered that the demonstrators be dispersed, and when they refused to move they were set upon vigorously by the Soviet military. Sixteen people were either clubbed to death by 'batons or spades', or died from the effects of the toxic gas used against the crowd. Later four other demonstrators died, bringing the death toll to 20, the majority of whom were women. The remaining demonstrators were dispersed, arrests were made, troops patrolled the streets and further rallies were banned. The authorities claimed that the troops had met with fierce resistance, and in the mass hysteria sticks, stones and metal objects had been thrown at them. This was denied by the demonstrators in this significant outburst of Georgian nationalism. There were conflicting versions, and considerable argument followed over the type of gas used and its possible effects.

The authorities in Moscow hastened to send messages of condolence to the relatives of deceased demonstrators, while the Georgian authorities declared the 11th a 'day of national mourning'. The event passed into Georgian folk history as the day the Russian troops beat Georgian civilians to death with spades.

Eduard Shevardnadze, the Soviet foreign minister and himself a Georgian, cancelled a visit to East Germany and hurried to Tbilisi to discuss the situation with Georgian Communist Party officials and opposing 'nationalist leaders'. He blamed the first secretary of the Georgian Communist Party, the senior Georgian with political and executive responsibility (an office he himself had held for some years), for the death of innocent people. The first secretary resigned.

Shevardnadze lectured his fellow Georgians and urged them

to end their nationalist protests, which he said were damaging President Gorbachev's policies of perestroika and glasnost. The curfew was lifted and the troops were withdrawn from the streets, but tension remained. In Moscow on the 23rd, police broke up a large Georgian demonstration supporting the 'victims of the 9 April massacre' (Tass). Later a commission that had been appointed to look into the incident found that the army was accusing the politicians and the politicians were blaming the commander of the Transcaucasian military district, who was alleged to be trying to cover up the use of gas. The commission's findings were indecisive.

Since the fourth century the ancient Christian kingdom of Georgia had been variously occupied by Romans, Turks, Arabs, Mongols, Persians and Russians. Although its boundaries fluctuated according to its fortunes and misfortunes, its kingdom status survived, although precariously at times. In 1801 Georgia was incorporated into the czar's empire, which for the first time brought Russian troops into fringe territory held by Persia. In 1804 the Shah of Persia began hostilities against Russia over the sovereignty of Georgia. This dragged on until Russia's defeat in 1813, when it had to surrender much of its territory in the Caucasus.

After a brief spell as the independent 'Georgian Democratic Republic' (1918–21), Georgia was occupied by the Bolshevik Red Army and wrapped tightly within the Soviet Union. However the Georgian people remained independent-minded, their own language with its own alphabet remaining in common use as well as being taught in schools. Many Georgians were natural traders and a merchant class continued to survive. It was said that Georgians played a prominent part in the hidden, black market economy that was rampant (but unpublicised) in many of the major Soviet cities.

Corruption was endemic in Georgia as many of its leaders and inhabitants worked the Communist system for their own benefit, rather than trying to buck it. An interesting insight was given into this state of affairs by *Zarya Vostoka*, the Georgian Communist Party newspaper, which, in April 1975, reported the dismissal of the chairman of the republic's State Committee for Oil Production on the ground of 'widespread embezzlement'; while the first deputy secretary and other officials were reprimanded for inefficiency; and the police chief of the city of Gori (Stalin's birthplace) was dismissed for corrupt practices. In August that year the minister of culture was dismissed for nepotism and patronage, and in October there were further dismissals of local Communist Party officials for misbehaviour of various sorts, and of police for corruption.

This may have been more or less commonplace, and probably was, but what was unusual was that the punishments were so openly and pointedly reported, when previously they had usually been shielded from external gaze by censorship to preserve the ideal of the purity of communism. There had been a spate of explosions and arson in Tbilisi and other Georgian cities the previous year, which had also been openly reported. This too was unusual as the CPSU's normal policy was to conceal disasters and other bad news, especially of a political nature.

Present-day Georgia is a Black Sea country whose southwestern frontier abuts Turkey, a traditional enemy. To the south lie Armenia and Azerbaijan; to the north the Russian Federation along the Caucasus Mountain range, Chechenya and the Black Sea; and to the east Dagestan. Georgia is crossed by a main railway line from Baku in eastern Azerbaijan, and also one from Turkey, the junction being near Tbilisi. The track then runs north-westwards to Samtredia, where a line branches off southwards to Batumi, a resort in the oblast of Adharia, the main line going on to Sukhumi and Gagra (both in the oblast of Abkhazia) and then into the Russian Federation. A disused oil pipeline runs from Baku across Georgia to Supsa on the Black Sea.

In 1989 Georgia had a population of 5.4 million (official census), of whom 70.1 per cent were ethnic Georgians with a formal Christian heritage. The Russian element was 6.3 per cent and other small groups included Muslim Abkhazis, Adzharis, Meskhetians, Mingrelians and Ossetes, plus Armenians, Azeris, Greeks and Kurds. In Soviet communist times Georgia had been the playground of the political elite, owing to its favourable climate and sandy beaches. Georgian wines, fruit and tea were exported to all parts of the Soviet Union, but like all the republics it was not allowed to become economically independent, for example it had to rely on fuel from external sources.

GEORGIAN NATIONALISM

Positive signs of nationalism in Georgia began to appear in 1987 with the formation of the Chavchavasde Society, which cautiously concentrated on Georgian culture. This provoked the Georgian Communist Party to establish the Rustaveli Society, which had a cohesive Georgian platform (Goldenberg, 1994). The following year, stirred by the effects of Gorbachev's reforms, which were beginning to take root and percolate into the outer republics, two decidedly political groups appeared. One was the Society of St Ilya the Righteous, which was formed by Zviad Gamsakhurdia for native Georgians and espoused an independent Georgia. The other was the National Democratic Party, formed by Georgi Chanturia, whose aim was also to gain independence.

In November 1988 a huge demonstration was mounted in the Rustaveli Prospekt in central Tbilisi against the Soviet Union's proposed amendments to the USSR constitution, which would be detrimental to the Georgian march towards independence. When the Kremlin authorities saw the depths of feeling being demonstrated on the Tbilisi streets, the proposed amendments were withdrawn. This gave budding Georgian nationalists a fresh impetus.

A series of rallies began on 25 March 1989, prompted largely by anger at Abkhazian demands to be separated from Georgia. At the rallies various Georgian nationalist demands were voiced, ranging from greater autonomy under Kremlin rule to independence from the USSR, then considered political heresy.

On 4 April some 150 Georgian nationalist activists began a hunger strike outside the Communist Party headquarters on Rustaveli Prospekt. They were demanding full independence for Georgia, and that the oblast of Abkhazia, which already had considerable autonomy, be fully integrated into the Republic of Georgia. Two days later over 100 000 people took to the streets to demonstrate their solidarity with the hunger strikers, causing Soviet troops to be deployed to keep order. On the 8th the demonstration whose tragic outcome was described at the start of this chapter included university students, transport employees and factory workers. Georgian nationalism was on the march.

A huge crowd of 200 000 or more Georgians marched through

the centre of Tbilisi on 26 April to mark the anniversary of the 1918 declaration of the independent Georgian Democratic Republic. Later, at a session of the Georgian Supreme Soviet (17–19 November 1989), the constitution was amended to declare 'Georgian sovereignty' and ownership of all natural resources within its boundaries, as well as reaffirming its right to secede from the Soviet Union, and asserting the right of the Georgian Supreme Soviet to suspend Soviet Union laws if they ran contrary to Georgian interests. A bold step to take, but in keeping with the rapidly changing times in the USSR.

A Georgian Commission, set up to examine the Soviet takeover of the country in 1921–22, declared that this had been a violation of a Treaty of 7 May 1920, whereby the Bolsheviks had recognised Georgia's independence, and that their entry into Georgia in February 1921 had been a 'military occupation' aimed at changing its existing political system. The Georgian Supreme Soviet declared on 9 March 1990 that the Treaties of 1921–22 were illegal, condemning them as an international crime and calling for the Moscow authorities to enter into negotiations on the issue.

On the first anniversary of the 8–9 April demonstration in Tbilisi, another well attended all-night vigil was held, when speakers called for Georgian nationalist groups to unite in the struggle for independence, and for Georgians to boycott military service.

PARTIES AND PERSONALITIES

Meanwhile active groups with distinct political characteristics had begun to surface, some of which set up small armed militias. Dominated by their leading personalities, there was little liaison between them, let alone unity. At this stage individual political manifestos, when made, were rambling and vague. Intense rivalry developed between leaders as the thirst for political power developed, the prize being an independent Georgia, so long a dream, but now seeming more attainable.

The predominant figure in this new political maelstrom was Zviad Gamsakhurdia, a long-time protester with good dissident credentials. He had first been imprisoned for his activities at the age of 17, and his father, Konstantin, had been a well-known Georgian poet; two factors that combined to boost his political status. Gamsakhurdia explained that he had been converted to the cause of Georgian nationalism during the suppression of peaceful demonstrations in 1956, after which he had become a prominent dissident demonstrator and writer. Like many national leaders who escape the international gaze until they achieve fame or notoriety, the accounts of the early life of Gamsakhurdia are contradictory, his biographers and publicists tending to disagree on details.

It may be sufficient to say that in 1974 he helped to form the 'Initiative Group for the Defence of Human Rights', in which sphere – speaking both English and French fluently – he gained the recognition of and endeared himself to the Western media, becoming a member of Amnesty International and the Georgian Helsinki Group. In addition he became an outspoken Georgian nationalist and frequently clashed with the Georgian communist authorities, especially the local KGB. After a period of incarceration in a Soviet labour camp, he emerged in the 1980s as the foremost nationalist leader. Gamsakhurdia developed the Round Table coalition, and his supporters became known as 'Zviad' or 'Zviadistis'.

Georgi Chanturia's National Democratic Party and the National Independence Party became part of the National Congress Movement coalition, which was led by Tengiz Kitovani and was in opposition to Gamsakhurdia's Round Table. Others were waiting in the wings but less was known about their leaders, who had yet to prove themselves politically, although it was suspected there might be ambitious and ruthless dark horses amongst them. The rough and tumble of Georgian politics was becoming really rough.

THE OCTOBER 1990 ELECTIONS

The first multiparty elections were scheduled for 28 October 1990, but there was some preelection violence and dirty tricks between competing groups to try to preempt the official elections by holding an impromptu, independent poll for a 'National Congress' on 30 September in order to overshadow, and influence, the official ones. For example on the night of 12 September members of the Society of St Ilya the Righteous, a member of the Round Table coalition, ransacked the offices of the local KGB headquarters, where some of its rowdy members had been detained.

The Mekhedrioni (Horsemen), a paramilitary group led by Dzhaba Ioseliani (described as a writer and literary critic by some, and who was reputed to have been imprisoned for robbery in his youth), was allied to the National Congress Movement. The Mekhedrioni developed as a dedicated Georgian group (non-Georgians were not invited to join) with a degree of military organisation and discipline, being extremely nationalistic and very prone to displaying Georgian insignia and symbols. The Mekhedrioni kidnapped Vazh Adamiya, a prominent Round Table leader, on 18 September and a gun battle developed between the two groups on the Rustaveli Prospekt the following day. Round Table supporters ransacked the buildings of both the National Democratic Party and the National Independence Party.

The unofficial rival poll was duly held on 30 September for a National Congress, in which the National Independence Party gained most votes and the National Democratic Party came second – but as the poll was boycotted by the Round Table coalition and other parties it was of little practical value, except to highlight the division between the two rival coalitions. An unknown gunman shot and wounded Georgi Chanturia of the National Democratic Party on 26 October.

PRESIDENT GAMSAKHURDIA

The first round of the official elections was duly held on 28 October 1990 for the 250-seat Georgian Supreme Congress. The round was won by Gamsakhurdia's 'Round Table–Free Georgia' coalition, which gained 54 per cent of the votes cast, but there was a partial boycott in Abkhazia and South Ossetia and an almost total one by the National Congress Movement coalition. The second round took place on 11 November, and the Round Table–Free Georgia coalition of nationalist parties increased its share to 64 per cent, gaining 155 seats but falling just short of the two-thirds majority required to alter the constitution. The Georgian Communist Party gained 64 seats and the Georgian Popular Front, another coalition, gained eleven, the remainder going to 'independents'. Gamsakhudia claimed that his support was based largely on rural voters, the less well off in cities and towns, and Georgians in Abkhazia and South Ossetia. It seemed that professionals and the intelligencia, who had previously been vocal in anticommunist and pro-independence activities, had been pushed aside.

On 14 November Zviad Gamsakhurdia, leader of the Round Table–Free Georgia coalition and veteran nationalist dissident, was elected president of the new Georgian Supreme Soviet by 232 votes to five. It was Gamsakhurdia's moment of triumph at the age of 51, but he sat on a very uncertain power base. He promised to work for complete independence, which he thought would take up to five years. Tengiz Sigua, a member of the same coalition, was appointed prime minister. The words 'Soviet' and 'Socialist' were eliminated from the country's title, which became simply the 'Republic of Georgia'. The old Georgian flag was flown in Tbilisi for the first time since 1921. Nationalism was beginning to triumph over communism in Georgia.

The Congress of the Georgian Communist Party declared on 8 December that it was seceding from the CPSU, and would in future work for Georgian independence (communist delegates from Abkhazia and South Ossetia boycotted this congress). On 30 January 1991 the Georgian Supreme Soviet voted to establish a 20 000-strong national republican army, to be raised by conscription, as part of its process towards complete independence.

GEORGIAN REFERENDUM

In March 1991 Georgia boycotted Gorbachev's all-Soviet Union referendum on whether or not to preserve the USSR, as this would tend to legitimate Soviet constitutional authority over it and negate its argument for independence. However, Abkhazia and South Ossetia did take part in the overwhelmingly affirmative vote. On the 31st Georgia held its own referendum on the issue of independence, the result being 98 per cent in favour (out of a poll of 91.5 per cent). Zviad Gamsakhurdia was elected executive President of Georgia by 87 per cent of the votes cast, defeating five other candidates for this office.

Gamsakhurdia was a native of Mingrelia (as was the notorious Lavrenty Beria), a comparatively poor and neglected region, based mainly on the city of Zugdidi, adjacent to Abkhazia. Although Migrelians were officially part of the Georgian nation, they were in fact outsiders, tending to be backward, isolated and isolationist. Mingrelia had developed as a Georgian principality with periods under Muslim rule, indeed the Mingrelians had sided with the Turks against Russia in the Crimean War (1854–56).

SOUTH OSSETIA

Meanwhile ethnic emotions had also been rearoused in the autonomous Soviet oblast of South Ossetia, nominally part of the Republic of Georgia and lying adjacent to the diagonal Caucasus Mountain range, on the other side of which was the autonomous Soviet oblast of North Ossetia, which lay within the Russian Federation. Ethnically the two parts formed one nation with one language, but they had been divided by Stalin. The population of South Ossetia was probably about 175 000, of whom some 50 000 were non-Ossetes. North Ossetia probably had a population of over 300 000.

The Christian Georgians and the Muslim Ossetes were traditional enemies, and in the nineteenth century the Ossetes tended to support the Russians in their colonial conquests, holding for them the region's only pass over the Caucasus Mountains. In Georgia's brief existence as a democratic republic it had put down several Ossete uprisings with great severity. Even so there were several Georgian-inhabited villages scattered inside South Ossetia, especially around Tskhenvali, its capital city. Under communist rule there had been a degree of amity and some intermarriage, but the inherent dislike continued. The Georgians contended that the Ossetes' real home was north of the Caucasus Mountains and usually referred to South Ossetia as 'Inner Georgia'.

In April 1988 there were unruly protest demonstrations in Tskhenvali that lasted three days. Initially the protests had been directed against the insanitary state of the city's water supply, which had caused an outbreak of typhoid fever, but then they developed political overtones, for which the Communist Party's first secretary of the Georgian regional committee for South Ossetia was dismissed.

In early 1989 an Ossete group called 'Ademon Nykhas' ('Popular Shrine') (Goldenberg, 1994), published a letter supporting the Abkhazian campaign to open an exclusive Georgian college at the Sukhumi branch of the Georgian State University. The letter also contained political demands. Clashes and friction between Ossetes and resident Georgians became more frequent, and elements of a Georgian militia appeared on the scene. Demonstrations occurred in Tskhinvali in September, when the Georgian Supreme Soviet ratified a decree that Georgian and Russian would be the official languages of South Ossetia.

During the summer, local industry had been crippled by a number of politically motivated strikes organised by the 'Popular Front of South Ossetia', which had been formed in 1977 and was campaigning for South Ossetia to be upgraded to the status of 'autonomous republic', and thus be freed from Georgian shackles. Protest demonstrations for greater autonomy swept through South Ossetia and were countered by groups of Georgians, some from outside the oblast. Ossete groups and residents were attacked and several people were injured. Consequently a detachment of Ministry of Interior troops was sent to South Ossetia to seal off Tskhinvali and protect its residents from rampaging Georgians.

On 20 September 1990 the Supreme Soviet of South Ossetia proclaimed itself a full 'Union Republic', completely independent of Georgia. The following day the Georgian Supreme Soviet ruled the declaration invalid. On 10 December South Ossetia reaffirmed its September proclamation of 'independence and state sovereignty' within the Soviet Union. The following day the Georgian Supreme Assembly stripped South Ossetia of its self-declared autonomous status, which resulted in clashes in Tskhinvali between Ossete militants and Georgian police – three Georgians and one Ossete were killed, and others were injured. Georgia declared a state of emergency in Tskhinvali and Dzhava (the second largest town), and additional Ministry of Interior troops were moved in to enforce it.

Anxious to crush these petty nationalist squabbles, Gorbachev issued a decree on 7 January 1991 countermanding both the South Ossete's September declaration and the Georgian legislation, and ordering all Georgian armed units, less Ministry of Interior ones, to withdraw from South Ossetia within three days. On the 9th Gamsakhurdia rejected Gorbachev's decree, saying he would reinforce the contingent of Georgian 'police' already in South Ossetia, and accusing Gorbachev of deliberately stirring up discontent so that he would be able to impose direct presidential rule on the oblast, and then progressively on the whole of Georgia.

However on the 28th Gamsakhurdia changed his mind about the reinforcements, and said that those remaining could patrol jointly with Soviet troops. By this time over 20 people had been killed that month by explosions and gun battles between militant Ossetes and Georgian militiamen. The two sides began to negotiate but the Georgians insisted the Ossetes must surrender their arms to the Georgian 'police'. The negotiations were interrupted by the arrest of Torez Kolumbegov, leader of the South Ossetia Supreme Soviet and self-proclaimed 'president', when on his way to the talks with the Georgian leaders. This caused protest strikes in Tskhinvali.

In response the Georgian authorities cut the electricity and water supplies to South Ossetia. A partial economic blockade had been in place against the oblast since December 1990, and this was now stepped up – Georgian militiamen prevented food convoys from reaching the Ossetes from North Ossetia through the road tunnel by blocking it. Tengiz Kitovani, an advocate of a unified Georgia, took an interest in events in South Ossetia, and elements of his National Guard became involved.

By this time Moscow TV was showing pictures of buildings and homes in Tskhinvali being ransacked by Georgian militiamen. Georgians were not popular in Moscow, allegedly because of their mafia connections. Soviet Red Cross and Red Crescent organisations reported they were dealing with some 8000 refugees who had fled northwards into North Ossetia, and some 3000 Georgians who had fled southwards into Georgia. On 11 February Torez Kolumbegov was arraigned by the Georgian government.

The Soviet minister of the interior, Boris Pugo, ordered Georgia to extend the state of emergency throughout South Ossetia and to lift the economic blockade. The electricity and water supplies were restored, but that was about all. Pugo stated that the death toll in South Ossetia since the beginning of January was 33 (14 Ossetes and 19 Georgians, Tass). Intermittent violence continued for much of the remainder of the year as Georgian militiamen tried to dominate Ossete militants. Then the age-old custom of hostage taking began to show its ugly face.

ABKHAZIA

In the autonomous Soviet oblast of Abkhazia in the north-western corner of Georgia, Georgians outnumbered the native Abkhazians. The 1989 census showed that 45.7 per cent of the population of just over 200 000 were Georgian and only 17.8 per cent Abkhazian, the remainder being Armenian, Russian and 'others'. On 18 March 1989 in the village of Lykhny, a large rally of Abkhazians called for the oblast's secession from Georgia and reinstatement as a Soviet republic (a status briefly held in 1920). A letter to Gorbachev on this issue was signed by Boris Adreyba, first secretary of the Georgian Communist Party Committee for Abkhazia, and other prominent Abkhazians. On the 25th a counterrally by 'thousands' of resident Georgians was held in Sukhumi, and on 2 April a large protest demonstration was held in the large, Georgian-majority town of Lesselidze, in which several people were injured.

Abkhazians are ethnic Georgians, Abkhazia being a former Georgian principality whose inhabitants were forcibly converted to Islam by Muslim overlords. Russia had attempted a policy of assimilation, which resulted in a steady seepage of emigrants and the immigration of other nationalities, which together with Stalin's arrests and deportations caused Abkhazians to become a declining minority in their own land. After being occupied by the Bolshevik Red Army, Abkhazia remained under central Kremlin rule until 1930, when it became an oblast within the Georgian republic. In 1941 a number of Abkhazians were executed for allegedly conspiring to form a Nazi state.

Abkhazia had come to be noted for the beaches of its Black Sea resorts of Gagra, Pitsonda, Sukhumi and others favoured by the Soviet Union's top political elite for their vacations, but it also had its dark side, which was historical interethnic and inter-religious strife and dissidence. Abkhazia first began to demand to become an autonomous republic within the USSR in 1978.

The next resurgence of interethnic rioting in Abkhazia occurred in July 1989, the catalyst being the controversial admission quotas to the Sukhumi Branch of the Tbilisi State

University. Disturbances began on the 14th, and during the following days escalated into street fighting in Sukhumi between Abkhazians and Georgians. When this spread to most parts of the oblast, additional Soviet Ministry of Interior troops were drafted in. Armed Georgians occupied a hydroelectric power station and deprived several districts of electric power. The Georgian population declared a general strike and a state of emergency was imposed throughout Abkhazia as mobs attacked police stations, releasing prisoners and seizing weapons. Clashes between armed Georgians and Abkhazians, sabotage and explosions continued until the the end of the month. Rail and road transportation was harassed by armed groups from both sides shooting at buses and trains, and from 18 July holidaymakers had to be evacuated by air and sea.

It was not until 8 August that the Soviet troops were able to report that they had the situation under control, whereupon special passes were issued to monitor the movement of people within the oblast. At the end of August the authorities reported that 42 had been killed and over 600 injured, that hundreds had been arrested for breaching the emergency regulations, and that over 5000 illegal weapons had been seized (Inter-fax).

The momentum may have slowed, but the tension remained and the Abkhazians continued to protest. Eventually, on 25 August 1990 their Supreme Soviet (with barely half their 150 deputies voting as the Georgian deputies boycotted the session) declared Abkhazia's full independence from Georgia and the restoration of its former republican status, accusing the Georgian government of illegal annexation. The Georgian Supreme Soviet denounced this move, which resulted in numerous Georgian protest rallies and a blockade of the railway into Sukhumi. This pressure caused the Abkhazians to rescind their declaration.

At the Supreme Council elections in Abkhazia on 23 June 1991 the Georgian Round Table–Free Georgia coalition won 48 per cent of the votes, while the Abkhazia Organisation of the Independent Party of Georgia, gained only 18 per cent.

THE MESKHETIANS

A group of about 200 Meskhetians (Shia Muslims) clashed with the police in the Georgian town of Borzhomi during a demonstration in favour of all Meskhetians being allowed to return from exile to live in the Meskhetian region near the Turkish border. During 1944 Stalin had deported the entire community of about 400 000 to Uzbekistan, since when less than 10 000 had been allowed to return. The Meskhetians, who regarded themselves as Turks, met continual hostility from the Georgians, who hoped they would go away. The Georgians constantly complained that more of their republic was taken up by 'minorities' than any other in the Soviet Union

PRESIDENT GAMSAKHURDIA

When Zviad Gamsakhurdia was elected President of Georgia he was probably the most popular man in that republic, but his popularity soon began to wane as, dictatorial and wilful, he became embroiled in intrigue, seeing enemies on all sides. His Round Table allies began to desert him, or were removed from positions of authority, as he began to place his own candidates on important committees and councils. Some of his original supporters began to distance themselves from him. Gamsakhurdia's election platform had been based on multi-party democracy and a free-market economy, but his administration tended to be just the opposite.

In early August he dismissed his prime minister (Tengiz Sigua), his deputy prime minister (Otar Kviliataya) and his foreign minister (Georgi Khoshtaria), having already assumed direct control of the Ministries of the Interior and Justice, as well as the KGB. Sigua moved to the Lake Tbilisi military camp outside the capital, which became a base for anti-Gamsakhurdia leaders. Growing popular discontent with Gamsakhurdia's dictatorial rule caused demonstrations to be mounted in Tbilisi to call for his resignation and that of his cabinet. Georgian politicians had mostly shed their former communist ideals and quickly devolved into quarrelling nationalist factions.

During the three-day crisis brought about by the attempted coup against Gorbachev, Gamsakhurdia dismissed Tengiz Kitovani, commander of the National Guard, from his government and ordered the National Guard to be disbanded. Some alleged that Gamsakhurdia was in league with the coup plotters, and that his newly appointed foreign minister, Murman

Omanidza, had held secret talks on the issue in Moscow prior to 19 August, which seemed to indicate he was backing the plotters. In any event, when the coup failed he turned against the Gorbachev government and rescinded his order to disband the National Guard, but his overhasty actions had alienated Kitovani and most of the guardsmen. It seems that Gamsakhurdia belatedly realised he had made a mistake and had little other military force to rely upon, so he sought to bring the National Guard under constitutional control, it now being of somewhat wavering loyalty.

THE NATIONAL GUARD

A huge, hostile demonstration took place in Tbilisi on 2 September 1991, which provoked Gamsakhurdia into ordering the National Guard to open fire to disperse it. An undetermined number of people were injured. This further dented Gamsakhurdia's waning image, thus encouraging his detracters, and hostile rallies became more frequent.

Gamsakhurdia broke off all relations with the Soviet Union on the 6th, declaring that Soviet troops stationed on Georgian soil were 'occupying forces', and refusing to sign either defence or economic agreements with the USSR. Genuine Georgian democrats, many of whom were seeking power, were dismayed, realising they could become entrapped and isolated in a small state that was tightly controlled by a dominant, self-centred president who was already restricting some personal freedoms and tightening his grip on the media. The previous day Gamsakhurdia had closed down all Georgian newspapers, the excuse being 'shortage of paper'.

On the 9th Gamsakhurdia announced the formation of the Georgian Defence Ministry, and ordered the 'rebel' elements of the National Guard, his nominal 'army', to return to barracks. In February he had arrested the paramilitary leader Dzhaba Ioseliani and a detachment of his Mekhedrioni, fearful of his military influence in the country.

The National Guard, originally planned to form the basis of the Georgian army, had been formally established on 1 January 1991 and had risen to a probable strength of over 5000 men, although no one seemed to know the precise figure at this confused juncture of Georgian evolution. It had originated as the private militia of Tengiz Kitovani, whose platform was to keep the Georgian republic united and who remained in command of it. Elements of the National Guard had been active in Abkhazia against the separatists, but it was now splitting into rival factions: the 'Zviadists' and the 'rebels', the latter led by Kitovani.

Gamsakhurdia threw down the gauntlet to his opponents, and on 15 September expelled the 64 Communist Party deputies from the Georgian Supreme Council, which caused another 40 deputies to walk out, leaving behind a democratic vacuum. The following day he arrested Georgi Chanturia, leader of the National Democratic Party, catching him at the airport before he fled the country. Apart from moving against other National Congress Movement groups and detaining leaders whenever he could, he also tackled the 'old guard' of the Communist Party (although these had been pushed from power, they remained influential and ambitious) and embittered mafia syndicates, which since 1985 had become powerful and all-pervading in Georgian society. Gamsakhurdia was setting Georgian against Georgian in an attempt to divide and rule. Meanwhile revolt festered in the Lake Tbilisi Camp, now the base for 'rebel elements' of the National Guard and opposition leaders.

ARMED REVOLT

A massive crowd of multifactional demonstrators swarmed around the Georgian Assembly, other government buildings and the TV station in the centre of Tbilisi on 18 September to interrupt a broadcast Gamsakhurdia was about to make. Three days later the TV station was occupied by the 'rebel' White Eagles militia, said to be several hundred strong, led by Georgi Karakashvili, the dismissed deputy defence minister. Karakashvili attempted to broadcast anti-Gamsakhurdia propaganda, but this failed as the government cut off the power supply. However Gamsakhurdia still managed to upstage the opposition as he was able to broadcast to the nation from the Assembly buildings, where there were adequate facilities.

Somewhat belatedly Gamsakhurdia came to realise the strength of popular opposition, and on the 22nd offered to meet an opposition spokesman for a televised discussion of future elections and other controversial matters. In Moscow Eduard Shevardnadze, who was shrewdly watching events in his native Georgia, urged Gamsakhurdia to 'restore dialogue with his opponents' (Tass). Gamsakhurdia immediately labelled Shevardnadze 'an enemy of Georgia'.

Gamsakhurdia declared a state of emergency on the 25th, because 'a military and civil putsch is under way in the republic' (Tass), demanding that all illegal weapons be surrendered – an almost impossible aim. He then established a National Security Council, chaired by himself. On the night of 24–25 September at least five people were killed in clashes between factional militias and government security forces, which caused Gamsakhurdia to threaten to impose presidential rule. An explosion outside the TV station gave him the excuse to cancel his promised discussion with the opposition spokesman, as the various factions had not laid down their arms. Another surrender ultimatum was issued on 1 October. The streets of the capital became the scene of glorified political gang warfare, watched passively by curious, uncommitted citizens.

The White Eagles militia evacuated the TV station on 3 October and the interfactional fighting moved to the area of the Lake Tbilisi camp, where opposing militias battled for two days. At least three were killed in the fighting and several were wounded.

At a closed session of the very much reduced Georgian Supreme Council on the 7th, the state of emergency in Tbilisi was confirmed and responsibility for the Soviet Ministry of Interior troops was transferred to the Georgian Defence Ministry, which was to take over all their establishments, buildings, equipment and facilities in the republic. The few Soviet military personnel remaining in Georgia kept a very low profile. They were almost completely inactive and stood well aside from the scuffling Georgian factions, seemingly regarding them with indifferent contempt, have neither affinity with them nor sympathy for their cause. Gamsakhurdia arrested a number of Chanturia's National Democratic Party leaders.

A MILITARY COUP

During four months of confrontation, huge crowds continually choked the wide Rustaveli Prospekt, often confining

Gamsakhurdia, his ministers and their staff to their government offices as many of them were unwilling to brave the hostile militias and populace. On 22 December 1991 'rebel' detachments of the National Guard, led by Kitovani, mounted an assault on the Assembly buildings, where Gamsakhurdia had been besieged for several days. The barricaded buildings were defended by a 'loyal' section of the National Guard and other militiamen, probably totalling about 1000 in all.

The attack failed but Gamsakhurdia remained besieged, operating from a large underground section of the building that came to be referred to as his 'bunker'. Many government buildings had 'nuclear shelters', relics of the Cold War that often proved useful in these troubled times. Hostile militias continued to bombard the buildings, mainly with mortar fire, although heavier weapons were later brought into action as well. Despite the daily bombardments and casualties, Gamsakhurdia, in a series of media interviews, including TV, insisted he would hold out and refused to negotiate with 'terrorists and bandits', nor would he resign as demanded.

On the 27th Tengiz Kitovani, commanding the besieging militias, was joined by Dzhaba Ioseliani, who had just escaped from arrest. The following day, three ministers deserted Gamsakhurdia, but he remained defiant. This siege in Tbilisi was given special billing on Moscow TV, being used as a political lesson to show what could happen to former constituent republics of the USSR if they did not join the proposed CIS.

On 2 January 1992 Kitovani and Ioseliani jointly declared that a Military Council had taken power in Georgia, that Gamsakhurdia had been deposed and his Georgian Supreme Council suspended pending new elections, which would take place within six months. A state of emergency was declared in Tbilisi, and all public gatherings were forbidden. The military junta was based mainly on the National Congress Movement coalition.

That morning the TV station was reoccupied by the White Eagles militia, and soon much of the centre of Tbilisi was under the control of the military junta. One junta leader tentatively suggested that its ultimate aim might be a constitutional monarchy (the Georgian royal family, the Bagrations, were living in exile in Spain), but this was not taken seriously. Once revolutionaries get their hands on political power it has to be prised away from them.

Unarmed crowds still milled around the centre of Tbilisi, some hoping that 'people power' might help resolve the issue to their respective satisfaction. One such gathering, said to be over 2000 strong and chanting in support of Gamsakhurdia, was fired upon by Mekhedrioni militiamen, killing at least three people and injuring over 30 others. One of the two gunmen was caught by the demonstrators and beaten to death. Ioseliani did not deny his men were responsible. The following day the Military Council reinstated Tengiz Sigua as acting prime minister, with the responsibility of forming a cabinet and assuming temporary power to govern. Sigua became the third member of the military triumvirate.

Meanwhile the bombardment of the Assembly building continued, but there seemed to be reluctance on the part of the military junta to launch a serious attack to overrun the defences and capture Gamsakhurdia. Kitovani said that if Gamsakhurdia resigned he would be pardoned for all the crimes he had committed, but Gamsakhurdia was not tempted. It seemed as though the junta was deliberately avoiding bloodshed and hoping that the constant mortar fire would drive him into surrender, but it did not.

The military junta wanted to solve this problem as soon as possible, so it resorted to deception tactics, reputedly arranged and operated by Nodar Georgadze, a former defence minister. Georgadze told Gamsakhurdia there was to be an all-day heavy barrage on 5 January, and that an all-out attack would be mounted at dawn the following day – after the all-day barrage had terminated, Gamsakhurdia and a small group would be allowed to slip away. Just prior to this arrangement most of the 'loyal' National Guardsmen defending the building deserted Gamsakhurdia and went over to the military junta, thus leaving him practically defenceless.

It worked as planned. In the early hours of the 6th Gamsakhurdia, his family and about 100 followers 'escaped' via the deliberately unguarded back entrance in three buses, a couple of armoured cars and a number of other motor vehicles. The convoy moved along a preselected 'open' route out of the city. Some firing broke out near a bridge over the Kura river, but the buses and armoured vehicles safely cleared the city's environs. However not all Gamsakhurdia's followers were so fortunate, for as the convoy spread out as it moved away, some of the motor vehicles blundered into side streets and were dealt with individually. The 'daring escape' of Gamsakhurdia has found its way into Georgian folk history (especially the Mingrelian one), suitably embellished and tailored. One version is that he took with him the contents of the treasury, said to exceed seven million roubles.

Military junta militiamen looted Gamsakhurdia's 'bunker' and the adjacent buildings, and the following day the Rustaveli Prospekt, which had been closed since 22 December, was reopened for citizens to walk along. They were horrified to see that the 'square mile' of handsome stately buildings had been devastated. The junta leaders held a victory conference for the media, confirming that the 'escape' of Gamsakhurdia had been deliberately planned to avoid 'unnecessary bloodshed'. Casualties for the 16-day confrontation were said by the junta to number 113 killed and 420 wounded.

The Zviadists called for Gamsakhurdia's return, and although demoralised by the failure of their leader to resist the military junta, they organised strikes and demonstrations wherever they could. A transport blockade temporarily closed down Tbilisi airport.

THE MILITARY JUNTA

Kitovani announced on 17 January 1992 that his National Guard, which he claimed was now over 4000 strong, had just occupied Kutaisi, some 160 miles west of Tbilisi, where he established his headquarters. Military junta reinforcements were sent to him and on the 28th he took the seaport of Poti, a Gamsakhurdia stronghold, and the following day Zugdidi, after hastily negotiated ceasefires with local officials had broken down. By the end of January the junta claimed control over the whole of Georgia.

In Tbilisi the situation remained uneasy and uncertain, as hostile groups continued to hover around, so public meetings and rallies were forbidden and a firm attitude was taken against them. National Guard militiamen dispersed one such crowd, killing two people and injuring others, and Ioseliani threatened that the Zviadistis would be 'shot on sight' if they demonstrated. Emotions cooled and the airport was reopened on 6 February, although periodic outbreaks of civil disobedience occurred in some other cities. On the 21st the Military Council announced it had restored the 1921 Constitution to the Georgian Republic.

Prime Minister Sigua visited Moscow with a begging bowl, complaining of the dire economic situation in Georgia and of acute shortages of food and fuel. He also attended the formal CIS meeting in Minsk on the 14th in the hope of coming to economic agreements with the CIS republics, but was not exactly welcomed. He was equally unsuccessful in trying to obtain aid and credit from the United States and elsewhere.

Meanwhile Gamsakhurdia had reached Chechenia. On 18 February in Grozny he held his first press conference since his escape from Tbilisi. He condemned the military junta and vowed to fight to regain his 'lawful authority'.

6 Chairman Shevardnadze

Eduard Shevardnadze returned to Georgia on 8 March 1992, and on the 10th the Georgian Military Council, which had ruled Georgia since the flight of Gamsakhurdia, transferred its executive and legislative powers to the newly created Georgian State Council, consisting of about 50 people, of which Shevardnadze became chairman. A four-man presidium (cabinet) was formed, presided over by Shevardnadze. The three other members were Tengiz Sigua as prime minister, plus Dzhaba Ioseliani, leader of the Mekhedrioni militia, and Tengiz Kitovani, leader of the National Guard.

Several people have remarked how puzzled they were that such a 'sophisticated Westernised statesman', so unlike his rough-hewn colleagues, who had operated on the international stage and been accepted as an equal by other foreign ministers, would want to step down from his pinnacle to administer a troubled, wayward backwater such as Georgia. They overlooked the fact that Shevardnadze was basically a nationalist whose heart had probably never left his native Georgia, and for years he may have planned this as his semiretirement job. For some 13 years Shevardnadze had been first secretary of the Georgian Supreme Soviet, which meant he had been the boss man, and he now wanted to resume his former good work, assured that he was the right man for the job.

Western statesmen, who regarded him with affection for 'handing over' Eastern Europe to them, assumed that Shevardnadze disliked the cut and thrust of Yeltsin's politics and was disillusioned by the collapse of communism and the disintegration of the USSR. It was probably true that the erosion of Gorbachev's power base and the emergence of the CIS had much to do with the timing of Shevardnadze's decision. Western statesmen may have been less surprised at his move had they been aware that in Georgia he was known as the 'White Fox', partly because of his white hair, but mainly for his Machiavellian operating methods.

Shevardnadze had resigned as Soviet foreign minister on 20 December 1990, warning of impending dictatorship under Gorbachev, to found a foreign policy study unit in Moscow.

He had also become involved with the Democratic Reform Movement, which strove to unite opposition groups within the CPSU. In November 1991 the Soviet Foreign Ministry had been reorganised and renamed the 'Ministry of External Affairs'. At the request of its staff (so it was said) Shevardnadze had become minister of foreign affairs, which had pleased his Western supporters, who were anxious about control of the Soviet nuclear arsenal. Shevardnadze certainly seemed to inspire Western confidence.

To say that the country to which he had returned was troubled and unstable would be a gross understatement. Civil wars were in progress in Abkhazia and South Ossetia, and much of the remainder of Georgia was split over the leadership, the Zviadistis having considerable grassroots support not only in Mingrelia but also in other parts of the country, while the central government lacked a reliable defence force.

Georgia had devolved into a lawless republic, infested with a myriad of tiny armed groups, some with political motives, others entirely dedicated to criminal pursuits. Parts of the country were rapidly becoming no-go areas for the government writ, barred by roadblocks. A practice known as 'bandit patriotism' developed as travellers and vehicles were stopped at roadblocks by people who allowed members of their own ethnic group or political faction to pass through, while others were often robbed. This also happened on the railways, so vital to movement due to the poor, unsafe roads. For example the daily Baku–Tbilisi Express was ravaged by groups of criminals, who robbed only those of opposing ethnic groups or factions. Georgians called them 'Muslim bandits'. Flights between Tbilisi and Baku were frequently suspended, mainly due to strikes at Tbilisi airport, but often caused by a shortage of aviation fuel.

GEORGIAN ARMED FORCES

Shevardnadze addressed himself to the question of defence. On 19 April 1992 he announced the formation of the Georgian army, to be 13 000 strong, maintained by conscription and under central command. His plan was to incorporate the larger militias and disband or disarm the others, by force if necessary. Slowly a nucleus of a defence establishment materialised, ex-Soviet weaponry accumulated and individuals with former Soviet military service enlisted; but it was a slow process with many hiccups. In fact Shevardnadze had only the National Guard and the Mekhedrioni to rely upon, both of which gave nominal loyalty but had mercurial leaders.

ZVIADISTI OPPOSITION

About 70 of the 250 former Georgian Supreme Council deputies met on 12 March 1992 in Grozny (Chechenia), and formed a government-in-exile under Gamsakhurdia. In a television interview he blamed Shevardnadze for the civil war that was developing an ominous momentum in Georgia. A wave of resentment had rippled through Gamsakhurdia's supporters in Georgia, especially in the Mingrelian region, when Shevardnadze was nominated leader of the republic.

Previously, on 6 January 1992, pro-Gamsakhurdia demonstrations had brought the seaport of Sukhumi in Abkhazia proper, a centre of Zviadisti support, to a standstill. Threats and negotiations had enabled Georgian military junta troops to regain control, but protest rallies had kept bubbling to the surface. On 2 March the Abkhazian Assembly had banned public rallies and ordered a curfew. An explosion on the 9th at the Zugdidi police station had killed three people; and on the 12th, the day of the meeting in Grozny, a helicopter carrying National Guardsmen was shot down near that city, the occupants being taken prisoner by the Zviadistis.

Some members of the National Guard positioned in Zugdidi refused to obey the orders of the government's military commander in Western Georgia, Colonel Georgi Karakashvili. Zviadisti militants took over much of the town, besieging the National Guard headquarters and other government buildings. Karakashvili (who had arranged Gamsakhurdia's escape), together with Besik Kututalaze, the deputy defence minister, visited the Zviadistis to negotiate, and with others were held hostage against the demanded release of Zviadistis in government detention. National Guard reinforcements were rushed to the area.

The government had second thoughts, and in view of the uncertain morale of the 'government forces' it was decided that loyal elements of the National Guard should for the time being be withdrawn from Western Georgia in case they were subverted or overwhelmed. Shevardnadze personally stepped in to enforce an unpopular temporary ceasefire agreement covering this withdrawal, which included an exchange of prisoners.

Tension was heightened in Tbilisi as TV presenters, backed by vivid pictures, alleged that six prisoners in Zugdidi had been tortured and then burnt to death. The Zviadistis claimed the prisoners had died in a fire at their headquarters and that there had been no torture. The captured negotiating delegation was only extracted from Zugdidi with some difficulty. The Zviadistis claimed this agreement allowed them to continue the struggle by political means. Most Mingrelians still regarded Gamsakhurdia as the lawful president.

The day after the ceasefire agreement had been signed the Zviadistis ambushed a National Guard patrol, killing six men. On the 21st Karakashvili was released, as were another 40 hostages on successive days, but not Kututalaze. The Zviadistis were left in possession of Zugdidi, and by the end of the month had taken control of other towns in Western Georgia.

The new Georgian State Council gave an ultimatum to the Zviadistis to lay down their arms by the 31st, which was ignored. Despite this adverse situation the Shevardnadze government insisted its armed forces were winning, and that the Zviadistis were in retreat in Western Georgia, which was by no means the case. Railways and many roads into Abkhazia remained blocked. However Shevardnadze only wanted a breathing space, and on 4 April in Poti, a seaport, Georgian troops repelled attacks by Zviadistis. The troops were reinforced during the course of the month and regained control of Zugdidi and several other towns, in the course of which over a score of people died, National Guard troops also prevented a large crowd of Zviadistis from marching into Kutaisi to proclaim it the capital of Georgia. Shevardnadze's ceasefire was a fictional tactic.

GEORGIA GAINS INTERNATIONAL RECOGNITION

Despite the Georgian State Council's precarious hold on its domain and the fact that the civil war seemed to be getting out of hand, the very presence of Shevardnadze at the helm seemed to attract international confidence, and on 23 March 1992 the European Community (EC) recognised the independence of Georgia, as did Britain, the United States and the Conference on Security and Co-operation in Europe (CSCE). However, despite pressure from Yeltsin, Georgia remained reluctant to join the CIS, nor was it yet a member of the United Nations. It was internationally considered that Shevardnadze had made a promising start, and it was expected he would soon sort out Georgia's problems.

The German foreign minister, Hans-Dietrich Genscher, visited Georgia to establish diplomatic contact, as well as to offer some humanitarian aid. The wheeler-dealer James Baker, the US secretary of state, in furtherance of the US New World Order policy, visited Georgia on 26 May formally to open a new US embassy in Tbilisi. He also provided a small amount of aid, making any further contributions conditional on the holding of elections and the observance of human rights. Baker wanted to ensure that the United States gained and retained influence in Georgia. Shevardnadze also established diplomatic relations with Iran, and neighbouring Turkey, rather to the annoyance of Yeltsin, who was at odds with both countries.

Formal diplomatic relations were at last established between Georgia and Russia on 1 July, contact between Shevardnadze and Yeltsin having improved somewhat, and this was followed on the 31st by Georgia's acceptance as the 179th member state of the United Nations. Celebrations were held in Tbilisi, and the Georgian State Council declared that 31 July should henceforth be known as Georgia's 'reconciliation day'. The state of emergency imposed in Tbilisi since October 1991, together with its curfew, was terminated and amnesty was announced for all Zviadistis. International recognition and legality were thus satisfactorily established.

However Georgian independence had its downside as Moscow cut off its money supply, which meant no more state-funded enterprises or government involvement in industry, and also no more access to the huge former-USSR markets for Georgia's production of wines, fruit and tractors. Food became scarce, and as the collective farms were broken up queues for bread appeared, the first for many years. Capitalism brought crime well in excess of normal Georgian standards. Paper money had to be issued, disparagingly called 'coupons'.

In the meantime Zviadisti military activity had died down somewhat in Western Georgia, although in June the Georgian State Council had authorised the use of the Mekhedrioni militia to help restore order in Zugdidi. Small groups of Zviadistis had remained in Tbilisi, mostly underground and inactive, with one exception. On 24 June about 100 Zviadistis had seized the Tbilisi TV station, announcing a coup. Shevardnadze had just left the capital to sign an agreement with the South Ossetes. A five-hour battle had ensued between the 'rebels' and the National Guard, aided by the tanks and guns of the new Georgian army, after which all surviving 'rebels' had surrendered, to be eventually pardoned by the 31 July amnesty. This abortive coup had been badly organised and impromptu, and it caused prime minister Sigua to state that his government would demand the extradition of Gamsakhurdia from Chechenya. The rebel casualties were officially disclosed as three dead and 26 wounded.

SOUTH OSSETIAN REFERENDUM

During 1991 it was reported that up to 500 people had died due to interethnic disturbances in South Ossetia. Taking advantage of the distraction provided by the revolutionary events in Tbilisi, on 5 January 1992 a group of Georgian militiamen, alleged to include Georgian police, stormed the centre of Tskhinvali, capital of South Ossetia, seizing and damaging administration buildings. They were opposed by militant Ossetes, who manned the barricades. Fearful and feeling they were completely isolated by hostile forces, many Ossetes fled northwards through the road tunnel into North Ossetia, before an explosion, allegedly caused by a 'rock fall', temporarily blocked it. The state of emergency was extended from Tskhinvali to cover the whole of the oblast, as much of it was being ravaged by Georgian gangs.

The Georgian Military Council released Torez Kolumbegov, the detained South Ossetian leader, who agreed to negotiate. A referendum in South Ossetia on the 19th produced an overwhelming majority in favour of independence from Georgia, and its integration into the Russian Federation, in a reported 90 per cent turnout. The result was condemned by the military junta, which ordered a general mobilisation in Tbilisi on the

23rd. The amassing of Georgian troops near Tskhinvali caused the Ossetes to fear that a military assault was imminent, but the situation in Tbilisi was so unstable that the junta recalled its troops to the Georgian capital, which brought about a lull in South Ossetia. It was generally estimated that the Ossetes had about 3000 armed militants, but no formal command structure. Oleg Teziyev remained the nominal president, with Torez Kolumbrgov as his prime minister, but the two men differed on certain policy matters.

The South Ossetian problem was attracting attention in the Caucasus region, as well as a degree of sympathy for the Ossetes in several quarters. During late February a group of 'Russian volunteers' arrived in Vladikavkaz (capital of North Ossetia), ostensibly to protect Russia's southern borders, from where they were flown by helicopter to Tskhinvali. The Russian commander of Ministry of Interior troops in South Ossetia refused to allow them to mount attacks on scattered villages, which seemed to be their general intent, and persuaded them to return to Vladikavkaz. A variety of North Caucasian Muslim 'volunteers' were trickling into South Ossetia to protect them from 'Georgian nationalists'.

During April, Georgian nationalists continued spasmodically to shell Tskhenvali, so the Russian Ministry of Interior troops were withdrawn. On the 26th the Confederation of Caucasian Mountain Peoples met in Tskhinvali, officially to call for a reassessment of relations between South Ossetia and the Russian Federation, but privately to urge its members to encourage Muslim volunteers to fight alongside their Ossete brethren.

TRINATIONAL TALKS

Shevardnadze made his first official visit to South Ossetia as the Georgian chairman on 13 May to hold trinational talks between Georgian and South and North Ossetian leaders, which resulted in a temporary ceasefire in the oblast. This was violently disrupted on the 20th, when Georgian militiamen attacked a group of Ossetes travelling to North Ossetia, killing over 30 people. This caused the Supreme Soviet of North Ossetia to close the road tunnel, thus blocking the main highway northwards from Tbilisi into the Russian Federation, and to suspend the supply of gas Georgia received via the pipelines running through North Ossetia. Shevardnadze condemned both the ambush and North Ossetia. Another ceasefire was brokered, but again was soon broken. Intermittent fighting between rival militants and the shelling of Tskhinvali continued.

In Moscow, on 15 June Ruslan Khasbulatov, chairman of the Russian Supreme Soviet, stated that Russia might consider annexing South Ossetia, and a few days later Aleksandr Rutskoi, the vice president, accused the Georgian authorities of genocide against Georgia's Russian population. Shevardnadze grumbled that Russia was deliberately stirring up trouble against Georgia, with sinister designs.

Relations between Russia and Georgia deteriorated further, and in an effort to improve them Yeltsin and Shevardnadze met in the Black Sea resort of Dagomys in Ukraine. It was agreed there should be a ceasefire in South Ossetia; that Russia would withdraw its troops from around Tskhinvali; and that a monitoring commission be established to oversee the ceasefire. Gas supplies to Georgia through North Ossetia were resumed. At the beginning of 1992 there were about 20 000 Russian troops in Georgia, with about 850 tanks of various types, 680 other armoured vehicles, about 170 combat aircraft and 40 attack helicopters (IISS).

TRINATIONAL PEACEKEEPING FORCE

At a further high-level meeting in Vladikavkaz on 4 July it was decided to set up a 1500-strong trinational peacekeeping force, to be positioned along a 15-kilometre-wide buffer zone (yet to be defined), and that the personnel should come equally from Russia, Georgia and South Ossetia. The first Russian contingent of about 500 troops moved into South Ossetia on the 14th; other detachments were slow to appear and there were arguments about the buffer zone. In general the ceasefire agreement continued to hold in South Ossetia, at least for the time being; but no progress was made on the political front.

The trinational peacekeeping force managed to maintain an uneasy peace in South Ossetia until 19 November 1992, when the South Ossetian Assembly voted to secede from Georgia and join the Russian Federation.

ABKHAZIAN SOVEREIGNTY

On 23 July 1992 the 65-seat Abkhazian Supreme Council proclaimed 'state sovereignty' and restored its 1925 constitution (which had been annulled in 1978), but the 26 Georgian deputies, who had boycotted the Council since April, opposed this declaration. In Tbilisi the Georgian State Council immediately countermanded the decision.

On 11 August tension between the Georgian government and that of Abkhazia came to a crisis point when Roman Gventsadze (the Georgian interior minister) and ten other officials on a visit to Sukhumi (including Abkhazia Kavsadze, the South Ossetian Chairman) were kidnapped by a group of Abkhazian separatists. Despite negotiations the captors refused to release their hostages, so Shevardnadze sent an armed force to rescue them. On the 14th, after two Georgian soldiers had been killed during an exchange of prisoners, the rescue force marched towards the centre of Sukhumi but were resisted by armed Abkhazian groups who regarded them as an invading army.

The Abkhazia Assembly met, guarded by a ring of tanks. Some wanted to compromise with the Tbilisi government; others wanted to play for time, hoping for the arrival of the promised Caucasian Muslim volunteers; while yet other hardliners wanted to stand and fight. The Assembly chose to order a general mobilisation and the arming of civilians. Shevardnadze quickly dispatched troops to Abkhazia as he feared a large influx of Muslim volunteers, rumours indicating that thousands were swarming towards Sukhumi.

Then followed two days' hard fighting as Georgian troops pushed towards the Assembly building to take it by force, using tanks and guns. Helicopters and missiles launched from offshore naval craft completed the all-out blitz. At the same time vigilante Georgian groups stopped and searched all vehicles and people for arms. The Abkhazian flag was torn down from the Assembly building and replaced by the Georgian one, but the Abkhazians still resisted.

Farther south, Georgian troops entered the town of Ochamchire. The fear was that this bout of fighting, which was spreading to other parts of Abkhazia, would draw in the trinational peacekeeping force and split it along ethnic lines.

A temporary ceasefire came into effect on 16 August, when

Georgian troops in Sukhumi withdrew a short distance, but they continued to shell the Assembly building to force Vladislav Ardzinba to resign. The Georgian troops regrouped and again began to advance on the Assembly building, whereupon Ardzinba and his colleagues hastily left the building and fled north to Gudauta.

On 18 August Tengiz Kitovani, the Georgian defence minister, appointed a Military Committee to administer Abkhazia, reinstating Givi Lomanidize (the Abkhazian interior minister), who had been deposed in June. President Kavsadze was released. Kitovani explained that the Georgian military invasion had been necessary as the Abkhazian Assembly had illegally declared independence.

For a week or so there was an uneasy stand-off in Sukhumi, while all combatants licked their wounds and considered their next move. The brief respite was broken by a combined manifesto and declaration by the Confederation of Caucasian Mountain Peoples, which was reprinted in many Russian newspapers on 25 August. It declared Tbilisi a 'disaster area', threatened to launch a 'campaign of terror' in that city, and ordered local chieftains to send fighters to 'Abkhazia to repel the aggressors'. It also stated that all Georgians in Abkhazia should 'be viewed as hostages'. This caused some alarm in Tbilisi, and also in Moscow, which was concerned that something similar might happen in its North Caucasian republics, some of which were already discontented and troubled. The threat was real, but the numbers were greatly exaggerated, although a 'few hundred' Muslim volunteers had already trickled into Abkhazia.

The Russian troops continued to stand back from the interethnic fighting, but on occasions they were involved involuntarily, although Shevardnadze complained they were helping the 'separatists' and supplying them with arms from across the Black Sea. Conversely the Georgian chairman was obtaining large amounts of ex-Soviet heavy weaponry for his new army in order to fight the 'separatists'. Shevardnadze refused to withdraw his troops from Sukhumi and Gagra, insisting it was Georgia's right to station them there.

The Abkhazian Supreme Council split along ethnic lines on 31 August, when Dzhoni Khetsuriani (the minister of justice) called for its dissolution on the ground that its representation was unfair, as Abkhazians (who made up 17.8 per cent of the population) had 28 seats, while ethnic Georgians (45.7 per cent) had only 26 seats; the remaining eleven having miscellaneous platforms. The deputy president, Tamaz Naradeyshvili (a Georgian), called for the resignation of President Vladislav Ardzinba (an Abkhazian). There was confusion for a while.

Negotiations between all parties involved in the Abkhazian crisis took place in Moscow. Another ceasefire was imposed on 5 September, when a trinational monitoring and inspection committee was established. It was agreed that the Georgian troops should remain in Abkhazia, while Russia would prevent Muslim volunteers from entering Georgia to assist the Abkhazian separatists. Despite indignant denials that it was happening, further Georgian National Guard troops entered Abkhazia, as did Muslim volunteers to fight against them.

Colonel Karakashvili again threatened to attack Gudauta if Ardzinba did not surrender, but Shevardnadze stepped in to cool the situation, ordering him to negotiate instead. Even so the fighting continued, spreading to Gagra by the end of the month and then north to Gudauta. The Abkhazian health minister stated that between 14 August and 24 September the casualties amounted to 189 dead and 823 wounded.

A Russian resolution on 25 September condemned the Georgian leadership for using violence to solve their interethnic problems, while a second resolution suspended the transfer of arms to Georgia, including those already contracted for. The Georgians accused Yeltsin of interference. Russia, for its part, had already deployed an extra ten units of Ministry of Interior troops to the Northern Caucasian republics to 'protect its borders and maintain order'.

ABKHAZIAN COUNTEROFFENSIVE

Colonel Georgi Karakashvili said that unless Vladislav Ardzinba surrendered he would attack Gudauta, but the boot was on the other foot as the impromptu Abkhazian army, stiffened with Muslim volunteers and using armoured vehicles, mounted a massive counterattack and seized the resort of Gagra on 2 October 1992. Hundreds of Georgian troops and thousands of civilians fled before the successful Abkhazian advance, which on the 6th took the towns of Gantiasi and Lesselidze, thus enabling the Abkhazians to establish control over the whole of northern Abkhazia from Sukhumi to the Russian border. It was additionally disastrous as the Georgian government had to face a general election on the 11th.

The Russian-brokered ceasefire had come to an abrupt end and this displeased Yeltsin, who warned he would take 'appropriate measures' if Russian lives were threatened. The Georgian State Council replied that it would take possession of all Russian weapons and military equipment on its territory. It authorised a general mobilisation and ordered more troops into Abkhazia. The roads eastwards from Abkhazia became choked with fleeing Georgian refugees, the railways stopped running and roadblocks surrounded Sukhumi, flight from its airport remaining the only means of evacuation.

To Shevardnadze it seemed that Yeltsin was appeasing the Abkhazians, while Yeltsin accused the Georgian State Council of fomenting rebellion, alleging its intention was to secure control of the strategic railway line in Abkhazia. In fact Shevardnadze was striving to avoid civil war with Abkhazia, and was blaming hard-line Russian generals for allowing Muslim volunteers to flood into the oblast, and for supplying Abkhazians with weaponry. During this Georgian retreat, on the way Shevardnadze had a narrow escape in the 4th when the helicopter in which he was travelling was attacked and forced to land. Shevardnadze continued his journey to Sukhumi by road.

GEORGIAN ELECTIONS

Elections were held in Georgia on 11 October 1992. Thirty paries took part, and despite the fact that the Zviadistis were calling for a boycott, there was a claimed 75 per cent voter turnout. Shevardnadze, the sole contender for the chairmanship, led the 'Alliance of Former Communists' (said to have abandoned their former political ideology) and was elected leader of the Georgian State Council by 95 per cent of the votes cast. There had been anxiety that the polls might be disrupted by the Zviadistis, so Shevardnadze took the precaution of detaining '50 potential terrorists' (Tass). However the elections passed off relatively peacefully. Despite the adverse situation in Abkhazia and the Zviadisti opposition, Shevardnadze had won the confidence of the majority of his countrymen, thus discrediting Gamsakhurdia.

On 6 November the Georgian State Council confirmed Shevardnadze as head of state, with executive powers in conjunction with the cabinet (presidium) until the later implementation of a new constitution. Tengiz Sigua was reelected prime minister.

RUSSIAN INVOLVEMENT

On 2 November 1992 Georgian forces seized a Russian arms depot in the southern part of the country, and although Shevardnadze formally condemned the action, the defence minister (Kitovani) admitted he had authorised it. In Moscow General Grachev, the Russian defence minister, threatened to recover the arms by force.

Further peace talks were held on 13 November, but there was no agreement: the Georgian delegation called for the Abkhazian militias to return to the positions they had held prior to 1 October, while the Abkhazians called for the complete withdrawal of Georgian troops from their territory.

Pledging to the world that Russia would tolerate no human rights violations, Yeltsin singled out 'Abkhazia and Georgia as places where abuses were taking place. He insisted he was withdrawing the Russian forces from Georgia, but contradictorily said that Russia must control the strategic railway line through Abkhazia. The Abkhazians insisted that the Russian troops remain. Shevardnadze accused Yeltsin of losing control of his Trans-Caucasian armed forces.

On 6 November the Georgians accused the Russians of bombing their positions in Sukhumi. A ten-day truce was brought into effect on the 10th to enable the Russian troops to withdraw from Abkhazia, but this was broken on the 18th when the Georgians accused the Russians of aerial activity. In turn the Russians accused the Georgians of involvement in the murder of three Russian soldiers. Shevardnadze again visited Sukhumi, insisting that his new State Council was committed to ending the conflict in Abkhazia as soon as possible. But the fighting continued.

Meanwhile, on 14 November a Russian helicopter had crashed on its return journey from delivering humanitarian aid to the

Abkhazian town of Tkvarcheli, killing 64 people, including women and children (Tass). The Abkhazians alleged it had been shot down by Georgians, who denied this, but were not believed by the Russians, who threatened to take decisive measures' of a military nature'. Prime Minister Sigua spoke of 'crisis relations with Russia' but denied being at war. The Georgian delegation was withdrawn from the second round of the Russian–Georgian talks in Moscow. Subsequent Georgian investigations revealed that the crashed helicopter had been carrying weapons and combat personnel, as well as civilians, but attributed the cause to overloading, as 64 people had be carried in an aircraft designed to take only 24.

Fighting in Abkhazia continued during December, the Georgians claiming to seize Ochamchire on the 27th. Defence Minister Kitovani met Defence Minister Grachev in Moscow to discuss the presence of Russian troops in Abkhazia.

ABKHAZIAN ATTACK

On 5 January 1993 an Abkhazian attack was launched on Georgian-held Sukhumi. The Abkhazians lost the hard, one-day battle and had to withdraw in the evening. The battle was fought across the Gumista river, which partially shielded the city and had come to form the dividing line between the Georgian forces defending Sukhumi and the aggressive Abkhazian militias. So far neither side had seriously attempted to force their way across. Mount Zegan dominated Sukhumi to the south-east on the Georgian-held side of the river, and was a tactical prize. This first serious Abkhazian attempt to seize the mountain seemed to have faltered at the river-crossing stage of the operation, the Abkhazians claiming they had in fact crossed the Gumista and the Georgians insisting they had not.

The Abkhazians also claimed they had inflicted 150 casualties on the Georgians, and admitted to suffering 80 themselves. Battle casualties were invariably inflated by one side or the other, and while these figures were unverifiable, like most other reported battle estimates, the ratio in this case may have been more or less correct. The following day the Abkhazians openly admitted their defeat, but their artillery and mortars continued to bombard Sukhumi. Away from Sukhumi Georgian militias continued spasmodically to shell Gudauta, now the Abkhazian military headquarters.

Winter was harshly affecting the opposing military groups and the inhabitants of disputed areas, which covered most of south-eastern Abkhazia. A highlighted example was Tkvarcheli – a coalmining town with a population of over 50 000 (*Izvestiya*), about half Georgian and half Abkhazian – which was completely cut off by winter snows and the people were in danger of starvation. The Abkhazian authorities claimed they wanted to evacuate the non-Abkhazian residents, but were unable to obtain Georgian cooperation. Relief was provided by helicopters from North Ossetia. At least two Russian helicopters carrying humanitarian aid had to make forced landings under Georgian anti-aircraft fire. The Georgian authorities did not want ethnic cleansing to happen behind Abkhazian lines if it could be helped. The whole of Georgia was already suffering under heavy Russian economic embargos.

It was widely alleged that Russians were covertly helping the Abkhazian separatists, local Russian commanders presumably being under orders to do so. Many thought this was a piqued response to Georgia's independence and continued reluctance to join the CIS. Arms and ammunition were being taken from Russian depots by Abkhazians by mutual agreement, threat, theft or corruption.

The military authorities in Moscow stated that in the previous six months over 25 000 weapons had been stolen from military depots, the majority in the Caucasus region. Certainly some Russian soldiers were actively engaged in black market dealing that extended to arms. One example concerned a Russian sergeant in the Georgian town of Vaziani, who shot dead two fellow soldiers and two civilian accomplices after a series of thefts, the group quarrelling over the division of the half a million roubles obtained during the previous month's activities (Tass). Extremely poor military pay made black market activities, with their comparatively huge rewards, plus the existence of opportunity and demand, very tempting to many.

GEORGIAN REQUEST FOR UN INTERVENTION

Becoming uneasy about the Abkhazian crisis getting out of hand and his troops being driven back, Shevardnadze wrote to the UN secretary general asking for the deployment of a peacekeeping force, only to be told that the time was not yet ripe for such a project. However as the UN was always on the lookout for new opportunities to expand, a small UN exploratory mission arrived in Tbilisi on 20 January 1993.

PEACEMAKING ATTEMPTS

Russian–Georgian peace talks were resumed in Tbilisi on 25 January 1993 to discuss a draft friendship and cooperation treaty; and also the status and conditions of Russian troops remaining in Georgia. These were abruptly suspended after an armed attack was made on a Russian supply depot near Tbilisi and two Russian servicemen were killed. Yeltsin adopted a carrot-and-stick approach towards the Georgians to bring them into his orbit, but was still opposed by a clique of generals who wanted to punish them.

Yeltsin thought a formal friendship and cooperation treaty might be the best way to deal with Shevardnadze, who was touchy about equal status and was finding it difficult to marshal his supporters behind him on this issue. Most Georgian nationalists distrusted the Russians, whom they suspected, with good reason, of arming 'rebel' Abkhazians to fight against them. One reason for Shevardnadze's unpopularity amongst some Georgian nationalists was that when he was Soviet foreign minister he had championed Gorbachev's new liberal policies.

Two aircraft made a bombing raid on Georgian positions near the Gumista river on the night of 20 February, killing one person and wounding others. Georgia claimed the aircraft was Russian, which Russia denied, alleging that Georgian artillery had been firing on its own troops.

On the 24th the Georgian State Council judged that aggressive Russian action had taken place in Abkhazia, and Shevardnadze threatened total mobilisation if the Russian troops were not withdrawn. Shevardnadze's somewhat inflated pronouncement that '500 000 Georgians' were available for instant mobilisation was deliberately floated for propaganda purposes, and was thought to be based on the number of military-aged men who had previously served as Soviet military conscripts and could be available in theory, but the means of mustering and equipping such large numbers verged on the realms of fantasy.

Three days later Defence Minister Grachev visited Russian troops in Abkhazia without informing Shevardnadze, who complained of Russia's 'ultimatum-orientated' approach. On 4 March, when the fourth round of the peace talks opened in Moscow, there was little friendliness in evidence.

ABKHAZIANS ATTACK SUKHUMI

Abkhazian armed forces launched an all-out attack on Sukhumi on 14 March 1993. The attack developed into a major battle that dragged on for almost four days, with both sides using aircraft and artillery. The 1500-strong Abkhazian 'army' probably faced twice that number of Georgian soldiers and militiamen. It was a drawn battle in which over 100 people were killed, more than 1000 injured and over 800 buildings destroyed or badly damaged, according to Georgian military sources. The Georgian State Council openly alleged that the Abkhazians had been aided by Russia, which it accused of exacerbating the 'undeclared war' between them.

Georgia also claimed that Russian SU-25 aircraft had taken part in the battle, and indeed on the 19th a Russian SU-25 had been brought down in Abkhazia, documents indicating that the pilot was a Russian. A Russian air force spokesman said that the pilot had been checking out intelligence that Georgian artillery was about to bomb a Russian army base.

Russia and Georgia had previously exchanged a series of protests and denials after SU–25s had bombed Sukhumi targets, causing civilian casualties. On this occasion Grachev warned that Russia would strike again if Georgia did not stop shelling a Russian seismic laboratory on the coast near Sukhumi. This was the first open admission by Russia that its combat aircraft were aiding Abkhazia.

Shevardnadze angrily dismissed Grachev's charge that he was waging war against his own people, and that Georgian government forces had painted seven of their SU-25s with Russian markings and then bombed civilians. Much later, when I enquired into this allegation, the reply had been 'Perhaps not seven'. This undeclared war, a dirty tricks one, uninfluenced by Geneva Conventions, continued viciously in Abkhazia, with Russians fighting by proxy.

On 18 April Georgian radio stated that 1008 Georgian soldiers had been killed and more than 3500 wounded in the fighting so far. This was regarded as an exaggeration, but no one could check at the time, nor later. Certainly a great many people, military and civilian, were being killed or injured. Later Russia stated that '46 Russian soldiers had been killed and 10 wounded in 1992', which gave the other side of the casualty picture (Itar-Tass).

The population of the city, port and environs of Sukhumi, swelled by influxes of refugees, was said to have risen to some 120 000 people. After a comparative lull the Abkhazian bombardments recommenced on 29 April. Shevardnadze himself had another narrow escape in the battle zone, when the helicopter he was in was rammed by a hostile one in mid-air and had to land quickly. The Georgians threatened that if the artillery bombardment did not stop, they would shell Abkhazian towns and villages.

THE SOCHI DEMILITARISED ZONE

At a meeting on 6 May 1993 in the Russian Federation town of Sochi, a Black Sea resort just north of Abkhazia, Russian Defence Minister Grachev, Georgian Prime Minister Sigua and Defence Minister Kitovani agreed that a three-kilometre wide demilitarised zone would be set up between the Georgian and Abkhazian military forces. It was also agreed that all Russian troops would leave Georgia by the end of 1995. As the Abkhazian representative had failed to turn up for the meeting, negotiations for a formal ceasefire had to be delayed.

GEORGIAN DEFENCE MINISTER DISMISSED

On 6 May 1993 the Georgian State Committee dismissed Defence Minister Tengiz Kitovani in his absence at Sochi. Kitovani, leader of the National Guard, had been prominent in forming the new, unified Georgian army. Originally a keen supporter of Shevardnadze, he was now implacably opposed to him. He was replaced by 27-year-old Georgi Karakashvili, former commander of the White Falcons. Shevardnadze took this opportunity to abolish the Council of National Security and Defence, which had been jointly headed by Kitovani and Dzhaba Ioseliani, leader of the Mekhedrioni militia. At the Congress of the newly formed Young National Democrats, Karakashvili delivered the closing address.

On the 11th a group of Mekhedrioni militiamen raided a Russian military base in Kutaisi to obtain arms, and in the scuffle the Russians killed at least seven of the raiders. It was assumed that the purpose of this action was not only to obtain weapons, but also to embarrass Shevardnadze, and to try to prevent resumption of the Russian-sponsored Georgian–Abkhazian peace talks.

GEORGIAN–ABKHAZIAN PEACE TALKS

Despite the deliberate distractions, formal contact between Yeltsin and Shevardnadze continued, as both men wanted, but for different reasons. Yeltsin wanted to bring Georgia fully into his orbit, while Shevardnadze, realising there were decided limits to how long Georgia could withstand the tight, harsh Russian economic blockade without falling into bankruptcy and chaos, wanted a Russian friendship and cooperation treaty, after which he would be willing to enter the CIS on the best terms he could get. This policy put him at odds with many of his nationalist supporters. The stumbling block was Abkhazia, which Yeltsin would like to embrace within his Russian Federation, while Georgia insisted it remain within Georgia

The two leaders met again in Moscow on 14 May and arranged for a ceasefire to come into effect on the 20th, on which date a UN envoy for Georgia would arrive in Tbilisi. This was not quite what Shevardnadze wanted: he had hoped Yeltsin would agree to stop supporting the Abkhazian separatists, but Yeltsin did not intend to play all his cards just yet. On the 31st, making the best of what he had got, Shevardnadze said 'all the necessary conditions for peace talks are in place' (*Daily Telegraph*). On 9 June Andrei Kozyrev, the Russian foreign minister, visited both Tbilisi and Gudauta.

Shevardnadze's apparent conciliatory stance towards Russia brought criticism from his nationalist opposition, and also from the National Democratic Party, now his own mainstream political supporter, all being suspicious of Russian neocolonial expansion. The degree of protest became so great that on 14 June Shevardnadze huffily said he would resign if it was the people's will. From 16–22 June talks were held in Moscow between Kozyrev and representatives from Georgia and Abkhazia.

Shevardnadze quickly changed his mind about resigning, although he probably never had any real intention of doing so, his declaration being a dramatic public relations gesture to drum up personal support and stop the bickering amongst his supporters. Instead, on the 21st he called on the Georgian State Council to give him increased powers, arguing that Georgia urgently needed strong leadership. Many of his supporters, ardent nationalists who thought they had at last thrown off the Russian yoke, now suspected (correctly) that Shevardnadze was working towards a Russian friendship and cooperation treaty, removal of the Russian embargo and renewal of former economic links. Shevardnadze's ploy worked, and on 1 July the Georgian State Council granted him extra powers, including the authority to issue decree without Council approval and to dismiss any deputy or state official arbitrarily, the sole exception being the prime minister.

The Abkhazian separatists were unhappy with Shevardnadze's new policies which, if successful, would be to their detriment. Vladislav Ardzinba openly accused him of 'genocide', hinting that Abkhazia might opt out and join the Russian Federation, which was a practical geographic possibility. Infuriated young Georgian nationalists, hungry to retain their own independence, perversely objected to the Abkhazians having theirs.

7 Turbulent Georgia: 1993–94

The 'new model' Georgian armed forces, the strength of which was to be upgraded to 20 000, to be maintained by a two-year period of conscription, had been taking shape under Tengiz Kitovani, but progress had been slow. By spring 1993 it had probably reached a strength of about 8000, but no one knew exactly as no official figures were published. Security and deception were watchwords. The army was to consist of six brigade formations, within two corps, and some border guards. Subunits and units were emerging, but the command structure was still experimental, discipline ragged and the loyalty of some sections doubtful. Conscripts and volunteers were placed in the armoured, artillery or other technical arms and units. Effective Georgian military operations still rested mainly on the several 'cooperating' armed militias.

While infantry weapons were plentiful in Georgia, sophisticated ones such as missiles were scarce, the main source of supply being the local Russian army depots, from where weaponry was officially and unofficially transferred. One authoritative source (IISS) quoted that by mid-1993 the Georgian army had about 120 T-55 tanks, 180 other armoured vehicles and 60 guns and mortars, presumably all of which were 'export models', that is, none were sophisticated items. However there were also reports of fully computerised Soviet T-72 tanks being seen in Georgian barracks and camps. It was said that Shevardnadze had obtained them, together with other sophisticated weapons, including ground-to-air missiles, through personal links with Russian generals. He was a Georgian, and there were Georgian generals in the Russian army.

It had been planned that Kitovani's National Guard, still thought be be about 4000 strong, would be incorporated into the regular army, but this had not yet been effected, and although it was involved in fighting on the side of the Georgian government in South Ossetia and Abkhazia, it had remained a separate entity. Sections of it had a lingering loyalty to Gamsakhurdia, and now its leader was in open opposition to Shevardnadze.

The Mekhedrioni, led by Dzhaba Ioseliani and probably numbering about 1500, was also openly hostile to Shevardnadze, while the White Falcon militia, having 'some hundreds' of armed members, led by Georgi Karakashvili, was now firmly in the government camp. On the other hand the Mingrelian militia, led by Loti Kobalia, which probably had about 1500 armed members, was fiercely loyal to Gamsakhurdia, the ousted Mingrelian leader, and hostile to Shevardnadze. Other smaller militias and armed groups were scattered across the Georgian countryside. Most were anchored to a particular locality and dominated by a local personality; some had vague political preferences; and most were engaged in 'bandit patriotism', mafia or other criminal activities and were open to political bribery if it was to their advantage. The Georgian government's writ was a precarious one. The numerous small groups of impromptu Georgian militias operating in Abkhazia and South Ossetia were uncoordinated, undisciplined and only vaguely under government influence, so Shevardnadze's sword was a very blunt one.

In addition a small Georgian air force was taking shape, with Russian aircraft and technical assistance. It admitted to possessing 40 SU-25 and SU-15 aircraft and about 15 Russian helicopters. A small Georgian navy was forming at the Poti naval base, around a cadre of 100 men manning a few small coastal craft. This Russian support did not seem to waver, even when Russia was supporting Abkhazian forces in battle.

About 20 000 Russian servicemen remained in Georgia as part of the Transcaucasus Group of Forces, which basically consisted of two motor rifle divisions, while the Russian air force element had about 35 transport and other aircraft and a number of helicopters. The morale of Russian military personnel in the region tended to be poor, mainly because the men were unhappy about being so far from home, but also because the conscription period had been extended from 18 months to two years. The best of the conscripted manpower was commandeered off by the Ministry of Interior and other specialised bodies.

JULY 1993 OFFENSIVES

Although over two thirds of Abkhazia was under the control of separatists, this was mainly the thinly populated expanses of the

Caucasus Mountain area and its foothills, which were almost roadless, while the fertile coastal plain was inhabited by Georgians. An Abkhazian separatist strategy was to cut the coastal road and railway running from Sukhumi to Tbilisi, and so isolate the Georgian garrison. The only way this could be achieved was by a flanking movement through the mountainous area, which owing to lack of roads and the very rough terrain meant that they had to carry all their heavy weapons, including guns and mortars, and their very weighty ammunition, an almost impossible task. The other alternative was to make coastal commando raids to cut the road and railway, as the opposing forces remained bogged in their positions either side of the Gumista river.

On 1 July 1993 the Abkhazian artillery bombardment of Sukhumi and its environs recommenced, under the cover of which an Abkhazian marine commando raid, using local fishing boats and small Russian naval craft, was made on Tamish, a coastal village just south of Sukhumi. The commandos succeeded in occupying a section of the road–rail link, thus completely severing contact by land with Tbilisi. Shevardnadze immediately flew to Sukhumi. Georgia alleged that Russia had not only organised this Abkhazian operation and provided the naval craft, but had taken part in it, which was instantly denied by Andrei Kozyrev. Prime Minister Sigua demanded that Russia immediately 'end this undeclared war' and wanted to break off all relations with Moscow, but Shevardnadze, having other policies in mind, would not agree to this.

During the first week in July there was intense fighting around Ochamchire, about 40 miles south-west of Sukhumi, the so-called 'southern front', in which both sides claimed that 'hundreds were killed' (Inter-Fax). During this fighting Shevardnadze had yet another narrow escape. On the 4th he was travelling by car in the forward area when a nearby Georgian tank was hit by an Abkhazian rocket and exploded. Although there were casualties, Shevardnadze was unhurt and unruffled, which added to his growing reputation for personal bravery. Sukhumi was now virtually surrounded, and he could have been safely back at his office in Tbilisi without attracting undue criticism on this score.

Dramatically, Shevardnadze pledged he would stay in Sukhumi until the Abkhazian separatists were defeated, and that if the city fell he would resign. However his new defence minister, Karakashvili, announced on the 10th that the road–rail link to Tbilisi had been restored. A second coastal attack by the Abkhazians on the 13th was beaten back. Bombardment of Sukhumi continued, Abkhazian guns firing into the city from Mount Zegan about five miles to its north, their emplacements being amongst hillside villages.

Meanwhile Boris Pastukhov, a Russian envoy sent by Yeltsin to assess the Abkhazian situation, stated that Russia reserved the right to intervene with military force and could not 'stand idly by as cities, once gems of the Black Sea, were burnt to ashes' (Tass). This marked a new, and sharper, Russian attitude towards the Abkhazian situation. Pastukhov reported that it should be possible to enforce a peace accord on the combatants.

Kozyrev reinforced this change of attitude, emphasising that Russia had the economic levers to force the combatants to the negotiating table. He need not have emphasised this factor as Georgia was already in the vice-like grip of Russian sanctions, and was accordingly isolated. The trickle of US food aid was tiny and tenuous. Georgia had to come within Russia's economic sphere or devolve into starvation and chaos.

Nevertheless Shevardnadze addressed the problem boldly, and on the 13th issued an ultimatum to the Abkhazian separatists to abandon the siege of Sukhumi and withdraw their armed forces, or face a major assault by air and sea. Some international arrangements were in operation to evacuate refugees from the beleaguered seaport. For example, after secret preparations Greece activated 'Operation Golden Fleece', whereby 1200 ethnic Greeks were evacuated by ship (*Daily Telegraph*). Other similar projects followed. As the Georgian ultimatum was ignored, on the 16th an attack was launched on Abkhazian artillery emplacements on Mount Zegan.

Shevardnadze had long been concerned about 'foreign volunteers' flooding into Abkhazia. These were mainly North Caucasian Muslims, eager to fight Christian Georgians. So far he had been unsuccessful in persuading Yeltsin to seal off the Russian frontier with Abkhazia. During July the shadowy Confederation of Caucasian Mountain Peoples, which had long been supporting the Abkhazian separatists by sending Muslim volunteers to help them, reemphasised its stance, which was covertly supported by Russia during its anti-Georgian period. It issued a call for general mobilisation in the Muslim North Caucasus republics, so that more Muslim volunteers could be sent to Abkhazia.

CEASEFIRE

The Russian-sponsored Sochi talks were resumed on 27 July 1993 and resulted in a provisional ceasefire agreement being signed by Shevardnadze and an Abkhazian representative. Both Georgia and Abkhazia were to withdraw their heavy weapons, mainly artillery, and the ground forces were to break contact in the Sukhumi area. Russia seemed to have halted the civil war for the moment, although each protagonist was soon accusing the other of violations. Georgian artillery was withdrawn from Sukhumi, but the Abkhazians retained theirs alongside the Gumista river line.

GEORGIAN PRIME MINISTER RESIGNS

Prime Minister Sigua announced the resignation of his government on 5 August 1993 after the Georgian State Council failed to approve a draft budget. Shevardnadze became acting prime minister and was given a fortnight to sort things out and pull his country together. Sigua complained that 90 per cent of the people were living below the poverty line, the country's economy was in shreds, law and order was almost non-existent and the country was ridden with armed banditry. Some members of the government were against ratifying the Russian-sponsored ceasefire, with its unfavourable conditions, especially the military and the nationalists. This caused Shevardnadze to dither for a while over whether or not to declare an 'emergency regime' and rule by decree. Eventually, on the 23rd Shevardnadze appointed Otar Patsatsia as prime minister.

Shevardnadze and Yeltsin met again in Moscow on the 23rd, purportedly to agree on what they called the 'first steps to peace in Abkhazia'. It was reported that some Georgian guns and troops had been pulled back on schedule. Two days later, by decree, Shevardnadze established a special commission to produce the final settlement on the Abkhazian problem, without specifying what it might be. In the meantime the Georgian State Council formally gave permission for Russian troops to remain in Georgia.

UN INVOLVEMENT

On 8 August Boutros Boutros-Ghali, the UN secretary general, had proposed that a contingent of '88 UN Military Observers' be sent to Georgia, which was agreed to by the Georgian State Council. This would be the first ever UN mission established on former Soviet territory. But there was some hesitation.

MINGRELIAN ATTACK

On 30 July pro-Gamsakhurdia militiamen had seized the town of Senaki in Mingrelia, and this was followed on 28 August by a unilateral uprising by the whole of the Mingrelian militia, commanded by Loti Kobalia. The militia occupied a huge swathe of territory in Mingrelia that included the towns of Abasha, Khobi and Senaki. The following day Gamsakhurdia, from his exile in Chechenya, welcomed this 'liberation', predicting it would soon turn into a nationwide movement. A worried Shevardnadze admitted that the situation in Mingrelia was 'most difficult and complicated' (Tass).

CIA INTERVENTION

Rumours and speculation had been rife for some time that the US CIA was covertly operating in Georgia for its own devious, opaque purposes. Little evidence supported this supposition, that is until 8 August 1993, when a CIA operative, Fred Woodruff, was shot dead near Tbilisi. Woodruff, initially described as a diplomat, had been the CIA regional affairs officer, based in the US embassy in Tbilisi. He had been engaged in training and arming bodyguards for Shevardnadze and other Georgian VIPs thought to be in danger of assassination. Woodruff, who had been in Georgia since June, was returning in the evening after a tourist visit to some ancient monuments when his vehicle was stopped in the village of Natakhtari, some six miles from the capital, by a group of armed men, one of whom fired the single shot that killed him. Also in the vehicle was Eldr Gogoladze, Shevardnadze's head of intelligence and security, Vakhtang Gvaramina, the chief prosecutor, and two women. No one else was hurt. At first bandits were blamed for a 'chance shooting'.

James Woolsey, the CIA director, who was visiting Moscow at the time, flew to Tbilisi to take the body back to the United States and briefly met Shevardnadze at the airport. It was agreed there should be a joint US–Georgian investigation.

Within weeks of the collapse of the USSR, President Bush had sent diplomats and agents into the new republics of the former Soviet Union, where they had kept a low profile. When President Clinton assumed power in January 1993 it was becoming obvious that Russia was not seeing things from the American point of view, so he decided there might be a useful role for covert CIA operations. Like his predecessors, he had a soft spot for Shevardnadze, who was widely recognised in American circles as the architect of the liberation of Eastern Europe, and his administration seemed to feel it 'owed him one', especially when it became obvious that Yeltsin was supporting the Abkhazian separatists. Shevardnadze was considered to be a 'safe' and friendly Caucasian leader. Clinton wanted a foothold in Georgia, but then so did Yeltsin.

Clinton signed a policy directive to provide training, equipment and arms for the bodyguards of Shevardnadze and other Georgian VIPs who had received death threats from Zviadistis, Mingrelians, Abkhazians and others. This was probably the first covert US operation in the breakaway states of the former USSR.

Shevardnadze – who was said to have been a close friend of James Baker, a former US secretary of state, even though the United States had rejected Shevardnadze's suggestion for a 'security belt' of republics to surround Russia, of which Georgia would be a part – had taken a huge gamble by collaborating with the CIA. A covert struggle developed between the CIA, the GRU (military intelligence) and the successor splinters of the former KGB, intermixed with traditional Georgian intrigue. The CIA let it be known that in December 1992 over 13 billion roubles had been transferred from private banks in Moscow to Gudauta, the headquarters of the Abkhazian separatists, so that they could develop a 'rebel' army. About the same time the 245th Guards Paratroop Regiment, normally stationed in Azerbaijan, was secretly moved to Abkhazia (*The Times*).

Looking ahead on the Woodruff issue, it was not until 7 February 1994 that Anzor Shaimadze, a former soldier, was convicted of his murder and sentenced to imprisonment. At the trial Shaimadze claimed the confession presented by the prosecution was false, and had been extracted from him under torture. A fortnight or so later the American spy Aldrich Ames was arrested in the United States, and it was revealed that he had been in Tbilisi a few days before Woodruff's death. This does not clarify this particular mystery, but it does confirm the CIA's covert involvement in Georgian affairs.

SHEVARDNADZE RESIGNS

Despite Russian objections that he was contravening the July ceasefire agreement, on 6 September 1993 Shevardnadze imposed martial law on Abkhazia. Although he had few means with which to implement it, he nevertheless felt that a positive gesture was essential to prevent Abkhazia's independence stance from solidifying. The following day the Georgian State Council approved Shevardnadze's plan to reconstruct his government, and on the 11th a new cabinet was presented, in which he took the Interior Ministry portfolio for himself. On the 14th Shevardnadze asked the Georgian State Council to dissolve itself and approve a two-month state of emergency (as from the 20th), which would give him impressive dictatorial powers. He decreed that all armed militias must be disarmed or merged into the Georgian national army.

Shevardnadze was berated by Ioseliani for wanting to assume the role of the old-time communist boss he had once been, insisting that his Mekhedrioni fighters, who controlled parts of Western Georgia, would not disband. Shevardnadze, who had previously threatened to 'liquidate any opponents who took up arms' against him, angrily shouted that he would resign and stamped out of the Council Chamber.

Huge crowds assembled outside the Georgian State Council buildings in a massive demonstration of support for Shevardnadze. In fact Georgia seemed to be set on a more peaceful course. The Georgian–Abkhazian ceasefire was holding, and many knew that only Shevardnadze, no matter how unpopular he was in certain quarters or on certain issues, was the only leader who could hold Georgia together at this particularly stressful time: the alternative was too awful to contemplate.

The Georgian State Council reassembled, Shevardnadze's resignation was refused and his request for a two-month state of emergency was granted; but the Council refused to dissolve itself. His enemies alleged that his resignation threat was simply a public relations ploy to gain more power. It might have been, but he remained at the helm, after successfully dicing with public opinion once again. He insisted that Georgia join the CIS, a policy that Gamsakhurdia had persistently rejected, but only gained a narrow victory (just 120 out of 235 deputies voting in favour). Shevardnadze also took this opportunity to sign an economic agreement with Russia.

MINGRELIAN REVOLT

On 15 September 1993 the Mingrelian militia in Western Georgia sprang into action and seized control of the railways and roads in the Lanchkhuti–Samtredia region, which cut off Tbilisi from the port of Poti, into which US food aid still trickled. Around 800 rebels, some in armoured vehicles, attacked the government garrison at Samtredia. Shevardnadze rushed some of his new model army troops to that city, and also to Zestefioni, an industrial centre, to protect the road–rail links, which if severed would literally divide Georgia into two parts.

This was a disappointment for Shevardnadze, who had been hoping to persuade the Mingrelians to join him in any fighting against the Abkhazians; but the Mingrelians disliked him too much. The numerous abuses committed against civilians by the undisciplined Mingrelian militiamen, who ostensibly were allied to the government, made the province a hotbed of subversion and discontent. To worsen matters Shevardnadze's vanquished rival, Gamsakhurdia, spoke out again from his Chechen sanctuary, urging the Mingrelians to stage strikes and demonstrations, and once again calling on Shevardnadze to resign. He also called on members of the new Georgian national army to desert and fight for him, which a few did.

But outside Mingrelia, support in Georgia for Gamsakhurdia was weak.

THE BATTLE FOR SUKHUMI

Probably influenced by the Gamsakhurdia rebellion in Mingrelia, on 16 September 1993 Abkhazian armed forces launched a major advance on Sukhumi, taking the Georgian defenders by surprise and breaking the seven-week ceasefire. General Vladimir Chikovani, commanding the Abkhazian army, boasted that his soldiers, with tanks, had crossed the Gumista river and were rapidly moving towards Sukhumi.

Shevardnadze seemed to be surprised too, as after all he had kept his part of the Russian-brokered agreement by withdrawing his troops and most of his artillery from Sukhumi. On the 18th he met Grachev at Sochi airport, where he accused Russia of reneging on the July agreement and of deceit. He asked for Russian military assistance to defend Sukhumi, but Grachev refused. However he did agree to impose sanctions against Abkhazia if its troops continued to advance towards Sukhumi, to cut off electricity supplies and ban the sale of military equipment. This was the first indirect admission that Russia had been supplying the Abkhazians with weaponry.

Shevardnadze returned to Sukhumi, emotionally proclaiming he would defend it with his bare hands if necessary, but Grachev would not agree to accompany him. Two of Shevardnadze's bodyguards were killed by shellfire two days later. In Tbilisi, where disloyalty to the regime was the uncertain, hidden danger, the state of emergency was biting: private citizens were forbidden to wear military-type uniforms, service personnel were not allowed to carry arms in public, rallies and strikes were proscribed and censorship had been imposed on the media.

On 20 September Shevardnadze again appealed for Russian military assistance, saying that 'Abkhazia is the fuse that could detonate not only the Georgia of Shevardnadze, but also the Russia of Yeltsin', but was rejected by Grachev, who insisted that the use of buffer forces to separate the two sides was impossible, and that the only solution was for the Georgian troops to withdraw. The following day Russia closed its border with Abkhazia. By this time Abkhazian troops were entering the outskirts of Sukhumi, despite an alleged local agreement by both sides to break off contact with each other within 24 hours (Itar-Tass).

During the ceasefire period many Georgian refugees from Sukhumi had returned to the city, but as the bombardment recommenced many became refugees for the second time. Aircraft brought in Georgian reinforcements and left with a full complement of Georgian refugees, as Abkhazian militias began to overrun the south-eastern suburbs. Soon the Abkhazians were fighting their way towards the central railway station.

Abkhazian anti-aircraft weapons began to take a toll of Georgian aircraft, shooting down two SU-25s on consecutive days. On the 23rd a passenger aircraft was hit when taking off by anti-aircraft missiles launched from small naval craft lying just offshore. General Chikovani also claimed his militias had destroyed a major bridge near Ochamchire.

Fighting had extended into the streets of Sukhumi by the 24th, while the port area was flooded with refugees desperate to escape by sea. The siege was tightened by both land and air by the Abkhazians. A Georgian attempt to force a land exit to the south-east was thwarted. Lack of sufficient artillery was telling against the defenders. Hopes rested on a relief column advancing from the south, which was having to fight its way through hostile territory. However it was halted by the Kodori river, about 15 miles from Sukhumi. On the 26th Abkhazian troops gained the central railway station, which meant they now occupied half the city as well as holding the overlooking heights. The Georgians were out-gunned.

On the 27th Abkhazian troops entered the centre of Sukhumi, a large part of which had been reduced to rubble, and resistance waned: it was almost all over. Shevardnadze refused Russia's offer to evacuate him by sea. The following day a Russian-brokered ceasefire enabled the Abkhazians to complete the occupation of their capital city, while Russians monitored, as best they could, the evacuation of Georgian troops and refugees, said to number over 20 000, most of whom left by sea, many in Russian landing craft. Georgia alleged that Abkhazian soldiers had gone on the rampage and thousands had been killed, but visiting journalists could find little evidence of such atrocities. Tass reported only one prominent Georgian death, that of Zhiuli Shartave, the chief administrator, who had been taken prisoner on the 26th.

Shevardnadze escaped by plane on the 28th, but his honour was satisfied as the Georgian State Council, which he had pushed aside, ordered him to return to Tbilisi, supplemented by the pleadings of the Georgian patriarch, Ilya, and others. He was urgently needed back at base, as on the 24th his enemy, Gamsakhurdia, had returned to his home town of Zugdidi and was inciting revolution. By remaining so long and so defiantly in doomed Sukhumi, Shevardnadze's prestige had risen in many Georgian eyes.

On the 30th Abkhazian militias occupied the towns of Gali and Ochamchire, which gave them virtual control of most of Abkhazia. Later General Karakashvili claimed that some 200 000 people had been displaced by the fighting in Abkhazia, and that some 20 000 Georgians were stranded in the Savaneta mountain passes, risking death through exposure in the approaching winter. Russia said it had evacuated 14 000 by sea, and at one stage, with Russian permission, Ukrainian helicopters were allowed in to evacuate about 7000 stranded refugees. Conservative estimates are that at least 5000 people were killed in the 'Eleven Day War'.

A BLACK DAY FOR SHEVARDNADZE

On 1 October 1993 Poti fell to the Zviadistis, said to number about 10 000, who then swept eastwards to take the railway junction town of Samtredia on the 17th, at the cost of about 40 dead. The Gamsakhurdia revolt against Shevardnadze was in full swing in Mingrelia. On 18 October, back in Tbilisi Shevardnadze admitted that his armed forces had practically disintegrated. It was a black day for the doughty Georgian leader.

THE GEORGIANS FIGHT BACK

However Shevardnadze did not remain depressed for long, as he used policy changes to improve his fortunes. He agreed that if Yeltsin gave him direct military aid, Georgia would join the CIS, and in early October Russian heavy weaponry began quietly to appear among the Georgian military forces. Gamsakhurdia was now back in Zugdidi with a 'few hundred' ill-disciplined Zvaidists (although he claimed over 3000), which took full advantage of the Georgian military withdrawals and retreats to seep into areas of Mingrelia, including Poti and Samtredia.

Counterattacks began on the 20th – the Georgian force consisting mainly of the Mekhedrioni which suddenly appeared to be more disciplined and efficient than before – spurred on by rumours of Abkhazian acts of plunder, genocide and ethnic cleansing, to recapture Samtredia on the 22nd and Poti on 25th. By the end of the month only Zugdidi remained in Zviadisti hands. The new Georgian army had put the Russian armour and guns to good use. In order to 'clean up his act', Shevardnadze had set up a special force to deter his own Georgian troops from committing atrocities, and also anyone else's. He decreed that looters, for example, would be shot on sight, and many were, mostly Abkhazians, who backed away from confrontation with this new, vengeful force.

As a potential CIS member state, Georgia agreed to accept a combined Russian–Ukrainian task force, which landed at Poti from Russian warships on 4 November to secure and hold the road and rail links between Poti and Tbilisi. The Zviadistis were driven back from their position blocking a 15-mile stretch of railway line between Poti and Senaki. The Russian–Ukrainian force then moved to Zugdidi, from where it spread out along the road–rail network eastwards to Tbilisi, thus securing Shevardnadze's internal communications. On the 6th the Zviadistis departed from Zugdidi without firing a shot, most hastily withdrawing into Abkhazian territory to base their resistance headquarters in Gali, just inside Abkhazia. Gamsakurdia's revolt collapsed as Georgian tanks and guns were deployed on the Abkhazian border.

The Georgian offensive against the Abkhazians began on 18 November 1993, penetrating the Lata Gorge area, which contained a number of Georgian villages – although harassed and periodically attacked, these had successfully resisted the Abkhazian military pressure. But winter fell upon the combatants and the operation slowed almost to a standstill. By the end of the month the Tbilisi government was accusing the Abkhazians of carrying out ethnic cleansing, while Vladislav Ardzinba, the Abkhazian leader, stated that a referendum would be held in Abkhazia to determine its future.

In Tbilisi, Shevardnadze was planning to strengthen his political base, and on 21 November the inaugural Congress of the Citizens' Union of Georgia was held, Shevardnadze being its elected leader. Its stated aim was to promote 'democratic values' and its purpose was to seek mass membership. The Citizens' Union of Georgia advocated the restoration of all Georgian territory, including Abkhazia.

GEORGIAN–ABKHAZIAN AGREEMENT

In Geneva on 1 December 1993, under UN sponsorship a Georgian–Abkhazian Agreement was signed by Dzhaba Ioseliani for Georgia and Prime Minister Dokrat Jinjolia of Abkhazia. The agreement catered for a continuing ceasefire pending further negotiations, the employment of additional UN observers, the return of refugees to their former homes (estimated by the UN to exceed 200 000) and the exchange of all prisoners. The future status of Abkhazia was to be drafted by UN and CSCE 'experts'. Hopes of peace were based on two opposing and most unlikely premises – that the Georgian government would grant considerable autonomy to Abkhazia, and Jinjolia would not insist on secession from Georgia.

THE DEATH OF GAMSAKHURDIA

On 31 December 1993, somewhere in Mingrelia and seemingly overwhelmed by defeat and despair, having constantly been outwitted and outfought by his old enemy the 'Silver Fox', Zviad Gamsakhurdia, aged 54, shot himself. Various legends have sprung up about the precise circumstances of his death, but it seems to have been a plain case of suicide. A joint commission of Georgian and Russian investigators confirmed this verdict on 17 February 1994, after the exhumation of his body from a grave in Western Georgia. Gamsakhurdia's death deprived the Mingrelians of their motive to rebel, and the Zviadistis were left bewildered and purposeless, and at the mercy of an unforgiving Shevardnadze.

PEACEMAKING

The month of January 1994 was taken up with talk of peacemaking as the United Nations had at last got into the act and was vigorously turning its attention to the Georgian–Abkhazian problem. A request for UN peacekeeping forces to be sent to Abkhazia had been made earlier by both Yeltsin and Shevardnadze, but the UN secretary general had played hard to get, being reluctant to respond until a comprehensive peace settlement had been reached over Abkhazia. This process had tended to drag on, and it was not until mid February that the UN-sponsored second round of Georgian–Abkhazian talks began.

On 3 February President Yeltsin made a formal visit to Tbilisi to sign a ten-year Georgian–Russian friendship treaty, as well as several economic cooperation and trade agreements. This pleased both presidents. Yeltsin gained a virtual protectorate and enhanced Russia's influence in the Trans-Caucasus region. Shevardnadze was happy to renew economic links with Russia, the CIS markets offering a kiss of life to his ailing Georgian economy, while Russia's new stake in Georgia meant the end of its former hostility. Shevardnadze now hoped for an end to Russian military support for the Abkhazian separatists. He described the treaty as 'One of the major events in 200 years of history between our two peoples' (Inter-Fax). It certainly marked an attempt to improve relations between Georgia and Russia, which had deteriorated badly since Georgia's allegation that Russia was providing military support to the Abkhazians.

Both presidents signed a military memorandum to establish three Russian military bases near Tbilisi to 'protect the security of the CIS'. Russian Defence Minister Grachev envisaged the creation of a Trans-Caucasus military force of 23 000 Russian troops, of which 60 per cent would be stationed in Georgia. In return Russia would provide arms and training for the new Georgian army. This heartened Shevardnadze as this security fence would enable him to increase not only his economic and military strength, but consequentially his internal security situation too.

Shevardnadze pressed ahead with unifying his new model army. On 8 February the Mekhedrioni was officially disbanded, and on the 11th the resignation of Defence Minister Karakashvili was accepted. Yeltsin was now in a more friendly mood, and the presence of Russian troops in Georgia gave Shevardnadze the confidence to bring wayward militias to heel and disarm them. Nonetheless hiccups occurred. For example on 3 February the deputy defence minister, Nikola Kekelidze, and one other person were killed by a terrorist explosion at Kekelidze's home in Tbilisi, and Karakashvili was injured by a second explosion when he visited the scene. Kekelidze was suspected of involvement in criminal activities, an accusation that could be levelled at many Georgian VIPs, ministers and senior military officers.

ABKHAZIAN INDEPENDENCE

During the lull in Georgian–Abkhazian fighting in the winter months, on 10 February 1994 Abkhazia proclaimed its independence. It followed this up on 15 March by withdrawing from the peace talks in protest at the Georgian State Council's decision to abolish the Abkhazian State Council. Later that month fighting erupted in the Lata Gorge region of Abkhazia, where Georgian forces had become bogged down the previous November.

GEORGIAN STATE COUNCIL

In Tbilisi on 1 March 1994 the Georgian State Council met for the first time since its suspension the previous September to discuss the ratification of Shevardnadze's October decision to enter the CIS. It was an acrimonious debate that only narrowly resulted in a disputed majority.

On 20 April the deputy interior minister, General Georgi Gulua, his bodyguard and driver were killed by unknown gunmen firing from a passing car. This was rumoured to be a mafia-linked crime. The universal carrying and indiscriminate use of firearms caused concern that reached the door of the Georgian State Council, where on 3 May deputies were banned from taking them into the Council chamber.

THE MOSCOW AGREEMENT

On 4 April 1994 several agreements between representatives of Georgia and Abkhazia were signed in Moscow in the presence of the UN secretary general, the main one being a ceasefire that was to commence immediately. Another was to establish a committee to supervise the return of refugees, it being 'reestimated' that 250 000 had been driven from Abkhazia during the previous year's fighting. Yet another was an agreement in principle to create a republic of Abkhazia, with its own constitution, but still within Georgia. No change there. Both sides requested the deployment of UN peacekeepers, but the UN Security Council demurred until there was further political progress. The ceasefire agreement, which envisaged the deployment of Russian troops under the auspices of the CIS, was not concluded until 14 May.

Previously Boutros-Ghali had rejected Yeltsin's request for 'UN status' for Russian troops on peacekeeping tasks, insisting that all 'multinational forces must be under direct UN control'. On 15 April Georgia had agreed to Russian forces patrolling its borders. Meanwhile the Georgian deputy prime minister had announced that over 30 000 Georgians had been killed in Abkhazia during 1993 (Inter-Fax).

Russia sent 2500 peacekeeping troops, under CIS auspices, to Georgia on 24 June, most of whom were deployed along the line of the Inguri river, which marked the boundary between Abkhazia and Georgia proper for most of the way, an advance party having arrived earlier to begin mine clearing. On 21 July the UN Security Council had second thoughts and adopted a resolution approving the presence of Russian troops in Georgia, and increasing the number of UN observers. Vladislav Ardzinba, the Abkhazian leader, loudly complained that 'Russian troops' were continuing to shell the Kodori Gorge area, and so he reneged on the April peace agreement, by which Georgia had agreed to withdraw its armed forces from that area of Abkhazia by 30 July.

DECLARATION OF NATIONAL UNITY AND ACCORD

A declaration of national unity and accord was signed in Tbilisi on 26 May 1994 by representatives of 34 political parties and public organisations, inspired by Russia's April Treaty on Civil Accord (signed on 28 April) to 'ensure civil peace'. It was to provide the foundation of an independent democratic society, stressing the need for stability and consolidation, including repudiation of violence for political ends, rights for Georgia's minorities, observance of human rights and a pledge to abide by the constitution. Actually it was a placid, self-righteous and fragile fig leaf to obscure the vision of Western observers from the obvious. The Georgian Communist Party (banned since August 1991) held a revival Congress in Tbilisi on 25 June. Other left-wing opposition parties included the Georgian Communist Workers and the Alliance of Communists of Georgia.

Despite his increasingly tight grip on his country, Shevardnadze still faced considerable opposition, both in the Georgian State Council and on the streets. A massive demonstration in Tbilisi of a reported 200 000 people was mounted on 10 July to protest against Shevardnadze's policies. The demonstration was dispersed vigorously by the police and several ringleaders were arrested. That month Loti Kobalia, the former commander of Gamsakhurdia's Mingrelian rebel forces, was arrested in Ukraine and extradited to Tbilisi to stand trial. The following month the *Helsinki Human Rights Watch* issued a report accusing the Georgian authorities of widespread human rights violations, and especially condemned Shevardnadze's November 1993 decree authorising the summary execution of suspected rebels.

Persistent criticism and opposition once again caused Shevardnadze to threaten to resign. This time he had to face a no confidence motion in the Georgian State Council on 28 September, which he won. Even though many people and factions disliked him, he was the only man for the job at this difficult time.

RUSSIAN PEACEKEEPERS IN ACTION

Yeltsin and Shevardnadze met again at the Russian resort of Sochi on 19 September 1994 to consider the Abkhazian situation, and it was agreed that those Georgian units remaining in the Kodori Gorge area of Abkhazia, the only one where fighting continued, should be quickly withdrawn; that Georgian irregular militia groups, who allegedly had been harassing civilians, would be disarmed; and that Georgian refugees driven from Abkhazia in 1993 should begin to return home. On the 9th two Russian soldiers in the peacekeeping contingent had been killed by local gunmen at Gali. A Georgian commission was sent to the area – to which a number of Georgians had returned to administer under the protection of Russian guns – to investigate allegations of brutality by Russian troops against local residents.

The Kodori Gorge area had been the scene of sporadic clashes between Abkhazians and Georgian irregulars since April. Despite Shevardnadze's promise to withdraw the Georgian units, they remained, Shevardnadze insisting they were simply Georgians who had armed themselves for self-defence. On 4 October the Russian peacekeeping contingent launched a large sweeping operation through the Kodori Gorge area to clear out all remaining Georgian military units. On the 11th the Russian military commander reported that his mission had been accomplished, adding the rider that Georgian militias would be allowed to remain to protect Georgian residents until the 'last rebel Abkhaz units withdrew' (*Daily Telegraph*), a rather ambiguous statement that satisfied neither side. The purpose of the operation had been to disarm the Georgian militias. Military activity in this fringe area died down somewhat as winter began to close in.

Boutros Ghali visited Tbilisi on 30 November to a doubtful welcome, being faced by crowds of hostile nationalists protesting about the UN-approved Russian peacekeeping operation, which had over 100 UN monitors. Boutros Ghali's purpose was to assure them the contingent would remain in Abkhazia.

Tbilisi remained turbulent and unstable, with elements of armed militias, now unemployed, roaming restlessly. On 12 November a combined army, Interior Ministry and Security Service operation was mounted against a 200-strong, recalcitrant unit of the former National Guard at the Lake Tbilisi camp. Local radio reports stated that they were 'neutralised'. Tengiz Kitovani, their former commander, denied that he had been responsible for this.

On 3 December 1994 Georgi Chanturia, leader of the opposition National Democratic Party, was killed when gunmen opened fire on his car in Tbilisi. His driver was also killed, and his wife (Irina Sarishvili, a deputy and a former deputy prime minister) was seriously injured. The National Democratic Party blamed 'Russian imperialistic forces, and the mafia'. Chanturia had accused certain ministers of collaborating with Russia, and when some refused to be questioned by the Georgian State Council there were resignations.

GEORGIAN ENERGY CRISIS

With winter approaching Georgia ran into another energy crisis and the electricity supply had to be rationed. In addition the main Tbilisi power station occasionally broke down and the gas supply from Turkmenistan, which was delivered by pipeline through Uzbekistan, suddenly ceased. Georgia had not paid its bills and Uzbekistan was demanding a higher tariff for the transit of fuel across its territory. Turkey stepped in to supply electricity, as did Iran, which also promised to provide gas, but these sources were spasmodic and unreliable.

ABKHAZIA ADOPTS A NEW CONSTITUTION

Abkhazia adopted a new constitution on 26 November 1994, establishing itself as a sovereign state and instituting a presidency. Vladislav Ardzinba became the first president and appointed a cabinet. Shevardnadze denounced this move and alleged there had been irregularities in the voting system, and that non-Abkhazian deputies, meaning Georgians, had not been present to vote. On 2 December the UN Security Council expressed deep concern, saying that this violated all agreements made on its behalf.

8 President Shevardnadze: 1995

The plain unpalatable fact was that the Georgian troops had been driven from Abkhazia, and the winter weather, together with the Russian–Ukrainian peacekeeping troops, meant there was little the Tbilisi government could do at the moment to reassert its sovereignty. Inactivity rankled with many Georgian deputies and other restless leaders, one of whom, Tengiz Kitovani (former defence minister and former leader of the disbanded National Guard, now leader of the National Liberation Front), argued that Georgia was entitled to continue its military operations in Abkhazia to recover its formerly dominant position, just as Russia was doing in Chechenya to prevent that republic from breaking away from the Russian Federation. Shevardnadze was cautious – he had longer-term aims in mind and wanted time to unify and strengthen his national armed forces, and for his ailing economy to recover a little. In any case winter was not the time to launch a military operation. Kitovani thought otherwise.

Early in the morning of 14 January 1995 a contingent of Georgian security forces surrounded the Lake Tbilisi camp and disarmed 370 irregulars, all members of the 'disbanded' National Guard, who were preparing for military action against Abkhazia. Several people were injured in the scuffle. Later that day Kitovani was arrested, and was eventually charged with 'planning to reignite the civil war' in Abkhazia (Tass).

As a generality it can be said that Georgians disliked and distrusted Russians, to whom could be added Abkhazians, feelings that were reciprocated, and in frustration extremists on all sides became covertly active. In Moscow on 25 January, for example, unknown gunmen shot and killed General Paata Datuashvili, a former Georgian deputy defence minister, and wounded Georgi Karakashvili, a former defence minister. (The previous year a bomb had been discovered on Karakashvili's aircraft.) Responsibility was vaguely ascribed to Abkhazian nationalists, and as an afterthought, to the mafia as well.

In January attacks were made in Tbilisi on the headquarters of the Russian Transcaucasus Forces Group, and on that of the

Russian Border Guards. The buildings were damaged by explosions, but no casualties were incurred. The Russian embassy in Tbilisi demanded that the government provide better security for Russian personnel.

SHEVARDNADZE VISITS THE UK

Shevardnadze strove to make his country more internationally acceptable. He had hoped that his previous reputation as Soviet foreign minister might have prompted his 'Western admirers' to be more generous, but apart from fine words, few showed any generosity, or wanted to draw close to him. He knew that the British-Petroleum-led international oil consortium wanted a secure route for an overland pipeline to carry Caspian offshore oil to Black Sea terminals, and hoped he could persuade it to resurrect the long-disused Georgian one that ran from Baku to Supsa on the Black Sea. Transit tariffs would be a welcome addition to the Georgian economy, and it would also be a prize international asset that would attract Western investment. The problem was that the oil consortium required stability, which at the moment Georgia lacked.

In February Shevardnadze took his begging bowl to Britain, to tout for his oil pipeline. He was given a VIP welcome, but was sent away almost empty handed. Vague declarations of friendship, trade and investment, together with a promise to open a British embassy in Tbilisi, was all he could obtain. Shevardnadze lectured his hosts, depicting himself as a far-seeing statesman and accusing the West of being 'so intoxicated by the belief it had won the Cold War, that it failed to see that rampant nationalism posed threats comparable to a nuclear Armageddon'. Referring to his own civil war, he said 'I have seen a baby skinned alive', and described other horrors that were the price of self-determination (lecture give by Shevardnadze at Royal Institute of International Relations, London).

He also tried hard to improve Georgian–Russian relations, and on 23 March initialled an agreement confirming three Russian military bases in Georgia, asserting that in return Russia should support the reintegration of Abkhazia and South Ossetia, and assist in creating a unified Georgia. Although this met with intense domestic criticism, he survived.

More terrorist attacks were made against Russian buildings

in Tbilisi in April, when shots were fired at the headquarters of the Russian Transcaucasus Forces Group and an explosion occurred at the entrance to the Russian embassy. The 'Algeti Wolves', a covert nationalist organisation, claimed responsibility. Also that month, four senior security officials of the Abkhazian government were killed, which caused Vladislav Ardzinba to call for general mobilisation, warning that Georgia was preparing to resume hostilities.

GEORGIAN LINKS WITH RUSSIA

During March the Russian defence minister, Pavel Grachev, visited Tbilisi, accompanied by a large military delegation, the object being to tie Georgia into the joint Russian–CIS military framework. Grachev held talks with both Shevardnadze and his defence minister, General Vardiko Nadibaidze, to negotiate a new draft agreement on military cooperation and assistance. This produced two significant features: that Russian bases in Georgia would be increased from three (previously agreed in in February 1994) to four; and that there should be a Russian military presence in Georgia for at least 25 years.

Russia declared that, to be effective, regional security must be based on partnership, omitting to mention that Russia would be the senior partner and that it planned to create Joint Coalition Armed Forces in the Transcaucasus region by the end of the decade. As the first step, joint exercises were to be held in Georgia and Armenia, the next was to establish a joint CIS defence system, in which it was proposed that Georgia would become the predominant partner in an air defence system covering the whole of the Transcaucasus region. These agreements, which were initialled, tied Georgia further into its 'protectorate status'. As regards the Abkhazian conflict, Grachev reaffirmed that 'Georgia is one state, which in future should be constructed on a federal basis' (Tass).

Russia was prepared to give Georgia considerable military assistance in equipping, organising and training the Georgian national army, as well as other economic aid, which was badly required. In April Shevardnadze established a Military Collegium of the Defence Ministry of the Georgian Republic, on the Russian model, to be the armed forces' advisory and monitoring committee. It would review all aspects of the armed forces, make recommendations and be responsible for the implementation of presidential decrees. This was badly required to tighten the Georgian armed forces into a disciplined, unified body.

THE RESCUE CORPS

Accused by Shevardnadze of 'racketeering and extortion' (Tass), the Mekhedrioni, although officially disbanded in February 1994, had retained its entity and arms, changing its name to the 'Rescue Corps'. Based mainly in the town of Telavi in eastern Georgia, it continued to be accused of involvement in criminal activities, especially 'protection rackets'. Shevardnadze decided to crack down on this powerful, wayward militia, and issued a decree forbidding its members to carry arms. On 4 May he sent a contingent of army and security troops to disarm them. Quantities of weaponry and ammunition were seized and a number of its leaders detained. This disarmament process continued piecemeal at other Rescue Corps locations, and on the 20th Interior Ministry troops destroyed a base near Tbilisi, killing four members. It was officially reported that the last Rescue Corps stockpile of weaponry was destroyed on the 23rd. Despite threats from Rescue Corps members to mount terrorist operations against the authorities unless some of its detained leaders were freed, tension subsided. Ioseliani, who remained at liberty, protested loudly but lacked popular support.

Shevardnadze assumed this was a big step forward in his plan to disarm the militias, still regarded as loose cannons, and bring them to heel. But his satisfaction was premature as all was not quite as it had been portrayed. The commission charged with monitoring the handover of the Rescue Corps' weaponry reported on 14 June that, despite government claims to the contrary, the Rescue Corps had only surrendered a small proportion of its weaponry. Ioseliani brazenly said that retention of the weapons was justified 'as parts of Georgia are in continuing disorder' (*Daily Telegraph*), and so the matter was unsatisfactorily left as it was for the moment.

The Rescue Corps did not retain that title for long, for on 16 July it was changed to the Mekhedrioni Political Society

(Dzhaba Ioseliani remaining the leader), the intention being to participate in the forthcoming elections.

Despite criticising Russia for giving humanitarian aid directly to Abkhazia instead of channelling it through Tbilisi following serious flooding in June, on 10 July Shevardnadze signed a Georgian–Russian agreement for the return of some 300 000 ethnic Georgian refugees to the Gali district of Abkhazia. Yeltsin said that Russian peacekeeping forces were ready to guarantee their safety. However Vladislav Ardzinba objected, indicating that any such move would meet with sabotage. After further fruitless negotiations the issue was suspended. Later, on 11 September, Yuri Voronov, leader of the Russian community in Abkhazia and deputy prime minister, was shot dead in Sukhumi.

ASSASSINATION ATTEMPT ON SHEVARDNADZE

On 24 August 1995 a new Georgian constitution was overwhelmingly approved by the legislature to replace the 'Decree on State Power' of 1991, which had served as an interim one. It provided for an executive president, with considerable powers, of a republic 'with federal elements', and a single legislature of 150 deputies. Ardzinba openly objected.

On the 29th, as Shevardnadze's motorcade moved away from the Georgian State Council building in Tbilisi to the Palace of Youth, where as chairman he was due to sign the formal approval for the new constitution, a bomb was exploded by remote control and blew up the vehicle in which he was riding, slightly injuring him. Twelve other people were also injured.

Adjacent buildings were searched and arms were found in the offices of Ioseliani, who initially became the prime suspect, but not the only one as Shevardnadze had many enemies. Shevardnadze at first blamed the 'mafia that wants to run the country' (Tass), and the shadowy Algeti Wolves also came into the frame of suspicion. Tanks again briefly appeared on the streets of Tbilisi, and a police dragnet brought in over 300 suspects.

Allegations finally focused on Igor Giorgadze, the security minister and a deputy prime minister, who disappeared before he was formally dismissed and a warrant for his arrest issued. Giorgadze was accused of collusion with 'Russian reactionary forces', and although he was frequently interviewed by the media the Moscow police claimed they were unable to track him down. The object of the attempted assassination was to remove Shevardnadze from the scene, without whom, it was thought, the country would become more destabilised and the new constitution would not be implemented. The Georgian State Council decided against declaring a state of emergency so as to avoid giving an impression of instability, which would probably have been noted adversely by the Azerbaijan International Operating Company. Shevardnadze officially disbanded the Rescue Corps on 1 October, describing it as a haven for criminals. Serious efforts were made to root it out, leading to allegations from critics that he was detaining hundreds without trial.

RUSSIAN BASES

The Russian prime minister, Chernomyrdin, visited Tbilisi on 15 September 1995 to signed a series of cooperation agreements, negotiated in March by General Grachev, in exchange for economic assistance. The four Russian military bases were to be in Akhalkalaki, Batumi, Gudauta and Vaziani. It was also agreed to establish a joint Russian–Georgian military operation to 'restore Georgian territorial integrity', a fig leaf for Shevardnadze to use against domestic opposition, and an excuse for turning his country into a virtual Russian protectorate. However, shortly afterwards this statement was rescinded by the Russian Defence Ministry, which had little intention of helping Georgia regain control over Abkhazia.

STABILITY

A flickering sign of approaching stability occurred on 25 September 1995, when the much maligned 'coupon' was replaced by the 'lari'. Credits were provided by the IMF to support the new currency, and the exchange rate was provisionally fixed at 1.3 laris to one US dollar. Inflation had been rampant, the previous rate being 1.3 million coupons for one US dollar. The first IMF loan to Georgia had been granted in December

1994, and this one showed there was increasing confidence in the country.

Meeting in Moscow in October, the Azerbaijan International Operation Company, the eleven-member British-Petroleum-led oil consortium, confirmed it had gained the contract to explore and extract Caspian offshore oil deposits. It was decided to have twin overland pipelines to pipe the oil to the Black Sea terminals, one of which was to run across Georgia. The prospect of rehabilitating the disused oil pipeline from Baku to Supsa gave hope, encouragement and a boost to the Georgian economy, as it would undoubtedly attract much-needed international investment and provide the benefits of transit tariffs and ancillary occupations.

GEORGIAN ELECTION

The new Georgian constitution came into effect on 17 October 1995 and elections were held on 5 November. The electoral register listed six candidates for the presidency, and over 40 parties or groups were permitted to compete, several having been barred. Those deputies who intended to take part in the election resigned, but were asked to continue in office. Shevardnadze was supported by the Union of Citizens of Georgia and the Socialist Party.

Shevardnadze obtained over 75 per cent of the votes, thus becoming Georgia's first executive president, a title he had long coveted and now at last had gained. His supporters formed a majority in the Georgian Assembly, indicating that while many still disliked and distrusted him, most Georgians knew he was the only man who could hold their country together and improve conditions. On being sworn in as president he promised to continue his reforms, restore the country's integrity, reinforce democracy and protect citizens' rights – grandiose pledges guaranteed to please both domestic and international ears. He also offered to resume talks with the Abkhazians, who did not respond.

ADHARIA

Not to be forgotten is Georgia's tiny Black Sea semi-independent oblast of Adharia, tucked away in the south-western corner of the country, adjacent to Turkey. Throughout Georgia's turbulent times, Adharia had shone in contrast with the troubled regions elsewhere. Batumi, its capital city, had been a favourite holiday resort of the former communist elite. Aslan Abashidze, chairman of the Adharia Autonomous Council since 1991, claimed that his tiny fiefdom of some 450 000 people, of whom about half were Georgian Muslims, seemed to be the only peaceful and prosperous region in Georgia, without organised crime or politically rapacious armed factions. Perhaps this was a little overstated, but he had the reputation of being a strong-armed ruler and admitted to having survived at least ten assassination attempts.

It was rumoured that Shevardnadze had asked him several times to become prime minister of his government in Tbilisi, but it seems that Abashidze felt safer on his home ground. His stated ambition was 'to create European capitalism in Batumi, our free port', claiming that his trains ran on time (*The Times*). Georgian sovereignty rested lightly on Adharia, which Shevardnadze agreed should be a base for Russian troops.

SHEVARDNADZE'S GEORGIA

By December 1995 Georgia had virtually become a Russian protectorate and Abkhazia had broken away, sheltering behind Russian and Ukrainian troops with UN observers posted along the Inguri river border, to the west of which Vladislav Ardzinba was organising his administration and forming his small defence force. The remaining Georgian residents (once a 47 per cent majority but now much reduced in number) were trying to adjust to the new situation. Russia still wanted to incorporate Abkhazia into the Russian Federation, but owing to its Chechen problem this would have to be postponed for a while – but not forgotten. Meanwhile the Russian authorities were doing their best to keep their peacekeeping force on station and Georgian troops out of Abkhazia.

The ceasefire still held in South Ossetia, which Russia also wanted to incorporate into the Russian Federation, attracted by the significance of the vital pass over and tunnel through the Caucasus Mountain range, the route southwards into Georgia. Shevardnadze also wanted to resume sovereignty over South Ossetia. One suspects that Russia will continue to ensure that separatists in both Abkhazia and South Ossetia are supported in resisting pressure from the Tbilisi government.

In Tbilisi President Shevardnadze, nowadays more firmly in the saddle, determinedly presides over a mafia- and armed-faction-ridden country that is basically nationalist and anti-Russian in attitude, and in which separatist cracks still show. Some Georgian nationalist political leaders have been itching to march into Abkhazia before the opposition becomes too strong, but Shevardnadze is putting his economy first. In any case his close intertwining with the Russian military has handicapped any adventurous thoughts of this nature.

Georgia remains a powder keg, but Shevardnadze is probably confident that, even at 67 years of age, he is still the man to govern the once turbulent Georgia. He still has problems, including developing efficient and loyal defence forces, disarming some political militias, crushing mafia gangs and improving the run-down national economy. He has some advantages, and receives economic aid and assistance from Russia, which needs him as much as he needs it. The IMF has smiled cautiously on Georgia, international commercial interest has been awakened, the promised Caspian oil bonanza is the grail ahead, and a full and flowing oil pipeline the prize that could bring prosperity. Optimists have seen signs of a decrease in armed factionalism and instability in Georgia, but pessimists are not so sure. Much depends on Shevardnadze, the Russian government and the advent of Caspian oil.

9 The Chechen Syndrome

During January 1995 Russian armed forces gained control over most of Grozny – capital city of the 'separatist' autonomous republic of Chechenya in the Russian Federation – by a heavy aerial and artillery bombardment that turned a major part of the five-square-mile area, previously home to a population of over 350 000, into a scene of desolation and destruction. On the 19th they gained possession of the badly damaged presidential palace, and then drove Chechen resistance forces back across the Sunzha river, which winds its way through central Grozny, making it the demarcation line between opposing battling forces.

Chechen fighters were driven from the centre of Grozny to its eastern part, literally inch by inch, making occasional successful counterattacks. Their spirit of resistance surprised Russian military commanders and the watching world. It was a 'TV war', with TV camera teams in forward positions amid shot and shell, often relaying pictures of bombardments as they were happening, and their deadly results, into millions of homes, not only in the Western World, but also in Russia, the Commonwealth of Independent States and other parts east and south. The casualty figures were uncertain but rumour placed them above the 20 000 mark. Probably some 70 000 inhabitants remained, many marooned and sheltering in cellars. Many perished under the rubble, while the bodies of dead Russian soldiers lay scattered around in the snow, their corpses nibbled by roving dogs in the frozen landscape. The Chechens mainly recovered the bodies of their dead comrades; the Russians seemed unable to do this.

The Russian armed forces showed no sign of slackening their military offensive, nor of negotiating, while on the eastern side of the Sunzha river Chechen fighters, despite their inferior numbers and weapons, showed no sign of surrendering or fading morale. Both were locked in a murderous struggle, the ferocity of which appalled Western leaders, who were trying hard to help President Boris Yeltsin survive in power in Moscow, and to think well of him in his attempt to liberalise Russia and develop a free market economy. How did this appalling situation come about?

CHECHENYA

Chechenya is a small, landlocked, autonomous republic of the Russian Federation in the North Caucasus region. In 1993 its population stood at about one million. Covering an area of just over 6000 square miles (about the size of Yorkshire), it is somewhat rectangular in shape and is bounded on the east and north-east by the autonomous republic of Dagestan; on the north-east by the autonomous republic of North Ossetia; on the east by Ingushetia (with an uncertain constitutional status); and on the south by the fully independent Republic of Georgia. Oil was discovered in Chechenya in 1823 and the British built Chechenya's first oil refinery. Much later, in 1928, the Soviets opened their first petrochemical research institute there.

Grozny, founded in 1824 as an outpost on the Cossack 'Terek River Line', developed as a major USSR training centre for oil technicians of all types. By 1994 it was estimated that Grozny was producing about 3.5 million tonnes of petroleum annually, its refining centre processing about 6.5 million tonnes of crude, much of which arrived by pipeline from Tyumen in the Urals (*Financial Times*).

As Chechenya only required about one million tonnes of oil a year for its domestic needs, the surplus should have provided a strong basis for economic development, but this was against Soviet policy as it could further aspirations of separatism. The Chechen oil reserves were thought to amount to only 30 million tons, located in three oilfields (Khayankort, Malgobek-Voznesen and Starogroznensk), which produced 3.6 million tonnes of oil in 1992 but only 2.6 million tonnes the following year. By the end of 1994 many oil wells were not working. Chechenya had two large oil refineries, which refined quantities of oil from adjacent republics, but with the advent of the CIS and the collapse of the centralised Soviet oil distribution system the volume declined. The only legitimate outlet for oil and allied products from Grozny was still through the Russian Federation, but a great deal was illegally being syphoned off (*Financial Times*).

Chechenya's major strategic importance lay in its oil resources, its considerable oil refining capacity, and the fact that it was an 'oil pipeline corridor and junction' between the Caspian Sea ports of Makhachkala (Dagestan) and Baku

(Azerbaijan), northwards into the oil pipeline system in the Russian Federation. Russian troops had been ordered to secure the oil pipelines and refineries, and to prevent local sabotage of these facilities. A very busy railway line crossed Chechenya, in an area generally devoid of good all-weather roads.

HISTORICAL BACKGROUND

The North Caucasus region was long inhabited by about six major tribes, most of which were of Caucasian stock. Some eventually came to be dignified as 'minor nations', including the Chechens. Apart from the intrusion of Islam, they were generally left alone in their wild, remote, mountainous and comparatively barren region. Islamic missionaries came to convert the people, but then retreated from this now strategic backwater, which assumed no international importance until the Christian Russian Empire began to expand southwards.

The Chechens were prominent in resisting Russian colonisation. In the late eighteenth century one chieftain, Imam Mansour, known as the Lion of Dagestan (he was a Dagen, but led a majority Chechen army), became a traditional Chechen hero who hindered Russian expansionism. By this time the Chechens had come under sway of the mystical Sufi branch of Islam, a way-out Shia sect, and the Naqshbandi, a semisecret Muslim brotherhood order that was alienated from the mainstream of Islam.

At the beginning of the nineteenth century Russia resumed its colonial advance into the Northern Caucasus, at first building defensive forts against attacks from Islamic forces from the south, but soon besieged within hostile territory. Russia changed its tactics and inflicted heavy-handed pacification measures on the inhabitants. When Russian soldiers were murdered, villagers massacred and local tribesmen expelled, their lands being allocated to the Cossacks, who formed a frontier gendarmerie for the expanding czarist empire.

The next Chechen warrior leader of note was Imam Shamil (also a Dagen), a legendary resistance fighter who became known as the Mahdi of the Caucasus. He was eventually captured by the Russians in 1859. In the course of these colonial campaigns much of Chechenya and Dagestan was deforested.

In 1864 Russia formally annexed the Caucasus Range, after which open rebellion amongst the mountain nations tended to subside, although there were periodic outbreaks of dissidence in the latter part of the nineteenth century and the beginning of the twentieth, which resulted in the mass deportation of indigenous peoples. The North Caucasus region also suffered from a small but continuous reduction in the size of its population through emigration, as much for economic reasons as any other, while occasional epidemics extracted a toll on life.

The Russian Revolutions of 1917 and the resultant civil war between the White and Red Armies had repercussions in the North Caucasus region, as elsewhere, especially when the newly formed Red Army began its 'reconquest' of czarist colonial territories. In 1918 some of the North Caucasus nations formed the United Mountain Republic, recognised briefly by Britain and France, but harassed by both the Red and the White Army it soon fell apart. This was followed in 1921 by the Mountain Autonomous Republic, which incorporated the Chechens, the Ossetes, the Ingush and four other nations, but not the Dagens, who unlike the others were of Turkic origin. One by one these nations were weaned away from the Mountain Autonomous Republic, being individually granted autonomous status as provinces. This happened to the Chechens in 1923, and the following year the Mountain Autonomous Republic ceased to exist. Then followed a decade during which the Soviets realigned the administrative boundaries between these autonomous provinces to reduce republican nationalist power. The strength of these nations was rooted in their rugged terrain, language and local culture.

The Soviet policy of 'divide and administer', using rivers and mountain ridges to fragment and reduce national power, brought about the formation of 'Ingushetia–Chechenya' (sometimes written as Checheno–Ingushetia) autonomous republic in 1934. The Soviets had already begun an anti-Islam campaign in this region in 1928, when mosques and shrines were closed and many destroyed, Sharia (religious) courts were abolished, the use of the Arabic language forbidden, and many Muslim clergy were killed or deported to faraway camps.

During the Second World War the North Caucasus mountain nations suffered from Stalin's mass deportations. In February

1944, almost overnight some 200 000 Chechens and 90 000 Ingush were packed on to trains and taken off to a long exile exile in Kazakhstan and Kirgistan. They were not allowed to return until 1957, when they found that their homes and jobs had been taken by Russians, especially in the industrial sphere, which caused ill-feeling. The excuse for this mass deportation, as if Stalin needed one, was that the Chechens and Ingush were alleged to have collaborated with Nazi German troops, whose forward advances had in fact ceased by 1943, the foremost German soldier not setting foot within 50 miles of Grozny.

GLASNOST AND PERESTROIKA

After the Second World War the Northern Caucasus remained fairly stable until March 1985, when Mikhail Gorbachev became first secretary of the Communist Party of the Soviet Union. While Gorbachev was quick to launch his glasnost and perestroika policies, they were slow to penetrate the inward-looking North Caucasus region, where in Ingushetia–Chechenya the communists remained in power, with only very slight superficial adjustments. Despite separatist events in adjacent Georgia and Azerbaijan, Gorbachev's replacement by Yeltsin and the formation of the Commonwealth of Independent States, the Supreme Soviet of Ingushetia–Chechenya tried to remain steady on its old course.

DZHOKHAR DUDAYEV

On to the Ingush–Chechen scene strode the small, dapper figure of Dzhokhar Dudayev, the first Chechen to be promoted to general in the Soviet air force. Born in February 1944 and swept up in Stalin's mass deportation, he spent the first years of his life in exile in Kazakhstan. On return to his homeland he joined the Soviet armed forces and graduated from the Gagarin Air Force Academy, after which he served as a fighter pilot in Siberia and Ukraine. He married a Russian and eventually commanded the Soviet air force base at Tartu in Estonia, where in 1989 he allowed the Estonian national flag to be raised.

This seems to have been the first overt sign of his inclination towards nationalism.

Dudayev resigned from the air force and returned to Ingushetia–Chechenya, with grandiose political ambitions both for himself and his fellow Chechens. In November 1990 he attended the founding meeting of the All National Congress of the Chechen People, which later became the Chechen National Congress (CNC). Dudayev was elected chairman, and under his energy and guidance the CNC became the most lively and influential political group in the republic, where several Islamic, national, cultural and other parties, groups and gatherings had sprung into existence in the glasnost era. A CNC executive committee of some 60 influential clan leaders or their representatives was formed – but no Ingush were included. Dudayev belonged to a comparatively minor clan, and some assumed that this helped him to enlist, and ostensibly unite, some of the more powerful clans, which were often at odds, and sometimes at blows, with each other over power and prestige. Almost immediately the CNC began to call for the disbandment of the Ingush–Chechen Supreme Soviet and Assembly, which had been elected in 1990.

THE CNC GAINS INFLUENCE

When the August 1991 coup attempt was made against Gorbachev in Moscow a period of political suspense ensued in Ingushetia–Chechenya, as many wanted to see how the situation was resolved before committing themselves to one side or another. The communist leader, Doku Zavgayev, was in Moscow at the time, where he quietly remained, while his deputy in Grozny went to ground and could not be found for a while. Thus the authority was lacking to convene the Ingush–Chechen Supreme Soviet and Assembly, which Dudayev was loudly demanding. In Grozny the local TV and radio station remained silent and uncommitted on this issue.

Dudayev seized his opportunity, and as news spread of the attempted coup he organised demonstrations in favour of Yeltsin, calling for mass disobedience and an indefinite strike. When the coup was over, Zavgayev returned to Grozny and convened the Ingush–Chechen Supreme Soviet and Assembly, which condemned Dudayev's actions. Dudayev responded by organising a rally in Freedom Square and denouncing the Zavgayev leadership for cowardice.

Dudayev called for the disbanding of the Ingush–Chechen Supreme Soviet, demanding that it transfer its powers to his CNC Executive Committee, pending fresh elections and the appointment of a special commission to investigate its negative stance. The CNC-instigated general strike continued. On 7 September Zavgayev resigned and was replaced by a Supreme Council.

On 15 September Dudayev's National Guard, the armed branch of the CNC, seized certain government offices and the telephone exchange, surrounded the combined radio and TV station and then stormed the Assembly building to oust the new Supreme Council while it was in session. At the same time his followers took control of the airport to prevent any deputies escaping to Moscow to retain a legal entity in exile. Dudayev and the CNC Executive Council took over the presidential palace, declaring that Dudayev would take charge until elections were held in October.

At first Yeltsin – leader of the RSFSR, of which Ingushetia–Chechenya was a constituent part – was grateful to Dudayev for his early support, and smiled on him, but Dudayev's seizure of power changed this attitude. On 8 October 1991, on the urging of Vice President Aleksandr Rutskoi, a resolution was passed condemning the illegal assumption of government of Ingushetia–Chechenya, and ordering that illegal armed Chechen formations should be detained as criminals and their arms confiscated. It also ordered that elections in Grozny be held according to the existing constitution, that is, a month after Dudayev's proposed election date.

The RSFSR Supreme Soviet sent a delegation to meet Dudayev in Grozny, and it was said that Rutskoi, who had given Dudayev an ultimatum to disband his National Guard by the 10th, also gave approval for Dudayev to hold elections on 27 October. Dudayev reacted by ordering a general mobilisation of all males aged 16–55, later claiming that some 62 000 had responded. A few volunteer groups also began to appear in his support from other parts of the North Caucasus region.

Yeltsin condemned the action of the CNC Executive Committee, ordering it to submit to the former Supreme Soviet within three days, and then banned all organisations and media campaigns that 'violated the integrity of the Russian Federation', indicating that any election held by the CNC on Dudayev's proposed date would be illegal.

At the general election in Chechenya, held on the 27th, most competing parties could be classed as either 'Islamic' or 'greens'. They were poorly organised, having no previous experience of democratic elections. Dudayev's own party, 'Vainakh' (Our People), swept the board and won almost 85 per cent of the all-male vote. Dudayev was then sworn in on the Koran as chairman, something that had not been done during the many Soviet secular years, and immediately granted himself emergency powers for a month. The Soviet troops in Ingushetia–Chechenya stood aside. To strengthen his National Guard Dudayev recruited released Chechen prisoners, who had mainly been convicted of carrying arms, an act considered by Chechens to be a right, not an offence.

CHECHEN INDEPENDENCE ANNOUNCED

Dudayev announced the independence of Chechenya on 2 November 1991, which Yeltsin ignored – in response Dudayev refused to recognise the newly forming Russian Federation. The following day Dudayev reordered general mobilisation in Chechenya, claiming a share of the former Soviet weaponry and military equipment remaining in the republic.

On the 8th Yeltsin declared a state of emergency in Ingushetia–Chechenya, and on the 10th he dispatched a detachment of Interior Ministry troops to Grozny to restore constitutional order, reputedly at the suggestion of Ruslan Khasbulatov (a Chechen), but they were surrounded by armed Chechens, and after some exchanges of fire were forced to withdraw across the border to Mozdok in North Ossetia. However the Supreme Soviet rescinded Yeltsin's state of emergency order, hoping this would cool the situation, instead imposing a weapons blockade, although the Chechens had plenty of infantry arms. On the 18th Dudayev assumed the office of prime minister, as winter strengthened its grip on the breakaway republic.

INGUSHETIA BREAKS AWAY

The Chechens' republican partners, the Ingush – then numbering about 350 000 (precise figures are not obtainable as they had been lumped together with the Chechens in former census returns) and mostly inhabiting the western edge of the republic – wanted to remain in the proposed Russian Federation, mainly for economic reasons, and did not wish to stand alongside the Chechens in this adventure. On 2 November 1991 the Ingush voted on this issue and decided to leave the Ingushetia–Chechenya autonomous republic. Dudayev accepted their decision, perhaps a little disappointedly, but he had a narrow Chechen national philosophy. The border between the two separate territories remained unmarked except for road checkpoints, and Nazran became the Ingush capital city.

Although the political parting of the Ingush and the Chechens seemed to be amicable, it caused a tremor of alarm in Yeltsin in Moscow, who feared it might spark off a rash of similar mutually agreed divisions of republics. He immediately imposed a state of emergency on North Ossetia and Ingushetia. An underlying reason for Yeltsin's alarm was that the Ingush regarded parts of North Ossetia as their historic homeland, from which they had been severed by Stalin, to be replaced by Ossetes. Although the majority of the Ingush, being an homogenous race, remained where they were, some of the more politically motivated began to march towards Vladikavkaz, the South Ossetian capital. Russian Federation Interior Ministry troops were rushed to Vladikavkaz, where a curfew was imposed, to patrol the streets. Ingush–Ossete tension continued, necessitating a heavy security presence.

In March 1992 the Ingush constitutional situation was discussed by Russian and Chechen delegations, which recommended that negotiations on this issue should begin the following month, at which time a draft law was approved by the Russian Federation Supreme Soviet, envisaging a two-year formation process for an Ingush autonomous republic, thus constitutionally splitting Ingushetia–Chechenya into two separate parts. A state commission would decide on border issues, Cossack (that is, Russian) interests, and the election of local bodies. The issue of the single Chechen autonomous republic would be considered after the settlement of its current crisis.

(The ethnic composition of Ingushetia–Chechenya was 57.8 per cent Chechen, 12.9 per cent Ingush and 23.1 per cent Russian: *Statesman's Year Book*, 1993.)

DISSATISFACTION WITH DUDAYEV

In March 1992 political talk in the North Caucasus region was mostly about the proposed new 'Russian Federation Treaty', which had to be signed by the end of that month. Not all Chechens were happy about severing all contact with Russia, and several groups suggested that a referendum be held on the issue. Nor were all happy about the way Dudayev was running the republic, some suggesting that he stand down.

Over 10 000 of the 200 000 resident Russians, mostly technicians in good jobs in oil-related industries, had already left Chechenya the previous year, and more were on the point of quitting owing to the lawless state of the republic and the reintroduction of Islamic customs, such as changing the weekly rest day from Sunday to Friday. Also, Dudayev seemed to be consorting with certain mafia clan barons involved in criminal enterprises.

Although Dudayev insisted he would not sign the proposed Russian Federation Treaty, it was widely rumoured that he would be prepared to do so if Yeltsin recognised his election as legitimate. It was said that secret talks were held on this issue, but that Yeltsin would not give way.

THE ONE-DAY REVOLT

The Russian Federation agreement was signed on 31 March 1992 by 18 of the 20 autonomous republics. The abstainers were Tartarstan, which was later tempted in by a special arrangement, and Chechenya. On the 31st there was a 'one-day revolt' against Dudayev in Grozny, when opposition forces captured the broadcasting centre, calling for Dudayev's resignation and a referendum on whether or not Chechenya should enter the Russian Federation. Dudayev immediately declared a state of emergency. The former Soviet military formations still in Chechenya remained passive, but later that day Dudayev's National

Guard recaptured the broadcasting centre and drove out the opposition.

The following day Dudayev accused the Russian Federation of manipulating the revolt against him and ordered an investigation. He also decreed jurisdiction over all former Soviet troops in Chechenya, but in later speeches he took a softer line and advocated military and economic cooperation with Russia – in short independence with all the former benefits but none of the former military ties.

General Boris Gromov, deputy commander-in-chief of the CIS armed forces, negotiated with Dudayev over the proportion of former Soviet weaponry to be left behind on a 'mutual security' basis. Later Yeltsin condemned Gromov for handing over 'half the heavy weaponry and ammunition of the tank regiment stationed at Shali' (Tass), rather than face an evacuation confrontion with armed Chechens. The Russian troops completed their withdrawal from Chechenya by 8 June, and on the 16th Dudayev announced the first intake of conscripts into the Chechen 'army'.

DUDAYEV THE AMBITIOUS

Dudayev proclaimed Chechenya's independence on 29 April 1992, now reckoning that he had surmounted the worst hurdles and would be left alone with his grandiose dreams, as Yeltsin was too fully engaged with problems of survival to mount a serious military operation against his small republic. He also calculated that Yeltsin, who was hoping to obtain a large amount of financial credit from the West, would not deliberately alienate Western opinion by initiating an old-fashioned and punitive colonial policy.

Dudayev's dreams included not only complete independence for Chechenya, but also the formation of a Caucasus federation, which he would domininate. A Congress of the Confederation of Caucasian Mountain Peoples, led by Musa Shanibov, a former university lecturer, was held in Grozny in October 1992, at which anti-Russian speeches were made and Dudayev urged all to resist the imposition of Russian Federation troops in their areas. However most shied away from his open independence stance. Shanibov's declared policy was that all Caucasus Muslim republics should strive to achieve independence under his leadership.

Standing as a Muslim leading a Muslim republic, Dudayev hoped for support from Muslim oil-producing countries such as Azerbaijan, Kazakhstan, Turkmenistan and others, but they wanted nothing to do with him. Chechens hijacked a Russian aircraft, which was flown to Ankara in Turkey to publicise their cause, but Turkish political support was lacking. He also touted for support from nominally Christian Armenia and Georgia, only to be again disappointed. Dudayev's claims of support from Saudi Arabia and the Arab Gulf States were bogus, as were others of a similar nature. The Russian economic blockade, while had been imposed in November 1991, was beginning to cause administrative difficulties, although Chechenya did manage to import essential items. Smuggling became big business.

DUDAYEV IMPEACHED

Meanwhile Dudayev met increasing internal opposition, particularly from his CNC Executive Committee, which backed away from him after being ignored and pushed aside by Chechen deputies who had been successful in the Dudayev election. It had become anxious about deteriorating civil order, the economic blockade, the split with the Ingush and lack of external recognition. Two days of violent protests in Freedom Square to demand Dudayev's resignation involved clashes between protestors and Dudayev's National Guard. Criticism of Dudayev in the Chechen Assembly on 17 April 1993 caused him to issue a series of decrees, which imposed virtual presidential rule on the republic, dismissed the government, disbanded the legislature and imposed a night curfew on the city.

The following day, in an emergency meeting, the legislature annulled Dudayev's decrees, except that of dismissing the government, and voted for his impeachment. On the 19th the Constitutional Court overturned Dudayev's 'presidential' rule. The situation seemed to quieten down into a stand-off, with opposition forces remaining in occupation of several government buildings.

A PREEMPTIVE STRIKE

Much of the opposition centred around two leaders, Khoza Suleymanov and Ruslan Labazanov, the latter a former aide of Dudayev's, each backed by a small militia. They called for a referendum to be held on 5 June over entry into the Russian Federation and the survival of Dudayev as 'president'. Suddenly, on the evening of 3 June Dudayev's National Guard launched a preemptive attack to clear the opposition militias from government buildings. The fighting, which continued for several hours, was won by the National Guard.

The following day Dudayev called the incident a 'Russian plot', claiming that opposition militias had been expelled from the republic, although it was said that several districts of Chechenya remained in opposition hands. A few major Chechen clans and former supporters remained hostile to Dudayev, some of whom were busily engaged in illicit operations. Others were having second thoughts about Dudayev, and yet others simply stood aside, waiting to see how long he could survive. Dudayev's dictatorial rule irritated many.

ASSASSINATION ATTEMPT ON DUDAYEV

An attempt was made on Dudayev's life when he was travelling in a car on 27 May 1994. He escaped without injury, but three others with him were killed. Dudayev alleged that the Russian KSK (the counter-intelligence service that succeeded the KGB) was responsible, but a spokesman of the Russian Foreign Intelligence Service denied any implication. Some days later Dudayev added that the KSK was planning to set off an underground nuclear explosion in Chechenya as part of a Russian plan to convince Western leaders that Chechenya had secretly tested a nuclear device, and thus isolate it internationally. Little notice was taken of this highly improbable allegation, which rebounded adversely on his public relations staff.

In Moscow Yeltsin stirred himself and extended the state of emergency already in effect in North Ossetia and Ingushetia to embrace certain Chechen districts. Dudayev responded by reimposing a night curfew in Grozny. He also ordered (on the

5th) that Ruslan Khasbulatov and other named individuals must leave Chechenya, accusing them of 'conspiring with Russian Imperial forces' against Chechenya (Tass). Khasbulatov, who had been involved in the White House incident in Moscow in October 1993, had returned to his native republic, where he had accumulated immense prestige. Establishing a base at Tolsoy-Yurt, his home town, and now supporting Yeltsin, he ranged himself against Dudayev.

On 11 July the National Guard hit back, at the two main resistance forces in Grozny. Khoza Suleymanov was injured in the fighting and taken prisoner, but Ruslan Labazanov, reputed to have 'several hundred militiamen', disappeared underground. At least ten people were killed in the struggle, which did not die down until the 15th. A Chechen spokesman accused Russia of supporting the 'rebels', and warned that this could lead to an all-out Russo-Caucasian war.

THE CHECHEN PROVISIONAL COUNCIL

Previously, in December 1993 Umar Avturkhanov, a Chechen and former Soviet oil minister, had formed the Znamenskoye-based Chechen Provisional Council, which contained members of the government ousted by Dudayev. He had appealed to Yeltsin to recognise the Council as the official government of Chechenya and talks had begun, but there was hesitation.

INTERNECINE FIGHTING

On 25 July 1994 opposition forces under Ruslan Labazanov occupied the town of Argun, some ten miles east of Grozny, and defied all attempts to eject them. In addition the 'Shalinsky Tank Regiment', based in Shali, about 20 miles south-east of Grozny, defected to Labazanov (Tass). These were severe setbacks for Dudayev, whose National Guard was not able to reoccupy Argun until 5 September, when it was reported that dozens were killed in the fighting.

The previous day Ruslan Khasbulatov, from his base in Tolsoy-Yurt, had announced he was forming a paramilitary group, with the intention of toppling Dudayev from power. He had admitted that he was being supplied by the Russian military, most probably meaning Yeltsin's KSK. The National Guard, even though it was supported by helicopters, tanks and guns, failed in its attempt to drag Khasbulatov from Tolsoy-Yurt. Khasbulatov's saboteurs destroyed two government transmitters, with consequent widespread radio and TV disruption.

Khasbulatov demanded that Dudayev resign by 30 September or face an all-out attack on Grozny. Dudayev ignored the demand and that day a group of commandos in a helicopter raided Grozny airport. Dudayev alleged they were Russian Spetsnaz (military special forces), which was denied; Khasbulatov claimed they were his supporters, but it was most probable that the KSK's hand was behind the exploit.

General Grachev stated on 5 September that units in the North Caucasus military district were on full combat alert to prevent any conflict in Chechenya from spreading beyond the region, and that Russian soldiers were standing by on its borders. Next, from the 20th to the 24th, a major Russian military exercise took place in the North Caucasus region under General Vladimir Semyonov, commander of the Russian Ground Forces. This was significant in that it was unusual for such a senior general to undertake such a comparatively routine, medium-level commitment.

OPENING SHOTS

So far Dudayev had been left alone by Moscow in his 'independence' stance for the simple reason that Yeltsin had been too involved in his survival struggle to launch a serious military campaign to restore Russian supremacy over Chechenya. However, after the 1993 Referendum had been approved by the Russians and he had gained a personal victory at the general election, which gave him more confidence in his own position, Yeltsin was able to turn his attention to the Chechen problem. Initially he decided that his new KSK should instigate and aid an internal revolt to topple Dudayev, so that it could be seen as a clan squabble and nothing to do with Moscow, something the KSK had been struggling to accomplish for some months.

Yeltsin's reasoning was based on the composition and inherent characteristics of Chechen society, which was organised on an interlocking religious, tribal, clan and family basis, with clans and families forever competing for supremacy. Soviet rule, for example, had been supported by the powerful Tyerekhskoi clan and its allies, which now formed the basis of the Chechen opposition, while Dudayev was supported by the powerful Myelkhi clan and its allies, which had gained influence over the oil industry.

Yeltsin hoped the fortunes of the dominant clans would change to his advantage, as they quarrelled over power and prestige, and in anticipation established a Chechen, Salambek Khadzheiv (a former Minister in the 1991 Russian government), as head of the 'Chechen Government of National Renewal (Renaissance)', based in Moscow, which eventually incorporated the Chechen Provisional Council.

Sergei Shakhrat, a Russian deputy prime minister, stated that Chechenya was part of Russian territory, must remain so, and that force may have to be used to quell unrest. This caused Dudayev again to declare martial law. On 15 October 1994 Khasbulatov's militia penetrated into parts of Grozny. The National Guard was unable to drive it out until the 19th, and in the fierce fighting each side claimed to have killed over a hundred of their opponents. Dudayev alleged that Khasbulatov's militia had been reinforced by Russian troops. The National Guard also successfully counterattacked opposition militia forces holding the town of Ulug Martan, about 12 miles south of Grozny, again claiming to have killed over a hundred of its opponents.

ASSAULT ON GROZNY

On the afternoon of 25 November 1994 Khasbulatov's militia mounted two attacks in Grozny. The first was against the airport by helicoptered troops; the second, the main one, involved about 200 armed men, with tanks in support, who attacked the presidential palace and adjacent buildings. There they unexpectedly met firm National Guard resistance, and after a fierce 12-hour battle the attacking militias withdrew. There were heavy casualties, although the claims made by both sides of '300 hundred killed on either side' (Russian Ostankino TV) were obviously exaggerated.

During the fighting Dudayev claimed his National Guard had captured 70 Russian prisoners. General Grachev stated (falsely) that no Russian military personnel had been involved in this exploit, and that any Russian prisoners must be mercenaries. On the 28th Dudayev replied that if Russia did not confirm that the captives were Russian soldiers acting under Russian orders, they would be treated as mercenaries and shot. Indirectly it was admitted that 19 were Russian servicemen.

Yeltsin now entered the picture, and on the 29th demanded that the Russian prisoners be released at once, and that all involved in the fighting must surrender their arms. He dismissed the deputy director of the KSK. Khasbulatov's militia agreed to lay down their arms, but Dudayev ignored Yeltsin's demand, so nothing moved on that issue for the time being. Khasbulatov's men either withdrew from Grozny or went to ground.

Four Russian bomber aircraft attacked Grozny airport on the 29th, destroying all Chechen civil aircraft and killing or wounding several people. One Russian plane was brought down by Chechen anti-aircraft fire. Yeltsin gave the Chechens a 48-hour deadline to release the Russian prisoners, but Dudayev remained defiant. The civilian population in Grozny became alarmed, and a stream of women and children began to leave the capital for the safety of outlying villages, while armed Chechens, supporting Dudayev, began to arrive to help defend it.

Russian aircraft flew over Grozny on 1 December to drop leaflets urging people to lay down their arms. The Russian military confirmed that troops were being sent to the Chechen borders, and Dudayev threatened to raid Russian nuclear installations if he was attacked, but this was regarded as another empty threat. Vladimir Zhirinovsky, the maverick leader of the Liberal Democratic Party, visited Grozny on the 4th and returned to Moscow with two released Russian prisoners. Sergei Yushenkon, chairman of the Russian Defence Committee, also arrived in Grozny for talks, but was unable to persuade Dudayev to meet Umar Avtorkhanov of the Chechen Provisional Council.

On the 5th the Moscow authorities admitted involvement in the 25 November incident, and key leaders, including General Grachev, Viktor Yerin (minister of the interior) and Sergei Stepashin (director of the KSK), flew to the Mozdok military base, where a military force was being assembled. Grachev declared Chechenya an 'air exclusion zone'.

The following day General Grachev met Dudayev in a border village and they discussed the release of the Russian prisoners, now admitted to number 19. Grachev stated that military force should not be used to solve the Chechen problem, but that all Chechen armed groups must be under central control. By this time the failure of Yeltsin's 'secret war' against Chechenya was causing detrimental comments in the Moscow media. Yeltsin extended his deadline until the 15th. Dudayev declared mobilisation.

In Moscow, on 7 December the National Security Council countermanded Grachev's promise to take no military action against the Chechens, and Nikolai Yegorov, the nationalities minister, was appointed to coordinate the restoration of legality to Chechenya. Yeltsin ordered troops to close off the borders of Chechenya, and secure the strategically important road–rail link and oil pipelines crossing that republic. Dudayev replied that this amounted to a declaration of war. The following day the Russian Federation Council condemned the covert KSK action, and the dispatch of troops against Chechenya, but many were hoping that a simple show of military force would bring Dudayev to heel.

REASONS FOR MILITARY ACTION

Yeltsin had several good reasons for using military force, the first and probably most compelling of which was that Dudayev had called his bluff, having no intention of yielding to threats or promises, while covert methods had disastrously failed. Ostensibly his main reason was an urgent constitutional one, as Dudayev's election and declaration of independence were illegal. Yeltsin was being criticised for shelving the Chechen problem for so long, and his seeming toleration to date had been seen as weakness, as well as a bad example to other autonomous republics within the Russian Federation, especially those with considerable national resources that were unhappy about the distribution of and recompense for those resources.

Another reason for the use of military force was to ensure the free flow of oil through the Chechen corridor. For the previous three years Dudayev had illegally syphoned off huge quantities of oil from the pipelines crossing Chechenya, having the means to regulate or even terminate the flow. This strategic stranglehold was affecting the economy of the Russian Federation, and so had to be removed. Alternative oil pipeline routes, some of which were already being planned, would be extremely expensive, politically complicated and would take time to lay. There was also a fear that an independent 'Muslim Chechenya' might form alliances with adjoining oil-rich Muslim republics, or even Christian Georgia, which would raise disputatious international issues.

A further reason was that Chechenya had become a bandit state, a thieves' kitchen, the habitat of drug smugglers, criminals and hijackers, and the home of crime syndicates and mafia groups that operated in Moscow and other major Russian cities across the Russian Federation. In the summer of 1994 a spate of major robberies and kidnappings, involving dramatic helicopter chases, made the headlines of the international media. Perpetrated by Chechen criminals, these crimes were giving the Russian Federation a lawless reputation.

Speaking on TV, Yeltsin described Chechenya as a 'powerful crime-breeding zone'. Under Soviet rule the Caucasian nations had been notorious for their black-market activities, and when the USSR collapsed these flooded over into the Russian Federation. The Moscow police department stated that the 'Chechen mafia has expanded to about 60 gangs, involving some 2000 members, trafficking in drugs, prostitution and stolen cars, from the Baltic to the Pacific' (*Nezavisimaya Gazeta*). North Caucasian visitors were very unpopular in Moscow and other major cities.

However Yeltsin made three miscalculations. First, he badly underestimated the degree of Chechen resistance that might be encountered if the military option was used. (Chechens boasted that during the Afghan Campaign the Afghans had been unable to take a single Chechen prisoner, a boast that no other Soviet nationality could make.) Second, he overlooked the fact that while the Chechens might fight amongst themselves, they might unite in the face of a foreign invasion, especially if it was by the old Russian Imperial bogeyman. Third, he forgot an important Russian strategic doctrine that stemmed from bitter historical experience: never launch a military campaign in the Caucasus in winter. Blame for other major mistakes and miscalculations seems to lie with the military, although both the politicians and the military vigorously blame each other for them.

10 Operation Wave: December 1994–January 1995

Before dawn on 11 December 1994 about 40 000 Ministry of Interior troops and army paratroopers mustered to invade the Russian Federation's tiny mountain republic of Chechenya, their orders being to move 'to restore constitutional authority and disarm illegal militias'. As the Russian authorities announced there was no intention of attacking Grozny, it was assumed that the invasion was simply an intimidating show of force, which it was hoped would bring about the downfall of Dzhokhar Dudayev. They should have researched better.

President Yeltsin had authorised 'Operation Wave' on the 9th, reputedly saying use 'all measures available to the state', after which he entered a hospital for a minor operation, and so was removed from the public scene for several days. Politically this military adventure was a very unpopular one, which provoked a flood of criticism in the state Duma and from Yeltsin's rivals and enemies, despite their general indifference to the fate of Chechenya and its unpopular (in Moscow at any rate) people. Later Prime Minister Chernomyrdin made it known that he had not obtained Yeltsin's permission to exercise the military option in Chechenya, and that he had kept a low profile on the issue and eventually (on 16 January 1995) called for a ceasefire.

The main tasks of Operation Wave were first to secure surrounding areas that were regarded as nominally loyal to Moscow (taken to mean Ingushetia, Dagestan and the north-western toehold in Chechenya held by the Moscow-backed Chechen Provisional Council, led by Umar Avtorkhanov, and loosely backed by Ruslan Khasbulatov, Khoza Suleymanov, Ruslan Labazanov and others), and then to impose a tight blockade around Grozny to prevent arms and military supplies from reaching the defiant Chechens.

The Russian invasion force was split between three divisions, one forming up in Dagestan, immediately east of Chechenya;

another in the breakaway territory of Ingushetia, immediately to the west; and the third in the northern part of the autonomous republic of North Ossetia. The force's headquarters were at the former Soviet military base in Mozdok, North Ossetia. All divisions were to converge on Grozny. In an attempt to win over the local population it was given out that the Russian columns were bringing in tons of grain, pasta, meat, butter and sugar for the people, all items in short supply, while troops using loudspeakers called on the population to keep calm and hand over their weapons.

This military operation had been mounted in a slipshod, hesitant, half-hearted manner, and things soon began to go wrong. The Eastern Column – that is, the Russian division in Dagestan, starting from near Khasavyurt, on the main road into Grozny from the east – moved off but was soon stopped by swarms of local people, who dragged the Russian soldiers from their vehicles and took some of them prisoner. This was the first of Moscow's miscalculations: assuming that because the Dagens had accepted integration in the Russian Federation, they would not take hostile action against Russian federal troops. Dagestan, with a population of about two million, was much more of a 'national mix' than Chechenya or Ingushetia, having at least eight national minorities.

The Western Column suffered a similar setback in Ingushetia. Soon after leaving Nazran it was held up near the large village of Yandere, where groups of local people, including women, immobilised the military vehicles by removing their batteries and severing their fuel lines. Shots were exchanged and vehicles damaged, in the course of which five Ingush were killed and several others wounded. After several hours' delay the column resumed its advance. It entered Chechen territory, only to be again halted by crowds of Chechens blocking its route outside Davydenko. The following day General Grachev accused Ruslan Auger, president of Ingushetia, of effectively declaring war on the Russian president. Auger insisted he had not been involved and that his people's actions had been spontaneous.

The main Russian body, the Northern Column (or northwestern to be exact), consisted mainly of the the 19th Motor Rifle Division, with '30 tanks, 50 armoured personnel carriers, ten self-propelled guns and 70 personnel-carrying trucks'

(Reuters), and helicopters flying overhead. It crossed into Chechenya at dawn through Znamenskoye, which housed the headquarters of the Chechen Provisional Council, and moved eastwards, eventually reaching the crossroads town of Tolsoy-Yurt, about 15 miles north of Grozny. There it came up against entrenched Chechen positions and was forced to halt, having already come under rocket fire from Dolinskoye, a large village to the south of the main road.

If the Russian military authorities were hoping this initial show of force would be sufficient to awe the Chechens into submission, someone had badly miscalculated. The opposite reaction occurred, and in Grozny hundreds of armed people rallied to support Dudayev, who was promising to turn Chechenya into a 'second Afghanistan' if military force was used against him. He declared that a Russian military invasion of Chechenya would 'throw a bloody blanket across the whole Caucasus region' (Chechen TV).

During the next 48 hours or so the Russian columns remain static, meeting resistance mainly from peaceful demonstrators. But soon Russian aircraft were brought into the action to bomb the airport near Grozny, then Shaami-Yurt (20 miles south-west of the capital), and then some villages near the capital; while Russian guns spasmodically shelled the town of Pervomaiskoye and other Chechen positions. A Russian helicopter was shot down by Chechens. The battle for Grozny was about to begin.

RUSSIAN HESITATION

The day after the Russian invasion of Chechenya Russian negotiators arrived in Vladikavkaz, in adjacent North Ossetia, to be joined by Dudayev's representatives, but the talks proved fruitless and the Chechens refused to disarm. Russian aircraft and artillery continued to make sporadic attacks, the Russians announced their first casualties (9 killed and 14 wounded), and in Dagestan negotiations continued for the release of 47 Russian prisoners, displayed to the media. The authorities in Ingushetia and Dagestan were passive and did nothing to aid or hinder the military invasion, but the sight of Russian troops arriving in battle array aroused old emotions and fears and caused some groups of people to react against them.

The Russian troops seemed bewildered, hesitant and unprepared for a serious military campaign. There was doubt as to who was in command. Yeltsin had nominated Oleg Soskovets, a first deputy prime minister, to coordinate the operation, and under him were General Pavel Grachev (the defence minister), Viktor Yerin (minister of the interior) and Sergei Stepashin (director of the KSK), all of whom had separate forces in the field. A *Komsomolskaya Pravda* opinion poll indicated that 58 per cent of Russians were against sending troops into Chechenya, and only 22 per cent in favour. People in Moscow feared that the Chechen mafia might take violent terrorist reprisals on individuals and government targets in Moscow.

On 13 December 1994 General Ivan Babichev, commanding the Northern Column (his regular appointment was commander of the Pskov airborne division in Moldavia), agreed to halt his advance when Chechen civilian protesters blocked his way. The general was summoned to the operational headquarters in Mozdok, but instead of being dismissed for disobeying orders as expected, he was returned to his field command, seemingly still without positive directions. Negotiations between Russian and Chechen officials on the 13th and 14th came to nothing.

Senior Russian generals began to criticise the launching of the operation, which dented morale, while Georgi Kondratyev, a deputy defence minister, declared the Chechen problem could not be solved by military means. Another senior general, Aleksandr Lebed (commander of the 14th Army in Moldavia and a former commander of Soviet armed forces in Afghanistan), said the operation was foolish, and that young, poorly trained soldiers should not have been used.

It was thought that up to half the Russian force had received no combat training at all, and that the only properly trained personnel were the 2000 paratroopers. A rumour spread that units in Russia had disobeyed orders to deploy to Chechenya, thus forcing the Defence Ministry hastily to conscript less well-trained elements into the task force.

In Grozny the scene was one of surging nationalism and a grim determination to defend the capital to the death, and plenty of arms were in evidence. From the Czarist days the Chechens had had a reputation as fiercesome mountain guerrilla fighters. The Chechens' military strength was not known with any certainty, but it was initially assumed that Dudayev's Presidential

Guard was about 1000 strong, supported by numerous, hastily raised groups of people's volunteers that were high on morale, weak on discipline and lacking sophisticated weaponry. Many Chechens had served in the Soviet armed forces, and so there was a font of basic military know-how, and as most male Chechens possessed a weapon of some sort a hard fight ahead was indicated. Speaking on Chechen TV, Dudayev said 'It is a war for life or death. The soil must burn under the feet of the Russians', and he called off the proposed negotiations.

The active armed militias of Khasbulatov, and others in opposition to Dudayev, passively secure in their own supportive areas, were undecided about which enemy to fight, and in fact did nothing for a while. However some anti-Dudayev factions immediately agreed to fight with him against the invading Russians. It was a moment in Chechen history when every Chechen had to decide whether or not to fight for his native land. Most eventually opted to fight the invaders – old scores could be settled later.

By the 14th the Northern Column had reached the outskirts of Grozny, where it was halted by the Terek river until the military engineers could bridge it. Despite his bravado, Dudayev offered a ceasefire and to pull his forward troops back 1000 yards to break the close contact, but to save face Yeltsin advanced the deadline for the Chechens to disarm – the US secretary of state was in Moscow at that moment.

Dire threats continued to emanate from Moscow, while the Russian soldiers in Chechenya listlessly shuffled their feet. On the 18th, with armoured support, they pressed forward again, but their progress was slow and Chechen resistance hard. On the 19th Russian aircraft began to make night-time raids on Grozny, striking Chechen positions near the oil refinery, while Russian artillery fire continued intermittently. By this time the Chechens were firing back, having brought into use heavy weaponry left behind by Soviet troops. Dudayev was ill-prepared to resist a full-scale military invasion, presumably being overconfident that Yeltsin would never fully commit himself to the military option, so the Chechen defences were impromptu. Once the Russian troops began to enter the outskirts of Grozny they found that many buildings were being used as Chechen strongholds to block their progress. Dudayev offered to renew negotiations, but Yeltsin brushed him aside. It was later ascertained from TV interviews of Russian soldiers that they had been surprised by the ferocity of the Chechen resistance, complaining they had been given hardly any orders, and that once the battle was joined, they had lost contact with their commanders.

Another Russian helicopter was shot down by the Chechens on the 20th. The volume of Russian artillery and rocket fire increased, tanks became mobile artillery posts, and Chechen casualties were beginning to mount. Russian aircraft made a daylight raid on Grozny on the 22nd, causing Dudayev to appeal, unsuccessfully, to the neighbouring Dagens to rise up against those Russian troops in their own country. As Russian aerial activity increased, so did the exodus of Chechen residents, eastwards and southwards, along whatever roads were still open to them. On the 22nd the Russian Defence Ministry claimed (falsely) that its troops had surrounded Grozny, saying that it was leaving just one southward route open for civilians to leave the city. The Chechens' defence philosophy at that stage was to harness the 'CNN Factor', meaning to show just sufficient armed resistance to attract media attention and bring their plight to international attention, hoping that Western pressure would be put on Yeltsin to halt his military operation.

The slow Russian progress gave the impression there was distinct reluctance on the part of of Russian commanders to order their troops to fire on civilians, as instanced by General Babichev's hesitation when confronted by Chechen women. This was explained by General Lebed, who said that on three previous occasions the Russian army had received verbal orders from Gorbachev to use force against nationalist crowds (in Tbilisi in April 1989, Baku in January 1990 and Vilnius in January 1991), and that each time Gorbachev had denied responsibility for the result, and tried to blame local commanders. The Russian commanders in Chechenya had their reasons for hesitating.

It was widely alleged that Yeltsin was doing much the same thing this time, having given his orders verbally before retiring briefly to hospital, so the generals were very wary, especially as many of them were dubious about the feasibility and morality of the project. As a result it was alleged that they too gave vague verbal orders to their colonels, who in turn took a similar precaution by simply telling their junior commanders 'to get on with it'.

General Edouard Vorobyov, deputy commander of the

Russian ground forces, was ordered to assume command of the halted 'Operation Wave', but refused and then resigned, a fact later confirmed in the Duma. Later Vorobyov spoke out, claiming that on 11 December he had not even heard of a planned intervention into Chechenya, but had agreed to one on the 19th, only to realise that the available Russian troops were in no fit condition to launch a blitzkrieg, and that time would be required to prepare them for battle. He blamed General Grachev for lacking the courage to put the facts before Yeltsin. Vorobyov said he had been ordered to resign. Rumours abounded of other senior military officers being 'removed' from their posts for non-cooperation. The command structure degenerated to such an extent that it was not really clear who was in actual command of the stalled operation.

The idea of a military invasion of Chechenya had been Yeltsin's, or rather that of his immediate advisers, his 'kitchen cabinet'. Both the Russian General Staff and the KSK were against the project, feeling that a quick military victory would only be the prelude to a long, unwinnable, Afghan-type campaign that would drain resources and attract international odium. They were overruled, and the pique of the military top brass showed through.

Sergei Kovalyov, the Russian human rights commissioner, returned from another visit to Chechenya, where he had spent several days with Dudayev in his bunker at the presidential palace. In the Duma he demanded that the bombing of Grozny be terminated, saying that of the estimated 80 000 people remaining in central Grozny, most were Russians who had nowhere else to go. Yeltsin's popularity rating plummeted. He refused Kovalyov's demand for a Christmas truce, overoptimistically saying he thought the fighting would soon end. President Clinton stated he supported Yeltsin in that Chechenya should remain in the Russian Federation, but wanted the problem to be solved by negotiation. Media reports put the Chechen strength at some 30 000 fighters.

RUSSIAN BOMBING OFFENSIVE

The Russian Northern Column bestirred itself on 23 December and unsuccessfully attacked Chechen defences around Argun.

The Western Column remained stationary over 25 miles from the capital, and the Eastern one had not yet entered Chechenya. Then followed a four-day, four-night bombing offensive against Grozny, during which the presidential palace was hit several times, but Dudayev and his war cabinet remained in their underground bunker to continue the struggle. Many buildings in the centre of the city were badly damaged, and many people, now unable to flee openly along the streets, took refuge in their cellars. The Chechen anti-aircraft guns ran out of ammunition.

The Russian bombing raids were wide ranging, for example villages around the town of Achkhoi-Martan, a full 20 miles from Grozny, became a target. On the night of the 24th the presidential palace was again struck and set on fire, while in the Argun area the Russian troops remained stuck by the Argun river and suffered losses from sniper fire. That day the divided Duma in Moscow appealed to Yeltsin to stop the war in Chechenya, although several deputies still supported the operation.

On the 26th the Russian State Security Council met, chaired by Yeltsin, making his first appearance in public since being hospitalised. Yeltsin had left hospital on the 19th, after which he had remained quietly in his dacha. His absence had led to Western speculation that he was not in control of events. The following day he made a televised speech to the Russian people, who were astounded and dismayed by the ferocity of the aerial bombing of a 'Russian city'. A Duma delegation visited Grozny, afterwards returning to Moscow to describe what was actually happening there, while TV teams continued to show dramatic scenes of the fighting, casualties and devastation. External criticism regarding lack of human rights considerations was flooding in from Western nations. Yeltsin had a lot of explaining to do.

He declared that the armed forces would continue their campaign against the Chechens to crush their bid for separatism and restore law and order. He urged the Russian soldiers to do their duty, pointing out that during the past year Chechens had 'plundered over 120 trains and committed bank frauds worth over one billion dollars' (Tass). He said the air force would not bomb civilians, but would use laser-guided munitions to strike only military targets. The following day Russian bombs hit an orphanage in Grozny.

There was top-level hesitation to push the army, and its

commanders, too hard in case it led to outright mutiny, which Yeltsin, after his White House drama of 1993, could not afford to allow to happen.

RUSSIAN OFFENSIVES

After moving unsuccessfully against Khanakala (about five miles north of Grozny) and its adjacent airfield on the 27th, the Russian troops withdrew again, having lost several armoured vehicles in the fighting. More Russian attacks took place on the 28th, and it seemed that at last they had got their act together and were moving with determination. The next day they took the town of Pervomaiskoye and occupied the Khanakala airfield, which had been deserted for several days, and also mounted day-long attacks into the outskirts of Grozny, which made some progress. Russian intelligence now admitted that Dudayev had over 4000 hardened fighters, plus hundreds more volunteers, while the Russian strength committed to the fighting, that is the Northern Column, was thought to be about 18 000.

Fighting in the suburbs, Russian troops blundered into booby traps, were harassed by sniper fire and, having to remain in forward positions overnight, were exposed to snow storms and freezing conditions, while many of the Chechen fighters were able to creep home at night for food, warmth and sleep, ready to return refreshed for the morrow's activities.

The centre of Grozny was now very visibly battle scarred by Russian bombing and bombardments. The remaining citizens, crouching shivering in their cellars, were mostly without domestic gas. Generally used to heat buildings, gas was normally distributed through external, overhead pipes and many of these had been punctured by shell fire, sprouting chains of flares that lit up the city by night. It should be remembered that all this was happening in the depths of winter. There was no running water, snow being the substitute, and frequent electricity cuts. The open markets that had flourished in the central areas until a few days previously were now deserted, the traders having moved to the outer southern and eastern suburbs.

On the 29th the major oil refinery and its oil storage tanks, said to hold some 50 000 tonnes of crude oil, were repeatedly bombed. They stood adjacent to a Chechen three-gun position on a prominent ridge overlooking the capital known as the Karpinsky Hills, which was bombed several times but no direct hits were scored. That day two bridges over the Argun river were destroyed by Russian bombers to block off Chechen infiltration routes. It was claimed that Dudayev's helicopter was hit by ground fire.

It was alleged that the Russian air force was deliberately disobeying Yeltsin's orders, and that he seemed unable to rein it in. Feeble excuses were made in Moscow, and as late as the 29th General Grachev was denying on TV that Russian troops would storm Grozny. A Russian ground attack was launched into the centre of Grozny on the 30th, but was forced back again, the Chechens claiming a victory. Also, the oil refinery was struck again, fires were restarted and billowing black smoke smothered the area for hours. It was said that the adjacent storage tanks contained 5000 tonnes of ammonia, causing the Chechens to allege they were poised on the edge of an environmental catastrophe.

THE MAIN RUSSIAN ASSAULT

The main Russian ground assault on the city centre, supported by up to 300 armoured vehicles, began on 31 December 1994. It penetrated almost to Freedom Square, close to the presidential palace complex, before having to withdraw, the Chechens again boasting of victory. A second major ground assault was launched the following day. This reached the outer buildings of the presidential palace to battle against Chechens armed with antitank weapons and flamethrowers, probably losing some 100 armoured vehicles in the process. Russian armoured vehicles that were trying to make encircling movements tended to get lost in the maze of side streets, and many fell victim to tank-hunting Chechens. Russians occupied the Oil Institute building, but were eventually driven out again. On 2 January yet another Russian push was made, this time reaching Freedom Square and virtually surrounding the presidential palace.

By this time the Sunzha river was becoming the dividing line between the combatants, and the Russians systematically blasted buildings with tank guns as they advanced to eliminate Chechen-defended points in central Grozny. The Chechens still held doggedly on to their positions around the railway station, their main defensive locality on the west side of the Sunzha river, although numerous small guerrilla groups operated behind Russian forward lines. Russian troops were now in central Grozny, but not yet in control. Freedom Square was littered with burnt-out Russian vehicles and corpses.

The Russians paused to regroup and count their losses. Just previously, on 31 December, the Defence Ministry had quoted its own losses in Chechenya as 50 dead and 132 wounded, a considerable underestimate. Later, on the 8th, Khamzat Yarbiyev, the Chechen deputy speaker, cited the Chechen civilian casualties as 18 000 killed, of whom 12 210 had died in Grozny, which was thought to be an overinflated figure. The Red Cross's estimate of refugees was about 350 000, of whom at least 150 000 had fled Grozny.

Russian bomber aircraft struck Shali on 3 January, causing Yeltsin to demand why his order of 27 December to cease the bombing had not been obeyed. Reputedly he was told that it had, and that the damage in Grozny had been done by Chechens to attract Western sympathy. On the 4th Yeltsin again ordered the air force to cease bombing, but again he seemed to be disregarded. Confusion was caused in Moscow by the government-controlled All Russian State TV and the independent NTV, which gave out conflicting reports. There were dark allegations that Yeltsin was leaning on unsympathetic periodicals.

On the 7th the director of the All Russian State TV was dismissed after broadcasting pictures of the devastation in Grozny, and on the 15th the director of NTV was warned that unless his policy of showing live battle scenes changed his station licence would be revoked.

In Grozny, for the first time the Chechens were forced back from positions protecting the presidential palace, the oil refinery was again bombed and black smoke again formed dark clouds over central parts of the city. Fighting continued around the railway station and the airport, while Freedom Square had become a disputed no-man's land. On the 7th General Viktor Vorobyov, commanding the Ministry of Interior troops in Grozny, was killed by a mortar shell. The official Russian death toll rose to 250.

A COMMANDO FAILURE

A 50-strong Russian commando group was landed by helicopter behind Chechen lines, some 20 miles south of Grozny on 3 January 1995, to carry out disruptive ambushes on Chechen supply routes. Put down without winter tents or food, the commandos found they could hardly survive, let alone operate, and in response to repeated radio requests to be retrieved, they were told the weather was too bad for helicopter flights. The commandos clashed with Chechen guerrillas near a village called Alkhazurovo on the 10th, when two Russians were killed and two wounded; the remainder were taken prisoner.

Another morale-denting incident, revealed by the Moscow media on the 10th after being denied by the Defence Ministry, was that a 100-strong paratroop unit from Yekaterinburg, Yeltsin's home town, had mutinied and abandoned their positions, complaining of lack of orders and food, and insufficient weaponry.

FIGHTING IN GROZNY

Much of east Grozny remained in Chechen hands, but in the western part Russian troops edged slowly forward towards the presidential palace, low cloud and bad weather limiting aircraft sorties in their support. The Oil Institute, the university and other buildings within blocks of the presidential palace were now in Russian hands. Russian artillery was targeting bridges across the Sunzha river, handicapping those Chechens who were pushing reinforcements and supplies forward, but the Chechens still held out in the railway station position on the west bank. Bodies of Russian soldiers and other debris of war lay scattered in squares and streets. By this time Russian military equipment and ammunition in quantity were being flown into the Mozdok and Bislan airfields, both in North Ossetia.

Dudayev withdrew his headquarters from the presidential palace on the 6th, just before a Russian cordon was drawn tightly around it. Dudayev moved out to the crossroads village of Galanchezh on the southern outskirts of the city, a good road communication location, while his security chief, Sultan Gelishkhanov, moved to Gudermes, north-east of Grozny, to prepare its defence.

A two-day truce, instigated by Kovalyov and arranged for 10 and 11 January, broke down almost immediately as Dudayev wanted to add extra conditions, including the opening up of supply corridors to his embattled positions. The basic Russian demand remained – that the Chechens lay down their arms – but they refused to comply. The Russians were also stalling a UN fact-finding team that was trying to enter the battle area. The latest official Chechen figures were 200 fighters killed and up to 400 wounded, with 19 000 civilian deaths, 12 000 of which were in Grozny (local TV).

YELTSIN TAKES OVER

Yeltsin assumed command over the Russian Army General Staff on 11 January 1995, or to be more accurate removed it from the Defence Ministry structure and placed it directly under his own presidency. General Grachev, the defence minister, who thought he was in command of Operation Wave, was pushed aside, but not dismissed as was generally expected. Yeltsin blamed him for the Chechens having heavy weaponry, as when he had been deputy defence minister (1991–92) Grachev had ordered the Soviet mechanised division in Shali to give half its heavy weapons to Dudayev, rather than face hostile confrontation with Chechens surrounding the base. When originally urging the military option to be used in Chechenya, Grachev had told Yeltsin that a Russian paratroop brigade could deal with the problem in a couple of hours. Yeltsin gave the Army General Staff the task of reorganising the army, and the Defence Ministry that of improving the combat readiness of the troops. For the first time the Russian (and former Soviet) armed forces had a civilian chief.

On the same day Dudayev, wearing the uniform of a general, held a press conference at the 'Minuta crossroads' (named after a popular café), near Galanchezh on the southern edge of Grozny. His preceding one had been on 23 December in the air-raid bunker of the presidential palace. He called for a halt to hostilities so that negotiations could begin, knowing that the Russians were about launch another offensive against him. He accused Yeltsin of killing innocent civilians and trying to destroy the economy of Chechenya.

At that stage Dudayev was having difficulty in rallying Chechen clans and retaining their loyalty, as the first flush of ethnic defensive enthusiasm was waning under the weight of heavy casualities. Some of the clans were backing away, having second thoughts about going all the way with him, and remembering suddenly that he led a corrupt and dictatorial administration, which had allowed the country to sink into a state of lawlessness.

The Chechen forces still did not seem to have any firm military organisation, or much discipline. People's volunteers, in small units, often family groups, still elected their own officers, who had independent ideas. Most wanted to fight, but to fight in their own way and in their own time, and a few would fight only on their own terms. Despite these seemingly ramshackle arrangements, individual Chechens fought extremely well, and their adversaries, the Russians, were the first to praise their courage. One of Dudayev's sons had died of his injuries.

The town of Shatoi – some 25 miles south of Grozny at the foot of the Caucasus range (the other side of which was Georgia) and the site of Imam Shamil's victory over the Russians many years ago – suffered air attacks aimed at bridges across the Argun river, which caused civilian casualties. The inhabitants, estimated to number about 8000 and already burdened with about the same number of refugees, showed a disinclination to become immersed in the guerrilla war that Dudayev was now demanding. Medical authorities in the town of Urus Martan, 12 miles south of Grozny, complained that Dudayev did not care about the health of his people, and instead was scaring Russian doctors and medical staff away from the hospitals and clinics, which were only managing to stay operational by assistance given by Red Cross and Medecins sans Frontiéres personnel. By this time much of Grozny west of the Sunzha river had been deserted by most of its inhabitants.

The famous Russian author, Aleksandr Solzhenitsyn, who had returned to his native Russia in May 1994, called for the fighting to stop, suggesting that Chechenya should be divided into two parts, the Russians to have the territory to the northwest of the Terek River, on the ground that it was traditional Cossack land, and the remainder to go to the Chechens, as it was their historic homeland. Few supported this Solomon-like wisdom.

THE PRESIDENTIAL PALACE FALLS

General Vladimir Semyonov, commander of the Russian ground forces, agreed with Yeltsin that the campaign in Chechenya should be pursued with renewed vigour, although other generals dissented. Fresh reinforcements of more seasoned troops were rushed into the Mozdok and Bislan air bases. Despite a 236–1 vote in the Duma on 13 January 1995 urging Yeltsin to stop fighting in Chechenya, the following day heavy artillery barrages fell on parts of Grozny still held by Chechens, and fighting intensified around the presidential palace and the railway station, the only remaining Chechen strongholds on the west side of the Sunzha river.

On the 14th Russian troops forced their way into part of the the presidential palace, a symbol of Chechen resistance, but it was not until the afternoon of the 19th that the Russian flag was raised over the building by the 276th Motor Rifle Regiment to denote a symbolic victory, claiming that it had been fought for room by room (Defence Ministry press release). The Chechens insisted they had walked out the previous night. There was no immediate news of the Russian prisoners believed to be held in the building.

Announcing the fall of the Chechen presidential palace, Yeltsin overoptimistically stated that the 'military stage' was over, and that the following one would involve the restoration of Chechenya's 'life support system' and the protection of human rights. He promised to send no more inexperienced recruits to Chechenya. Moscow newspapers had been making much of the allegation that some young Russian soldiers in Chechenya had only fired their automatic rifles once before being posted there. The sting was in Yeltsin's tail, as he dismissed three deputy defence ministers.

Chechen emissaries visited Moscow to ask for a ceasefire, seemingly encouraged by Prime Minister Viktor Chernomyrdin, but their proposal was sharply rejected by Yeltsin, who insisted he was in control of events and knew exactly what was happening, accusing Dudayev of genocide. Dudayev replied (through the media) that 'Moscow generals just want some kind of win to avoid shame and disgrace. They have said they will flatten our city, and mean to do it'.

After the unsuccessful request for a ceasefire, 'Colonel' Aslan

Maskhadov, the Chechen military commander, held a press conference in Nazran (Ingushetia), saying he had spoken by radio to General Babichev (still in command), who had told him he must surrender the presidential palace and its whole garrison for prestige reasons. Instead the Chechens had chosen to slip away by night rather than have to stage an ignominious surrender in front of the television cameras, with President Dudayev as the prize captive, as the Russians were demanding. Maskhadov admitted the Chechen headquarters had moved to the 'eastern part of the city'.

There was still no sign of the Russian offensive slackening off in Grozny, as heavy artillery bombardments continued and fighting raged around the railway station. Russian reinforcements continued to arrive, as did tanks and military vehicles on flatbed railway trucks. Official Defence Ministry statements indicated that some 5000 Russian troops were involved in the Grozny battle, but that the overall size of the force remained about the 40 000 mark, as reinforcements replaced those who had been in action for 40 days or more. Russian casualties were quoted as being 505 dead, but the Chechens claim they had killed over 3000. Somewhere within this wide bracket was the correct, but elusive figure.

The Western Column, which had remained static some 25 miles from Grozny near the village of Assinovskaya, was attacked by Chechens anxious to obtain vehicles and weaponry. Casualties were incurred in the scuffle. This column, which now had to be protected by Russian helicopter gunships, showed no inclination to advance towards the battle areas.

DIVIDED MOSCOW OPINION

Moscow was in the throes of indecision over the Chechen adventure, a greater part of the media being against Yeltsin. Some newspapers, funded by business concerns, were anxious that Russia would lose the promised Western credits to get the free-market economy working. Bankers certainly had no interest in the Chechen problem, considering it an obstacle to economic development. Western powers had certainly invested heavily in Yeltsin, and continued to back him, but urged negotiation. Secretly they were probably looking for an alternative Russian leader. Gregori Yavlinsky, head of the pro-reformist Yabloko bloc in the Duma, had been a 'probable', but as he had recently begun to criticise Western policies he obviously was not their future man.

Those in favour of Yeltsin's military option included the oil companies, which were desperate to regain control of the Chechen oil pipeline to the Baku oilfields and allied installations – this was out of the question while Dudayev remained in power. Despite rebellious mumblings by certain senior generals, the armed forces were in favour of Operation Wave, seeing eye to eye with oil companies on his issue. The armed forces had suffered severe cuts, feared more, and were looking for both extra funding and further employment, before their strength withered even further. The armed forces saw the Chechen war as an opportunity to reestablish some of their former prestige and status.

MILITARY STALEMATE

The Chechens abandoned their railway station positions on 21 January 1995, withdrawing to the east side of the Sunzha river, after which – although Russian units crept forward, block by block into suburbs surrounding the city centre, still leaving a southwards Chechen escape route open – ground action slowed down. Two Russian helicopters were shot down on the 25th while supporting ground activity, and all on board were killed. Russian artillery barrages concentrated on targets across the river, while bomber aircraft began striking at targets deeper in Chechen-held territory to the south and east.

THE COMMITTEE FOR THE MOTHERS OF RUSSIAN SOLDIERS

The Committee for the Mothers of Russian Soldiers, formed in Moscow to protest against their sons being sent to fight in Chechenya, was gaining considerable publicity, the media reporting that it had been successful in snatching back conscripted sons on several occasions. One small group managed to make it to Grozny, the rumour being that Dudayev had offered to release his Russian prisoners if their mothers came to collect them, although he later denied this on TV. A few brief mother-and-son reconciliations did take place in Grozny, but no Russian servicemen prisoners were freed on this score.

REFUGEES

Sylvana Foa, the UN High Commissioner for Refugees (UNHCR), complained that although being asked officially by the Russians for help, they were preventing her staff from entering Chechenya, even though they already had permission to operate in both Ingushetia and Dagestan. Refugee camps were being established in those two autonomous republics, but none as yet in Chechenya. Ingushetia was flooded with refugees, having already received some 90 000 Ingush ones from Chechenya. Russian refugees from Chechenya were sent to 'migration centres' in Russia, originally established to receive Russians from Muslim CIS countries. Individual movement within Russia remained difficult.

The Red Cross became active in Chechenya, mainly operating a 'messenger service', with official assistance, for individuals and families seeking to get in touch with one other, details being posted on noticeboards across the Russian Federation. Aid in the form of medicines, food and winter clothing, provided by the Red Cross and other organisations, was arriving in Dagestan. A human rights delegation from the Organisation for Security and Co-operation in Europe (OSCE – the renamed CSCE) arrived in Vladikavkaz in North Ossetia, the first official Western delegation to be allowed so far into this 'active service' region.

GENERAL GRACHEV SURVIVES

General Pavel Grachev was damned with faint praise by the Russian State Security Council on 25 January 1995 – being commended for his handling of the Chechen campaign and for 'the completion of military operations' – before being pushed aside. Grachev was allowed to continue as defence minister, and a later motion in the Duma failed to obtain a majority to remove him from office. Grachev was proving to be a survivor.

Oleg Lobov, secretary of the Russian State Security Council, explained that Interior Ministry troops were trained to deal with civil unrest, and would have a primary role in Chechenya in the future. The armed forces were ordered to supply aircraft, armoured and artillery support, and to send 'better trained troops'. Russian military intelligence now officially estimated that Dudayev had between 1500 and 2000 fighters, split into groups of 30–50 men. Nikolai Yegorov, a deputy prime minister and nominee 'governor of Chechenya' when it was brought to heel, was dismissed.

As January 1995 ended there was tension in Moscow between Yeltsin and the top brass of the armed forces, amid rumours and fears there might be a military takeover, perhaps led by Aleksandr Korzhakov, head of the State Security Service, and a clamour arose for the Russian offensive in Chechenya to come to a stop before it got out of hand. The three dismissed deputy defence ministers were said to be continuing to work in their offices.

On the last day of the month one authority (Inter-Fax), citing an informed source at the Russian Defence Ministry, quoted the casualty figures for Russian personnel serving in Chechenya as 606 killed and approximately 2250 wounded; while in the United States the Russian ambassador complained that President Clinton had committed a breach of protocol by formally meeting Shamseddin Yusuf, the Chechen 'foreign minister', whom he alleged was engaged in anti-Russian activities.

11 The Struggle for Chechenya

On 1 February 1995, under the cover of aerial bombing, the Russians crossed the Sunzha river to establish their first bridgehead. They also made a three-pronged attack on the small town of Samashki – lying about 20 miles west of Grozny and housing some 5000 refugees – which was left in flames, two days previously a small Russian armoured column had been badly ambushed near a river bridge at Samashki, and Russian bodies had been recovered by Red Cross personnel. In Grozny, artillery bombardments continued across the river, but the Russians were unable to prevent Chechens from reinforcing their forward positions along the east bank, while a number of small, roaming groups attacked Russian positions and troops within the inner city ring.

The KSK openly established a unit, thought to be about 800 strong, in Grozny to deal with 'rebels and criminals', crime continuing despite the hazards and handicaps of war. The Chechen Provisional Council complained of looting by Russian troops. A warrant for the arrest of Dudayev was issued by the Russian Prosecutor General, a hunt for him having been in progress for some days. A Dudayev show trial in Moscow might go some way to offset the harsh military activities.

In Moscow the media criticism of senior generals began to ease off, owing to their complaints that they were being 'shot in the back'. The official Russian casualty list had risen to 608 dead, minus those 'missing in action', the Interior Ministry admitting that 60 of its soldiers were included in that category.

General Grachev disappeared briefly into hospital, probably to avoid publicity, it now being openly said that his rift with Yeltsin had occurred on 25 January when Yeltsin had questioned the $20 million 'sleaze fund' that had been found in his Defence Ministry accounts. The matter of the Russian journalist Dimitri Kholodov, who had been killed by a bomb in October 1994 while investigating alleged corruption involving Grachev, was also raised. But Grachev was soon back at work at the Defence Ministry as though nothing had happened.

On 1 February General Anatoli Kulikov, who had an Interior Ministry security background, was appointed as the new coordinator of Russian forces in Chechenya. Russian troops closed in on the Minutka crossroads area, where Dudayev had established his headquarters. An attack mounted on the 3rd met with fierce resistance. After several hours, as his defences began to fail, Dudayev withdrew. By the 6th the Russians were in possession of Minutka, which had linked several Chechen positions in the southern suburbs, thus closing a southern access road into the city for Chechen fighters. Next the Russians moved against Greshy, three miles south-east of Grozny, but in the meantime the Chechens made two minor counterattacks. On the 14th Dudayev threatened to launch a campaign of terror against Russian cities as part of his struggle for independence, although he had previously stated he would not resort to terrorism.

General Kulikov's assessment of the Chechen resistance forces was that their strength was probably about 15 000, that they were 'well-prepared, well-trained and excellently armed men', and that Dudayev had 30 000 local militiamen (Tass). But what general does not overstate the strength of his enemy? He said his Russian force was about 60 000-strong.

CONFLICTING CASUALTY FIGURES

In Moscow the Defence Ministry claimed its troops had occupied the whole of Grozny, which was only partially correct. It updated its official casualty figures to 600 confirmed dead and 456 missing in action; also admitting that over 1000 Russian soldiers were being investigated for refusing to serve in the Caucasus. Lists of Russians being held prisoner in Chechenya were published in Russian newspapers, but Dudayev would not release any to the Committee for the Mothers of Russians Soldiers, offering only to exchange them for Chechens held by Russians.

On 8 February 1995 Dzhokhar Dudayev held a press conference in Shali, at which he declared that Chechen resistance would continue, claiming he had left 'special assault groups' behind in Grozny. The Russian 'guesstimate' was that he had about 6000 guerrillas defending Argun, about 5000 defending

Gudermes, about 6000 elsewhere in a guerrilla role in western Chechenya, and 5000 in its eastern part, the admission being that it was hard to differentiate between the National Guard, people's volunteers and other impromptu groups of armed Chechens.

Not long afterwards (the 21st) a completely different set of casualty figures was issued by Sergei Kovalyov, the Russian human rights commissioner, who stated that, between 25 November 1994 and 25 January 1995, 24 400 people had been killed in Chechenya, of whom 1920 were Russian military casualties. His breakdown included 3700 children under 15 years of age, 4650 women over 15, 2650 men over 50 and about 14 000 men between 15 and 50. Only 650 Chechen fighters, he said, had been killed in the whole six-week conflict. In particular the death toll of local Russian civilians, unable to flee to the countryside where they were unwelcome, was high because heavy weapons had been used, meaning bombs and shells. Many wounded in Grozny died because of the lack of instant medical attention, and many of the dead still lay under the rubble of collapsed buildings.

Meanwhile the fighting had tended to die down, but the lulls were shattered by occasional bouts of Russian shelling. Russian air raids were made on outer towns and villages, as were frequent minor Chechen counterattacks. The lulls developed into a ceasefire, instigated by the Ingush, which formally came into effect on 15 February for the purpose of exchanging prisoners. General Kulikov met Chechen Colonel Aslan Maskhadov at an Ingush border village. Kulikov stated that his troops would remain in Grozny until the three Chechen resistance areas of Argun, Shali and Gudermes were captured, or surrendered, but that in the meantime he had ordered the artillery bombardments to cease.

General Kulikov was trying to reach past Dudayev to the Chechen 'elders', who traditionally had considerable influence amongst the people, in the hope they would persuade the 'rebels' to give up the fight in return for a promise that Russians would not storm the remaining Chechen bases, would refrain from aerial bombing, and would concentrate on controlling the main roads, railways and oil installations. Kulikov also hoped that the 'elders' could persuade Dudayev to resign (it being rumoured that a comfortable exile was awaiting him in

Cyprus), and that Maskhadov, the army commander, regarded by the Russians as a 'moderate' with whom they could come to some arrangement, should succeed him. As the Russian idea of an arrangement would mean the virtual partitioning of Chechenya into a prosperous northern part and a barren southern one, this did not come to anything.

The battle for Grozny aroused old hatreds which overrode clear thinking and commonsense, as Chechen animosity towards their former colonial masters intensified. Those Russians involved reciprocated, while those not involved were indifferent. The current Russian military joke in Chechenya was 'What were Stalin's best and worst actions?' The answer was 'to deport Chechens, and then to allow them to return'. Mutual hostility festered.

Minor breaches of the ceasefire occurred, a major one being on the 18th, when a Chechen group using mortars and grenade launchers tried to break into Grozny from the west, near the oil refinery. Several fires were started, the Chechens were driven off, and both sides suffered casualties. Other previous ceasefire arrangements had been broken by the Chechens within hours, which led to the assumption that Dudayev was not in total command of his troops. Negotiators were due to meet on the 18th to exchange lists of prisoners held, but this did not happen and another ceasefire collapsed.

Yeltsin made a televised speech to the nation on 16 February, admitting for the first time the shortcomings of the Chechen campaign. He insisted on his right to use force, described Dudayev as the 'Grozny tumour', blamed the military for incompetence, and promised that decisive measures would be taken to reorganise the armed forces in 1995.

RUSSIANS RESUME THE OFFENSIVE

On 21 February 1995 the Russians in Chechenya launched a fresh offensive against 'rebel-held' towns, using bomber aircraft, artillery and helicopter gunships. A successful dawn assault was made on Alkhan-Kala, four miles south-west of Grozny. This, it was claimed, closed the Chechens' last major access road, thus completing the blockade of the whole city on the west bank, although as snows began to melt many unpaved roads became available for infiltration purposes. After this flurry of offensive activity an uneasy stalemate settled on the military scene in northern Chechenya for the remainder of the month.

On the 23rd, Russian National Army Day, Yeltsin made a somewhat pessimistic TV speech, admitting the army could be in danger of disintegrating and promising more money, but his words were not strong enough to quieten senior generals, who were now openly blaming the politicians. He tried unsuccessfully to dismiss Sergei Kovalyov over comments made on the possibility of a UN detachment being sent to Chechenya, alleging that Kovalyov was scheming to bring foreign troops into Russia.

SPRING 1995

During March 1995 these was talk of a Russian spring offensive, fuelled by General Grachev, who insisted that the campaign must continue and that paratroops and infantry must soon move against Argun, Gudermes and Shali, the three remaining major Chechen-held towns. He claimed that 90 per cent of Chechen armoured vehicles had been either destroyed or seized.

The centre of Grozny was one of devastation. It was thought that some 70 000 people still remained, mainly Russian, over whom the threat of cholera hovered. They were still without gas, as the frequently ruptured aboveground pipelines, some badly damaged by shell fire, were yet to be repaired, and as the snow disappeared, shortage of water became a problem. Mass graves were being excavated in the Russian Orthodox cemetery north of the city, while Russian troops still feared Chechen snipers hidden in devastated buildings. Some Chechens were allowed to return to their homes in central Grozny, but most, after retrieving what valuables and necessities they could, quickly departed again. There was talk of establishing a quarantine zone, and of mass vaccinations, while the Grozny sanitation department admitted there could be still up to 5000 corpses on the streets or in damaged or devastated buildings.

SHARIA LAW IN CHECHENYA

President Dudayev chaired a meeting of a Chechen People's Congress on 9 March 1995. Chechenya was placed on a total war footing, and emphasising the Muslim aspect of the struggle, Dudayev introduced the Sharia, the Muslim legal code, in areas under his control. Delivery of food and medicines to the Chechen-held areas was a problem, as Russians manning the road checkpoints were refusing to allow humanitarian convoys to enter 'enemy' territory.

On 17 March General Grachev faced the press at the Mozdok base, and was asked the reasons for military ground inactivity. He explained that, although the cost of the Chechen campaign was causing financial worries, the military option was not yet exhausted and he was pressing on with it. He admitted that the Russian border troops were having difficulty closing the routes in and out of Chechenya as they were undermanned and ill-equipped. In short he was admitting that Dudayev's forces were obtaining adequate supplies despite the nebulous Russian frontier blockade.

Yeltsin again declared he would not talk to Dudayev, emphasising he was supporting the Chechen Government of Renewal, based in Moscow and now with a tenuous link with the Chechen Provisional Council, which was still sitting in Znamenskoye, struggling to assert its authority locally and attract those opposing Dudayev. There was a certainly a ground swell of discontent against Dudayev, but this did not extend to the 'quisling' government, which had established itself in Grozny in the former Oil Research Institute, the only major building to have survived more or less intact. Popular appeal was lacking.

THE FALL OF ARGUN

The Russian offensive began on 21 March 1995 with an artillery barrage on Argun that lasted almost three days, while ground troops gradually encircled the town where Dudayev had his military headquarters. Argun had already been battered by previous air raids and shelling. On the nights of 21 and 22 March the Chechen garrison decamped, abandoning its few armoured vehicles and other equipment and leaving the town open for Russian troops to enter, which they did on the 23rd.

General Kulikov triumphantly proclaimed at a press conference that Argun had been 'captured without being flattened', although subsequent aerial photographs did not support this statement, and that his casualties were only 'one Russian soldier killed and nine wounded', which indicated an almost unopposed victory. He was silent on Chechen losses.

This gain encouraged the Russians and accordingly their aircraft and guns began to turn on Gudermes, now a main Chechen resistance base and reputedly being speedily prepared to withstand Russian attacks. Shali and Samashki, which were home to Chechen resistance garrisons, also came under bombardment and shell fire. Kulikov needed to subdue these bases before he could claim control of northern Chechenya.

GUDERMES FALLS

The Russian strategy was becoming clear. General Kulikov was going to saturate the country with artillery fire so as to drive the population southwards, and continuous shelling was accomplishing this aim. Large areas were virtually depopulated, apart from Chechen fighters and a few old or stubborn people clinging on to their family homes, or those who had nowhere else to go.

This policy was paying off, and by 30 March 1995 the Russian forces that had partially surrounded Gudermes, the second largest city in Chechenya, walked in without opposition, the Chechen armed forces having quit a few hours previously. The Chechens admitted they could not indefinitely withstand Russian shelling, and would have to abandon positional warfare. As the Chechen armed forces withdrew from Shali, Dudayev's headquarters moved southwards. Later General Kulikov admitted that his objective was to control 80–85 per cent of Chechenya by mid April, seemingly content to leave the remainder of the republic, mainly the central plains and the foothills of the Caucasus Mountain ridge, to Dudayev.

However, Chechen fighters still retained a hold on bases in Achkhoi-Martan and Samashki, which were heavily bombarded by Russian troops during the first days of April, whereupon they fell. By this time events indicated the war was taking a nasty turn for the worse, causing a statement to be issued on the 11th by the 'Chechen Defence Council', headed by Dudayev, complaining bitterly of Russian 'cruelty, atrocities and torture'. Suddenly, on the 14th General Kulikov was briefly replaced by

General Nikolai Yegorov, who also had an Interior Ministry security background.

Samashki, which had been bombarded consistently from the 6th to the 8th, fell when the Chechen fighters withdrew. Many civilians had been caught up in this battle and bombardment. Later the Red Cross alleged that a 'massacre of at least 250 people' (*Daily Telegraph*) had occurred on the 8th, at the taking of Samashki, and that Russian soldiers had been 'high on drugs' during the final attack, as the battle area was littered with discarded hypodermic syringes.

It seemed to the Russian authorities that although the first part of Kulikov's plan had been accomplished, it would be better to get him out of the way, at least for the time being, for public relations reasons if no other, before the second stage of the 'pacification' of Chechenya was put into effect. The chairman of the Moscow-supported Chechen Government of Renewal, now esconced in Grozny, warned that it was too early to say that the military operations were over. The Chechen fighters may have been driven back by overwhelming firepower, but they had not been beaten. The Russians were apprehensive, fearing not only a long-drawn-out guerrilla struggle on the Afghan pattern, which would be bad enough, but also a wider Chechen campaign of urban terrorism. For their part the Chechens alleged that the Russians had drawn up a 'death list', containing the names of Dudayev and his senior staff, and that Russian 'death squads' had been assigned to target and eliminate certain individuals. This was denied.

BATTLE FOR BAMUT

One of the last Chechen strongholds to defy the Russians on the 'plains' or in the 'low country' (in Russian military jargon) – that is, the strip running between Grozny in the north and the foothills of the Caucasus Mountains in the south – was Bamut, a former Russian nuclear base. The Russians had mounted an attack on Bamut on 13 April, but had failed. After a pause to regroup, a second attack was mounted on the 18th, but the attackers were driven back by heavy fire from the low, surrounding hills. Bamut briefly became a prestige symbol of Chechen resistance.

On 23 April 1995 the Russians began a heavy night-and-day artillery bombardment of Bamut, giving rise to the Chechen black joke that 'at last the Russian are giving us light'. Dudayev let it be known that he had ordered the formation of 'suicide units', to remain behind when locations were evacuated. Intermittent bombardment continued, and although Russian forces had almost surrounded the base and were seemingly preparing to attack yet again, they hesitated. It was later admitted that they did not want to risk incurring heavy casualties when they were trying to give the impression they had already 'liberated' Chechenya. The Chechens thought they were battle-shy and took heart, using the respite to organise their resistance forces into a cohesive army. Yet another assault on Bamut began on 28 April, only to stop suddenly again.

On 19 April the Interior Ministry had issued what was meant to be the last campaign statement on losses. It was claimed that the Russians had killed 300 Chechens at Bamut for the loss of only 14 soldiers; and that the total battle casualties since December 1994, when Operation Wave had begun, were 1500 Russians and over 9500 Chechens killed. Over 300 Russians were missing in action, and the total civilian losses were estimated at more than 24 000.

UNILATERAL RUSSIAN CEASEFIRE

Yeltsin declared that a unilateral ceasefire would take place in Chechenya from 28 April to 11 May 1995 – or longer if some agreement could be reached – to coincide with the commemoration ceremonies of the 50th anniversary of Victory in Europe. Many heads of state were due to visit Moscow on the 9th, and Yeltsin wanted to give them the impression he had settled his Chechen problem. The Russian guns stopped firing, but the Russian troops remained in their forward positions, which was much what they had been doing for some time. Commanders were told not to inflame the situation. Dudayev immediately rejected the unilateral ceasefire gesture, launching small-scale assaults to emphasise his point.

On 1 May small Chechen groups penetrated Grozny to clash with the security forces, 'dozens being killed' (local TV). These urban guerrilla-like tactics continued spasmodically in Grozny for the first part of the month, and on the 14th the Chechens launched their first artillery attack on the capital. During the latter part of May the Russian forces mounted an offensive designed to dominate the 'low country', which included yet another unsuccessful attack on Bamut.

PEACE TALKS

Peace talks between Russian and Chechen officials took place in Grozny from 25 May, under the auspices of the OSCE and against the advice of Defence Minister Grachev, but no progress was made. An abrasive stalemate grated along, with Russian aerial bombing and all guns blazing in the countryside. This was countered by a degree of urban terrorism in outer Grozny and elsewhere, resulting in a small but steady stream of casualties.

THE BUDENNOVSK EXPLOIT

Suddenly, in early June 1995 a group of about 100 armed Chechens, led by Shamil Basayev, launched an attack on the small town of Budennovsk (whose population was estimated at about 100 000), some 150 miles north of Chechenya in the Stavropol region of the Russian Federation. The attackers eventually barricaded themselves in the main hospital, having seized a large number of hostages. Basayev had suggested to Dudayev that raids should be made on Russian cities to publicise their cause and show their teeth, but Dudayev had rejected the idea as it would only bring increased military pressure against him at a time when he was building up, equipping and training his armed forces.

Moving north from Chechenya, Basayev had been able to get his convoy through road checkpoints by bribing Russian border guards, but his money ran out, and on 14 June Budennovsk became the chance scene of his violent exploit, which severely shook the Russian security services. Basayev had initially attacked several buildings in the town, including the headquarters of the FSB (Federal Special Service, the successor to the KSB) and the main police station. It was reported that in the fighting 41 people were killed, including six FSB personnel, and over

50 injured. Hundreds of people were rounded up by Basayev and marched to the main hospital, which the attackers decided to make their fortified base. There they assembled between 1000 and 1500 hostages, including staff and patients, and threatened to kill them unless Russia ceased its hostilities in Chechenya (local TV).

It was an impromptu expedition by a guerrilla band, the decision to activate it being taken just after the Chechen headquarters, then in Vedeno in the south-eastern part of the 'low country', had been overrun by Russian troops. Shamil Basayev's original intention had apparently been to strike directly at Moscow.

If Basayev's expedition was cavalier, opportunistic, badly organised and ill-thought-out, the response of the Russian government, which was caught absolutely by surprise, was much the same. A contingent of Interior Ministry troops was rushed to the scene, whereupon the Chechens killed five hostages to illustrate their determination. The Interior Minister, Viktor Yerin, flew to Budennovsk, murmuring vaguely but hopefully that the crisis would be solved peacefully. A deputy prime minister (Nikolai Yegorov) also arrived in Budennovsk. Yegorov went further and said that the Russian government was ready to meet any conditions to free the hostages, while in the background Defence Minister Grachev demanded military action. For a short while all paused, none knowing quite what to do and influenced by interservice rivalry.

Two separate assaults were made on the fortified hospital on the 17th, both of which failed disastrously. The first, launched at dawn by Interior Ministry troops, was crude and full-frontal. Despite white flags being waved out of windows by patients and hostages, troops fired automatic and heavy weapons at the building, reputedly killing several people, many of whom had been ordered by the Chechen raiders to become a part of a hostage screen. A section of the hospital building was set on fire. The event was closely covered by the Russian media, which reported that the troops involved were undisciplined and disorganised. In the confusion a journalist (Natalya Alyakina) was shot and killed by a soldier. The Interior Ministry's later excuse was that the dawn assault had been an emotional reaction by Russians troops concerned about the plight of the hostages. About 160 hostages had been freed so far.

The second assault, conducted later in the day by FSB

personnel, was also chaotic, although 100 or so hostages were rescued. But Shamil Basayev remained defiant.

On the 18th Prime Minister Viktor Chernomyrdin took personal charge and negotiated directly with Basayev by telephone, some of his conversations being broadcast by Russian TV. He promised to halt the war in Chechenya and return to the peace talks, offering Basayev and his group safe passage back to Chechenya in exchange for the release of the hostages. Basayev agreed. Chernomyrdin directly ordered General Kulikov, now back in command in Chechenya, to cease the military activity.

Basayev insisted on a 'human shield' to accompany his remaining '74' men. The shield was formed by 123 volunteers, including several hostages from the hospital, Russian deputies and journalists, and Sergei Kovalyov, the Russian human rights commissioner. Some 760 hostages were released and Basayev's convoy moved off under the glare of TV cameras. It eventually arrived in a Chechen border village on the 20th, where the human shield was released and the raiders dispersed into the Chechen hills (Tass).

Chernomyrdin's decision was not unanimously popular in some government circles, opposition coming from the defence and interior ministers. He had to promise that once the hostage takers were back in Chechenya they would be shown 'no mercy or leniency'. Grachev complained bitterly that they could have been 'liquidated either at Budennovsk or at any point along the route to Chechenya' (Tass). Dudayev agreed to arrest Basayev and hand him over to the Russians, but that was empty rhetoric. The regional authorities in Stavropol put the death toll at about 120, including 18 Interior Ministry troops and 14 army ones, but there seemed to be a degree of vagueness about the precise number of casualities. The Duma criticised the handling of the incident, provoking Yeltsin to reply on 22 June that 'if the Duma does not want to be disturbed, it should not try to disband the government' (Tass). Yeltsin made certain ministerial changes.

PEACE ACCORD

The Budennovsk episode brought the Chechen problem to national attention once again, causing the Russian people, already apprehensive of the activities of Chechen mafia groups, to become even more anxious about the situation in Chechenya, even though, despite occasional clashes, the Russian unilateral ceasefire was generally being observed. Talks were resumed between Russian and Chechen officials, again opposed by Grachev, which eventually led to a preliminary agreement under which the Chechen fighters would disarm in exchange for the withdrawal of all but 8000 Russian troops from Chechenya. It was also agreed that elections would be held in Chechenya.

At this point Chernomyrdin stepped in and took direct charge of the negotiations, which led to the Peace Accord of 30 July 1995. Designed to end the hostilities, this confirmed the ceasefire and catered for the gradual withdrawal of Russian troops in return for the disarming of the Chechen resistance fighters. It did not touch on the Chechens' demand for independence. Grachev complained that the accord would handicap the Russian troops while allowing Dudayev to reorganise his 'army'. On the 31st Russia's Constitutional Court declared that the Russian invasion of Chechenya had been legal, thus giving a moral victory to Yeltsin, whose critics were alleging that it had been both illegal and unconstitutional.

The Dudayev 'government', now esconced in a new headquarters in Roshni-Chu in the foothills, was left virtually unmolested, allowing its capable propaganda section to continue to operate. However it was thought that its political activities were not matched by its military muscle. Dudayev had failed to obtain tanks, guns or sophisticated weaponry in any quantity, and his ammunition supply was low. The Russian embargo and Russian pressure on adjacent republics were handicapping Dudayev, who had been hoping to build up effective armed forces and resume positional warfare. This was a disappointment to him, but as the Peace Accord implementation dragged negatively on, Chechen fighters crept northwards to reoccupy some lost towns and territory, to the exasperation of the Russians. On the other hand Dudayev had allowed a number of his mustered Chechens to return to their home towns and villages in order to reduce the military burden.

Chernomyrdin was trying to turn the July Peace Accord into a political settlement based on the Moscow-backed Chechen Government of Renewal, and wanted to push aside Dudayev and his 'rebels' completely. Grachev insisted that the Chechens be disarmed before they came to the conference table, which was another stumbling block.

The July Peace Accord catered for the exchange of prisoners held by both sides. The first exchange took place on 2 August. Being a purely symbolic one, just three Chechens were handed over in return for two Russians. A deadlock followed over incompatible lists of the numbers held and missing in action, the Russians listing 400 missing in action, and the Chechens 1346. There was disagreement over which were fighters and which were civilians. The Chechens allowed the Russians access to 14 of their Russian prisoners, but the Russians permitted no similar visits, which left 'hundreds of Chechens' unaccounted for. The Russians stated (falsely) that they had only one 'detention camp', but they had at least three, which later came to be known as 'filtration camps'.

The Chechen fighters were slow to respond to the July Peace Accord obligation to hand over their arms to the Russians, which on the 15th caused Chernomyrdin to produce a timetable for the process, which he demanded that Colonel Aslan Maskhadov, the Chechen army commander, sign and implement. Maskhadov refused, but when Chernomyrdin threatened to bomb Dudayev's Roshni-Chu headquarters a token surrendering of arms began in Grozny the following day. Only a few old weapons were handed over, so, in a face-saving exercise, the Russians offered cash rewards for Chechen arms. However, this too proved unsatisfactory, particularly as arms stolen from Russian forces were handed over, while others were sometimes traded in to obtain the release of Chechens held in the filtration camps.

During August the ceasefire generally held, the main exception occurring on the 20th, when a group of Chechens seized the police station in Argun. The following day Russian Interior Ministry troops launched a successful counterattack to recapture it, during the process of which '80 rebels' were killed (Tass).

CHECHEN GOVERNMENT OF RENEWAL

Due largely to the increasingly bad relations between the Chechens and the Russian occupation forces in Chechenya, Prime

Minister Chernomyrdin persuaded his colleagues to adopt a new policy of withdrawing into the background as far as possible, and pushing the Chechen Government of Renewal on to centre stage. He called this 'restoring constitutional order'. So far the Chechen Government of Renewal (now led by Umar Avaturkhanov, a former Soviet oil minister) had generally failed to attract any significant anti-Dudayev Chechen support and had been largely ignored. On 24 August 1995 Doku Zavgayev, a former chairman of Ingushetia-Chechenya, was confirmed as prime minister by the Committee for Reconciliation, Zavgayev stated that his main priorities would be to end hostilities and return to political stability. In Grozny, Dudayev's supporters organised protest meetings.

Zavgayev faced a formidable task. Members of the Chechen Government of Renewal were already complaining of the patronisingly hostile Russian attitude towards it, and towards Chechens generally. The Russians on their part had expected this 'government' to give them wholehearted and unquestioning support in the struggle against the Dudayev separatists, in which respect it had been found wanting. On the contrary, it seemed quick to support the rights of individual Chechens against Russian brutality, causing the Russians to accuse it of 'going native' and swerving from the Moscow line. When mass graves were opened in Grozny for individual Chechen identification and conventional burial, evidence of Russian maltreatment, torture and atrocities became apparent, whereupon the attitude of the Chechen Government of Renewal towards the Russian military hardened almost to the extent of non-compliance. Ironically the Council of Europe had congratulated Russia for its restraint towards the Chechen separatists during the campaign.

JULY PEACE ACCORD SUSPENDED

During September 1995, despite the formal ceasefire, '45 Russians were killed and 215 wounded' in Chechenya (Tass). Urban terrorism developed as Dudayev's fighters had percolated into the environs of Grozny and other northern towns. By the end of the month the situation was such that the Russian military forces controlled the towns only by day, when high-profile troops drove around in armoured vehicles while Russian planes and helicopters flew threateningly overhead. At night most of the Russians soldiers tended to withdraw into their bunkers and posts, simply patrolling the main streets, and then the Chechen urban guerrillas would appear to snipe, ambush military vehicles and set off explosions. Grachev chafed at the bit, prevented by the July Peace Accord from engaging in strong military retaliation.

The urban guerrillas became bolder, and on 6 October, in broad daylight, they attacked the convoy of the Russian military commander, General Anatoli Romanov, in an underpass in Grozny, killing three of the escort and ten bystanders, and wounding the general. Romanov had been an advocate of the peace process and was thought to have struck up a good relationship with the Chechen negotiators – not all Chechens were in favour of Dudayev's policies. Russia immediately stated it would cease to observe the restrictions of the July Peace Accord, and on the 8th bomber aircraft struck at Dudayev's headquarters in Roshni-Chu, killing '28 villagers and injuring over 60 others' (Tass).

Dudayev stated on the 11th that Chechen participation in the July Peace Accord implementation negotiations would cease, and that hostilities against the Russians would resume as soon as fog and rain reduced Russian air effectiveness. On the 12th, also in Grozny, a Russian colonel was kidnapped in broad daylight. Grachev tried to persuade Yeltsin to declare a state of emergency in Grozny to override the restrictions of the Peace Accord, and so allow him freedom of military action. But Yeltsin stayed his hand, saying that this would indicate a failure of the peace effort, so despite military advice he decided to 'give peace one more chance' (Tass). On the 26th Yeltsin was hospitalised again. He remained under medical care for the remainder of the year, leaving Prime Minister Chernomyrdin to handle the Chechen problem.

THE OIL PIPELINE DECISION

Meanwhile, in the preceding months rubble had been cleared from roads in central Grozny, and certain damaged buildings had been made habitable to house Russian administrators, officials and those working on communications and in the oil and related industries. Oil was once again being extracted from the Chechen oilfields, oil from Baku was again flowing through

Chechen pipelines into the main Russian oil distribution system, although only a trickle as yet, and trains were again running across northern Chechenya.

Russia had paid special attention to the security aspects of these assets, which showed tiny signs of reviving their economic potential. Russia still had its eyes on the Caspian offshore oil deposits, and wanted to dominate the distribution of the oil by channelling it through the Chechen pipeline system into that in the Russian Federation running to Novorossiysk on the Black Sea. If was therefore anxious to give an impression of stability.

Russia's efforts were rewarded on 9 October 1995, when the Azerbaijan International Operating Company announced in Moscow that the 11-nation oil consortium planned to have two overland pipelines to carry crude oil from the Caspian Sea to the Black Sea terminals, one of which would run through Chechenya and the other through Georgia. Little was said about the instability of Chechenya, it probably being assumed that this would soon be sorted out. It certainly gave a morale boost to the Russians in Chechenya, and also to the many Chechens whose thoughts and hopes were on the economic future of Chechenya rather than separatism. There was plenty of time to improve the political situation, as the potential oil bonanza was still months away.

CONTINUING INSTABILITY

Although heavily overshadowed by pro-Dudayev separatists and other strong-arm groups, life in northern Chechenya was slowly returning to normal. In Grozny, for example, street markets, formally a feature of the capital, were reappearing in the suburbs. Former employees of the oil and related industries, the railways and the administration were attracted back to work. Under selective Russian distribution, food and other essentials became more plentiful. A main barrier was that the Chechens invariably avoided all other than necessary contact with the Russian authorities, as ethnic attitudes were clashing.

The Russian military forces thought of themselves as 'liberators', and expected the 'liberated' to be grateful, while the Chechens thought of them as 'military occupiers', and worse. A general Chechen complaint was that the Russians were arrogant in behaviour and attitude. In addition it was commonly alleged that Russian soldiers shot first and asked questions afterwards, for example, Russian night patrols, often the worse for vodka, would fire indiscriminately. Mutual respect was absent, and mutual dislike was developing into something stronger.

In the south, in the Dudayev camp things were not going well, as Dudayev had been unable to obtain the hoped for international support. Winter was approaching and food was becoming a problem as the Russian embargoes against him were pinching tight. However, Dudayev remain defiant, and told BBC2 television that he had '3000 men with no jobs, with nothing to do, as they are fighters only', adding that 'he could use a small war' to keep them occupied. This was bravado, as a note of pessimism was detected by the interviewers, who sensed war-weariness in the mountains and an unwillingness to resume large-scale military activities. Turkey, a traditional rival of Russia, gave some aid and assistance, but it was only a pittance, although a number of Chechen children, for example, were sent away to Turkish schools. A tiny stream of emigration was detected.

Urban terrorism remained a problem in Grozny, for example on 20 November 1995 Doku Zavgayev, the Chechen prime minister, was slightly injured by a bomb explosion, and on 4 December a bomb explosion occurred near the Chechen Assembly building, injuring several people.

Another problem to develope was that of discontented Russian people resident in Chechenya, once quoted as forming 31 per cent of the population. They had suffered very heavy casualties in the Battle for Grozny, and many of their homes had been devastated. The Moscow authorities had promised aid and rehabilitation, and indeed large sums of money had been allocated for this purpose, but little had materialised. It was alleged that much of this money had gone into the pockets of Chechen entrepreneurs. Several aid and reconstruction projects had been started, only to be abandoned for lack of funds. Resident Russians complained they were being treated like 'Chechen rebels'.

INCREASED CHECHEN AUTONOMY

The Moscow authorities, counting on Chechen war-weariness and deprivation – both doubtful premises in view of the hard and bitter separatist element – to further their cause, gave the Chechen Government of Renewal a boost on the 8th, when an agreement was signed in Moscow between Prime Minister Chernomyrdin and Prime Minister Zavgayev to increase the autonomous status of Chechenya by allowing it to have its own foreign consulates and trade missions. In addition an amnesty was decreed for all 'rebels' who laid down their arms. In theory this gave Chechenya greater autonomy than that of any other constituent autonomous republic in the Russian Federation.

CHECHEN ELECTIONS

Chernomyrdin, wanting the Chechen Government of Renewal gradually to accumulate popular support and authority as the economy began to recover and thrive and Dudayev's influence declined, decided there should be a general election in Chechenya for a president and a government. The date was set for 17 December 1995, to coincide with general elections in Russia. Electioneering began in Chechenya.

Early in December Raslan Khasbulatov returned to his native Chechenya and put himself forward as a candidate for the presidency, being regarded as the only credible alternative to Doku Zavgayev. However, he soon backed down, declaring that 'fair and orderly elections under existing conditions' were impossible, adding that he would not take part 'in this blood-stained game called an election' (*Daily Telegraph*).

On 11 December a huge demonstration was held in the centre of Grozny to commemorate the Russian military invasion a year previously. The demonstration was rowdy and vocal, but caused little disorder, the Russian security forces standing well back to let the demonstrators voice their protests.

Suddenly the date of the general election in Chechenya was advanced to 14 December, the reason being given that it was 'an attempt to keep the process on course'. The decision was obviously influenced by the thought that the shorter the electioneering period, the sooner it would be over, the fear being that tension might escalate into mass violence. Dudayev opposed the election on the ground of illegality, and his supporters did their best to persuade the Chechen people to boycott it.

Several shooting incidents occurred in and around Grozny

on the 13th by separatists trying to intimidate would-be voters, but the main incident took place on polling day. At dawn on the 17th the town of Gudermes was invaded by a group of Chechen fighters, initially said to number about 600, who occupied the police barracks, the railway station and other buildings. Russian armed forces, supported by rocket-firing helicopters, rushed to eject them but met stiff resistance. First reports indicated that over 30 Russians were killed and more than 50 wounded. No figures were given on Chechen resistance casualties (Inter-Fax).

Pockets of fighting continued in Gudermes, and a few other armed attempts on a much smaller scale were made in a few places to disrupt the elections. A heavy Russian military presence rested on Grozny and its environs. Intimidation seemed to be more limited that had been feared, the media reporting, for example, that long queues formed outside polling booths in many northern towns and several on the 'plains'. However the reports also mentioned irregularities, including multiple voting.

The Chechen Electoral Commission reported the voter turnout to be over 70 per cent. As expected, the Chechen Government of Renewal was proclaimed the victor, and then claimed the election gave it a democratic mandate to govern Chechenya.

UNFINISHED BUSINESS

Despite the elections the struggle for Chechenya continued. The turbulent and hectic thirteen months had cost the Russian armed forces over 2000 dead and more than 24 000 wounded. The Chechen casualties could only be guessed at. Dudayev would not admit his losses in detail because he could be detrimental to morale. Although the violence had subsided somewhat since the July ceasefire, it had by no means ended. Three main factions remained in the struggle: the Russian security forces, which held military might; the Chechen Government of Renewal, the weakest element but which was expected to unite the republic and start an autonomous administration; and the pro-Dudayev separatist fighters, estimated to number about 3000, who although beaten back into the southern foothills, were by no means defeated, having recently given an example of their long-range military striking capability. In additional Dudayev threatened further forays into Russia to strike at nuclear targets. As 1995 ended the situation in Chechenya was that of an abrasive armed truce, with no sign of an outright winner.

Future variables include another all-out Russian military campaign in southern Chechenya in the spring of 1996, if the Moscow authorities lose patience and realise that time may not be on their side. Another is to try to tempt Dudayev into the Moscow camp, with bribes and offers of high office, in fact anything except total sovereignty. Dudayev may yet fall for this, regarding it as a first step that could perhaps later be turned to his advantage in obtaining his ultimate objective – to be president of an independent Chechenya – rather than see his cause wither away through embargoes and lack of allies. Yet another could be a KSK-instigated plot to topple him from his leadership position by raising the more powerful Chechen clans against him through intrigue and bribery (it will be recalled that Dudayev comes from a minor clan). This is a possibility, as Dudayev's popularity rating with some of them is not high.

In the meantime Chechenya remains a powder keg that could explode at any time.

12 Retrospect and Prospect

Suddenly, and somewhat unexpectedly, as the Soviet Union dissolved national independence fell into the laps of the Soviet Socialist Republics of Armenia, Azerbaijan and Georgia. They achieved this political pinnacle without the need to fight a long and hard resistance war for freedom, gaining it by a quirk of history. The stifling cloak of communism rapidly fell away, to be replaced by rabid nationalism and adventurism. Instead of concentrating on creating viable, liberal, democratic nation states on the approved Western pattern, with trade and cooperation between them, they instead chose isolation, aggression and ethnic cleansing.

It was as though an evil genie had suddenly popped out from a magic bottle to do its worst. Ideals of good government and tolerance were forgotten. Long suppressed tribalism and petty nationalism predominated, civil wars within civil wars flared up, old prejudices and suspicions were reawakened and old enemies resurrected, while thoughts of domination, acquisition and revenge motivated the political leaders. The clock in the Trans-Caucasus had simply been turned back half a century or more. Soviet communism had contained these violent emotions, but had failed to irradicate them.

Armenia and Azerbaijan vigorously fought against each other over the constitutional status of Nagorno-Karabakh and Nakhichevan, Stalin's leftover tinderboxes. The tide of battle ebbed and flowed. Landlocked Armenia, with its Christian heritage, suffered embargoes from Muslim countries, and from its larger and more wealthy Muslim opponent. A tenuously held ceasefire was eventually achieved, as the exhausted combatants prepared for the next round. The territorial questions remained just as stark and unsolveable as when Stalin had designed them. Timid international attempts at peacemaking and peacekeeping made only limited progress. Both countries adopted a crude form of democracy, electing presidents and Assemblies, but power bases remained uncertain as warlords and political contenders lurked in the background jostling for dominance.

Georgia, also with Stalin-bestowed, built-in tinderboxes, while accepting independence gladly, but not gratefully, refused to allow its subordinate oblasts similar freedom. Civil wars erupted almost concurrently. In one Gamsakhurdia became president, only to be overthrown by Shevardnadze, who in turn was thwarted by separatist Abkhazians and South Ossetes, both latterly supported by Russia, which virtually turned Georgia, suffering from banditry, lawlessness, economic woes and embargoes from fellow Caucasus republics, into a Russian protectorate.

Russia eventually absorbed these three republics into its Commonwealth of Independent States, mainly by economic blackmail, although the fear of falling to aggressive predators helped. Apart from occasional mischief making and embargo breaking, adjacent Turkey and Iran stood back, content for the time being with an unspoken policy of containment, neither wanting to become involved in hostilities that could escalate. The instability of the Trans-Caucasus region discouraged foreign investment, which hindered economic recovery.

In the North Caucasus Chechenya was in a different category, being a constituent republic of the Russian Federation that wanted to break away and become completely independent, under the leadership of Dzhokhar Dudayev. Owing to major problems and distractions in Moscow, Dudayev's assumption of independence was put on the backburner, allowing Chechenya to degenerate into a 'bandit state'. In December 1994 Yeltsin, after trying other methods without success, launched a colonial-type military invasion that began with the Battle for Grozny. The fierce, determined and continuous Chechen resistance surprised all. Russia was relearning the military lesson that it is easy to put troops into a hostile situation, but it is difficult to withdraw them again, especially when the enemy will not accept defeat. Chechen resistance devolved into guerrilla warfare and terrorism.

THE PROSPECT

The future prospects of the three Trans-Caucasus republics, all of which wallow in a degree of instability, will depend up several factors. In the short term increased stability and the maintenance of internal order, both priority essentials, depend on President Ter-Petrossian of Armenia, President Aliyev of

Azerbaijan and President Shevardnadze of Georgia, or if they are removed from office, their successors. As long as instability prevails, so does the danger of malevolent intervention by outsiders, the temptation for contenders for power to use violent means and subversive activity by embittered groups. Failure means resumption of civil war and unrest.

Much will depend on Russia and what action it takes to bring stability to the region over which it is trying to reassert its influence. If Russia continues to ensure that existing ceasefires are maintained, that arms deliveries are commensurate with modest republican defence requirements, and that ammunition is kept in short supply, this will contribute to improved stability. If Russia continues to sponsor and promote negotiations between hostile republics and factions, and if international peacekeepers are brought in to stand between the armed factions, this could bring the constitutional stumbling blocks of Nagorno-Karabakh and Nakhichevan into a wider forum where any equitable solution, and any frontier rearrangement, could be influenced by the force of international opinion.

Trade would follow stability, so the next important measures will be to remove the economic embargoes between these three Trans-Caucasus republics, and to ensure that vital oil, natural gas, electricity and other resources become available according to basic needs. This will require some give and take, some hard bargaining and some deprivation, but the alternative is more war and more misery.

Due to economic poverty, Armenia has been forced to bring into use an old nuclear power station to provide desperately needed electricity, thus endangering the whole Caucasus region. Azerbaijan's superior wealth and industrial prosperity could be wiped out in an instant by a Chernobyl-type disaster, so any aid and other forms of accommodation given to Armenia could be regarded as sound insurance, rather than blackmail. Stability, harmony and nuclear safety are prerequisites for Russia, the Azerbaijan International Operating Company and foreign investors. The Trans-Caucasus region could be a fruitful field for the OSCE and other international peacemaking and peacekeeping organisations to work in.

In the longer term much depends upon whether, or when, the promised bonanza of Caspian offshore oil materialises. The deposit is thought to exceed in volume that of Kuwait, and is expected to replace the declining output of Arabian oil by about the year 2010. This means that the Caucasus region will become a centre of international commercial interests, pressures and rivalries. In short, a whole new ball game.

Not to be forgotten is the ongoing civil war in Chechenya, which Yeltsin does not seem able to terminate. Russia is striving to dominate the distribution of the anticipated Caspian offshore oil bonanza, having repaired and heavily guarded its pipeline through Chechenya for the purpose. It may be months before the Caspian oil flows from Azerbaijan through either the Georgian or Chechen overland pipelines, or both, to Black Sea terminals and thence westwards, which will give Russia some time to resolve its Chechen problem.

Maps

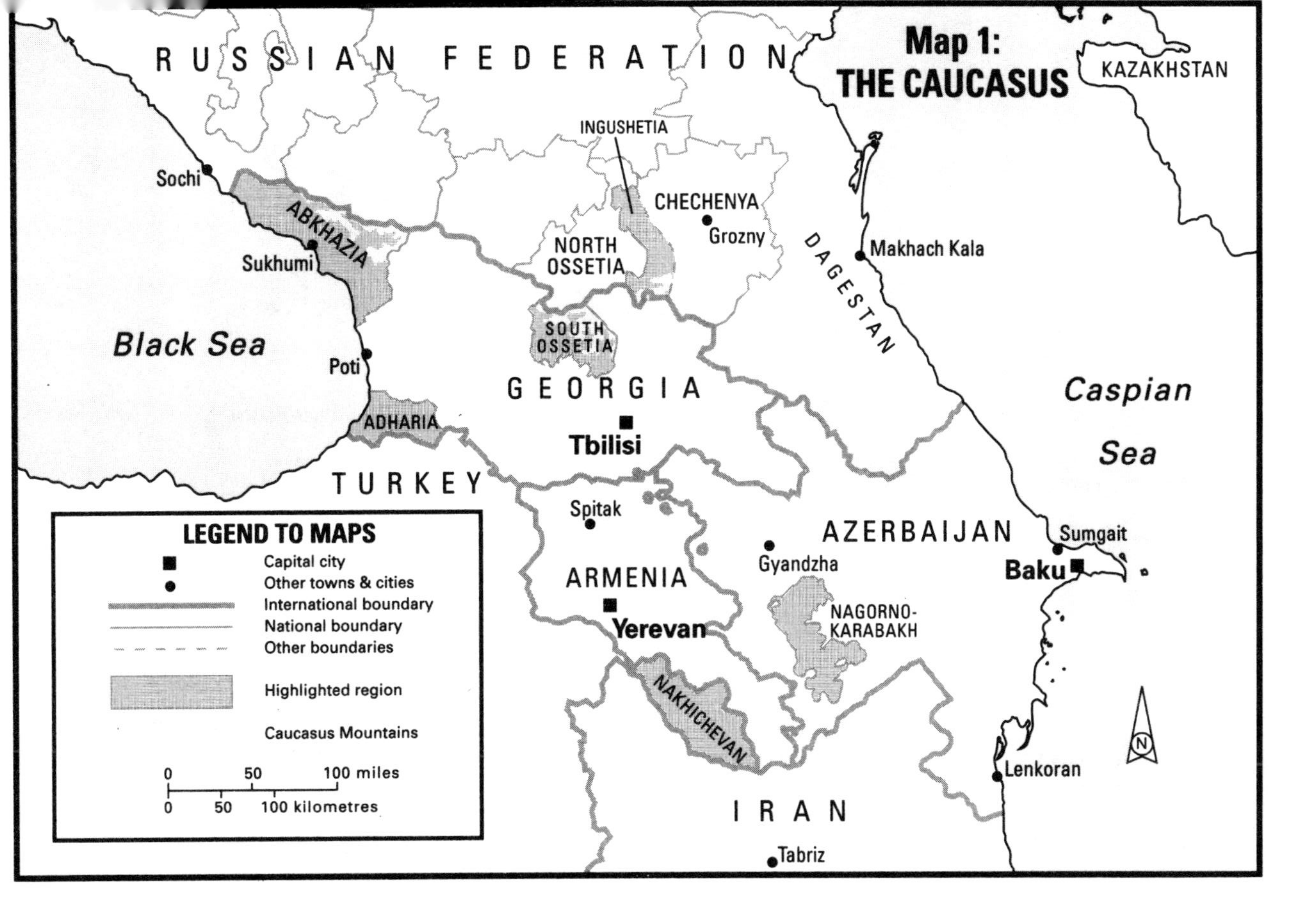
Map 1:
THE CAUCASUS
RUSSIAN FEDERATION
KAZAKHSTAN
INGUSHETIA
CHECHENYA
Grozny
NORTH OSSETIA
SOUTH OSSETIA
DAGESTAN
Makhach Kala
Sochi
ABKHAZIA
Sukhumi
Black Sea
Poti
ADHARIA
GEORGIA
Tbilisi
TURKEY
Caspian Sea
Spitak
ARMENIA
Yerevan
AZERBAIJAN
Gyandzha
Sumgait
Baku
NAGORNO-KARABAKH
NAKHICHEVAN
Lenkoran
IRAN
Tabriz
N
LEGEND TO MAPS
Capital city
Other towns & cities
International boundary
National boundary
Other boundaries
Highlighted region
Caucasus Mountains
0 50 100 miles
0 50 100 kilometres

Map 2: ARMENIA and AZERBAIJAN
GEORGIA
Tbilisi
DAGESTAN (RUSSIAN FEDERATION)
Spitak
Gyandzha
AZERBAIJAN
ARMENIA
Yerevan
NAGORNO-KARABAKH
Agdam
Stepanakert
Shusha
Lachin
Fizuli
Sabrail
Sadarak
NAKHICHEVAN
TURKEY
IRAN
IRAN
Sumgait
Baku
Caspian Sea
Lenkoran
0
50
100 miles
0
50
100 kilometres

Map 3: GEORGIA
RUSSIAN FEDERATION
Sochi
Gagra
Gudauta
Sukhumi
ABKHAZIA
Black Sea
Mozdok
Grozny
Vladikavkaz
DAGESTAN
LEGEND TO MAPS
Capital city
Other towns & cities
International boundary
National boundary
Other boundary
Railway
Highlighted region
Caucasus mountains
Zugdidi
MINGRELIA
Khobi
Kutaisi
Poti
Samtredia
SOUTH OSSETIA
Tskhinvali
GEORGIA
Telavi
Tbilisi
ADHARIA
Batumi
TURKEY
AZERBAIJAN
Spitak
Kumairi
ARMENIA
Gyandzha
0
50
100 miles
0
50
100 kilometres
N

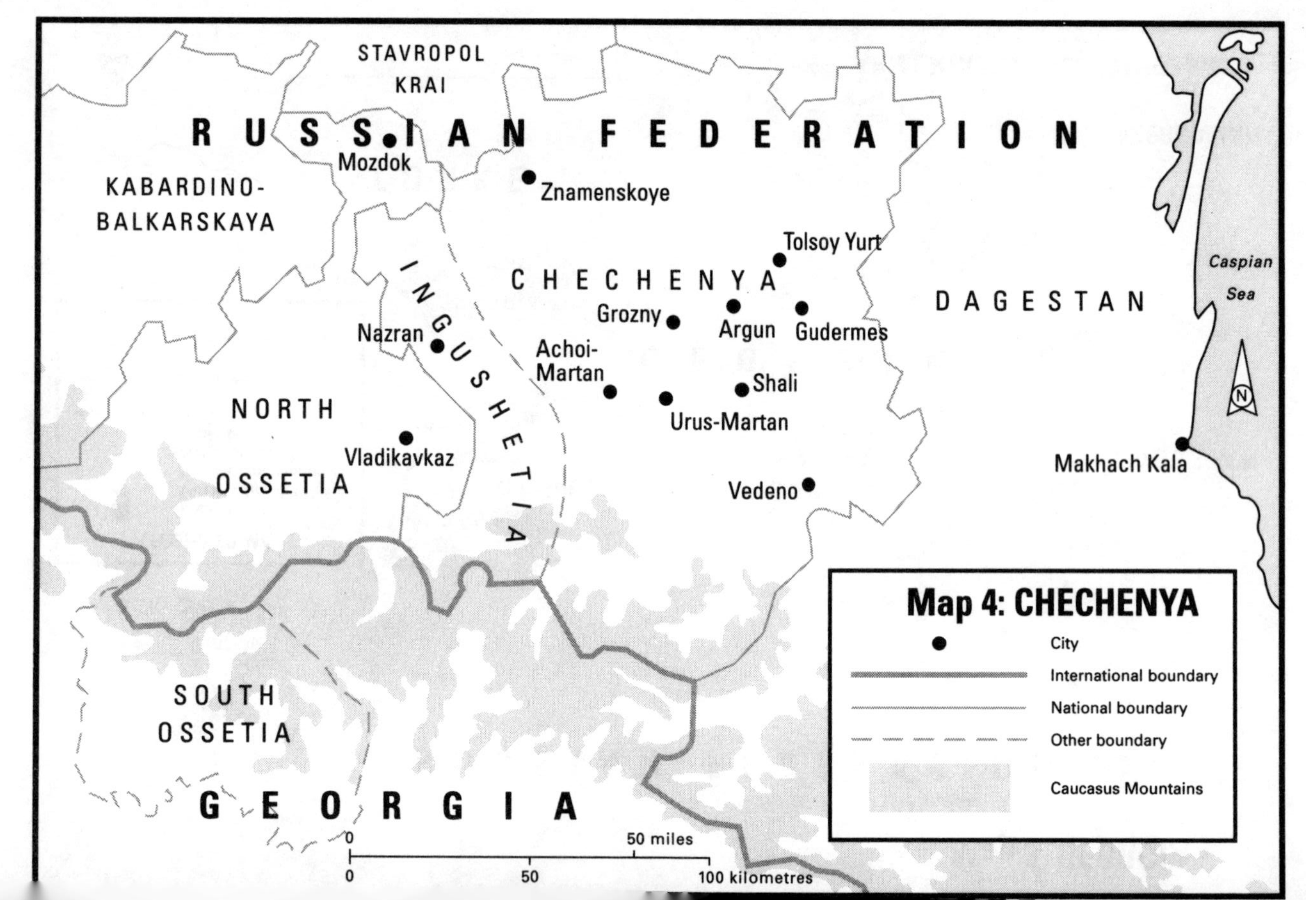
Map 4: CHECHENYA
City
International boundary
National boundary
Other boundary
Caucasus Mountains
STAVROPOL KRAI
RUSSIAN FEDERATION
Mozdok
KABARDINO-BALKARSKAYA
Znamenskoye
Tolsoy Yurt
CHECHENYA
INGUSHETIA
Caspian Sea
DAGESTAN
Grozny
Argun
Gudermes
Nazran
Achoi-Martan
Shali
Urus-Martan
NORTH OSSETIA
Vladikavkaz
Makhach Kala
Vedeno
SOUTH OSSETIA
GEORGIA
0
50 miles
0
50
100 kilometres

Bibliography

The following works are among the several consulted and I would like to record my sincere thanks and appreciation to the authors, editors or compilers. Where quotations or other matter have been used, appropriate credit is given within the text.

Altstadt, Audrey (1992) *The Azerbaijan Turks: Power and Identity under Russian Rule* (California: Hoover Institution Press).

Broxup, Marie Bennigsen (ed.) (1992) *The North Caucasus Barrier: The Russian Advance Towards the Muslim World* (London: Hurst).

Charvonnaya, Svetlana (1995) *Conflict in the Caucasus: Georgia, Abkhazia and the Russian Shadow* (London: Gothic Image).

Conquest, Robert (1978) *The Nation Killers: The Soviet Deportation of Nationalities* (London: Macmillan).

Goldenberg, Suzanne (1994) *Pride of Small Nations: The Caucasus and Post-Soviet Disorder* (London: Zed Books).

Nasmyth, Peter (1992) *Georgia: A Rebel in the Caucasus* (London: Cassell).

Nevers, Renne de (1994) *Russia's Strategic Renovation*, Adelphi Paper 289 (London: IISS).

Statesman's Year Book (1993–4) (London: Macmillan).

Suny, Ronald Grigor (1989) *The Making of the Georgian Nation* (London: I.B. Taurus).

Walker, Christopher (1990) *Armenia: The Survival of a Nation* (London: Routledge).

Walker, Christopher (1991) *Armenia and Karabagh: The Struggle for Unity* (London: Minority Rights).

Yeltsin, Boris (1994) *A View from the Kremlin* (London: HarperCollins).

Index